T0361122

RURAL-URBAN INTEGRATION IN JAVA

Rural-Urban Integration in Java
Consequences for regional development and employment

VINCENT L. ROTGÉ
Consultant to the European Commission, Brussels

with contributions from
IDA BAGOES MANTRA and RYANTO RIJANTA

Routledge
Taylor & Francis Group

LONDON AND NEW YORK

First published 2000 by Ashgate Publishing in cooperation with The United Nations Centre for Regional Development, Nagoya, Japan.

Reissued 2018 by Routledge
2 Park Square, Milton Park, Abingdon, Oxon, OX14 4RN
52 Vanderbilt Avenue, New York, NY 10017

Routledge is an imprint of the Taylor & Francis Group, an informa business

Publisher's Note
The publisher has gone to great lengths to ensure the quality of this reprint but points out that some imperfections in the original copies may be apparent.

Disclaimer
The publisher has made every effort to trace copyright holders and welcomes correspondence from those they have been unable to contact.

A Library of Congress record exists under LC control number: 132848

ISBN 13: 978-1-138-35226-1 (hbk)
ISBN 13: 978-0-429-43482-2 (ebk)

Contents

PART I: REGIONAL DEVELOPMENT ASPECTS

PART II: CASE STUDIES

List of Figures

List of Tables

List of Contributors

Vincent Rotgé, was born in France in 1959. He is the holder of a Ph.D in Geography with a specialization in economic geography and regional development from Sorbonne University (Paris IV), and he studied at Yale University, USA, where he was granted a Masters Degree in Environmental Design. He was also granted a M.Phil (DEA) in Development Studies with a specialization in geopolitics by the School for Higher Studies in Social Sciences (EHESS), Paris, in 1987, and a professional diploma in architecture and physical town planning in Paris in 1983. Since 1998, he has been the Operations Project Manager for a EC-sponsored decentralized cooperation programme, which focuses on urban development projects in South and Southeast Asia. Prior to this, he was involved on behalf of the European Commission with the Commission's programmes for the revitalization of European inner-cities (Urban Pilot Projects - UPP) and the employment of youth, and he was the Team Leader of the Rural Towns Development Study (RTDS) appraisal mission in Bangladesh. As a Visiting Assistant Professor at the National Institute of Oriental Languages and Civilizations (INALCO), Paris University, he taught courses on Indonesia and Southeast Asia between 1996 and 1997. In 1993, he was a Visiting Assistant Professor at Gadjah Mada University in Yogyakarta, Indonesia. Between 1989 and 1992, Vincent Rotgé was a researcher at the United Nations Centre for Regional Development (UNCRD) in Nagoya, Japan. While at UNCRD, as the team leader of 10 assistants and university counterparts within the framework of a 4-year programme initiated by UNCRD and the Government of Indonesia, he designed and implemented fieldwork in villages of Yogyakarta Special Region, Indonesia, on the implications of the strengthening of rural-urban linkages for the development of hinterland communities. This included the study of forward and backward economic linkages, local resources and demographics, agricultural and nonagricultural income, income disparities, labour mobility and remittances.

Vincent Rotgé has published and presented papers on metropolitan development and land-use policies in industrialized countries, and on rural-urban linkages, employment, and regional integration in Asia.

Ida Bagoes Mantra, was born in Bali in 1931. He graduated from the Faculty of Geography of Gadjah Mada University (FG-UGM), Yogyakarta, in 1964, and was granted a Ph.D. in Population Geography by the University of Hawaii in 1978. Ida Bagus Mantra holds a chair in Population Geography at Gadjah Mada University, and is a senior researcher at the Population Research Centre (PPK) of the same university. He was appointed visiting professor at the Universiti Kebangsaan Malaysia in 1994.

Prof. Mantra has presented papers in various conferences on Population Mobility and published his work in Indonesia and abroad, such as: *Population Movement in Wet Rice Communities* (Yogyakarta: Gadjah Mada University Press, 1981), and *Urbanization in Indonesia* (Nagoya: UNCRD Working papers series, 1990). His work on demography is published in textbooks, which are widely used in Indonesian universities.

Ryanto Rijanta, was born in Yogyakarta in 1962. He graduated from the Faculty of Geography of Gadjah Mada University with a specialization in Population Geography in 1986, and obtained a Masters of Science Degree on Survey Integration for Aerospace Survey and Earth Sciences (ITC) in Enschede, The Netherlands, in 1990.

He is a permanent staff-member of the Department of Rural and Regional Development Planning at the Faculty of Geography of Gadjah Mada University (FG-UGM), and a researcher at the Centre for National Development Planning Studies at the same university. Ryanto Rijanta has published articles in national academic journals in Indonesia.

Preface

- by Vincent Rotgé -[1]

Background of this Work[2]

In 1989, the United Nations Centre for Regional Development (UNCRD) and the Ministry of Public Works, Government of Indonesia, established a joint-programme in development planning. The Special Region of Yogyakarta (D.I.Y.), one of the most densely populated and oldest settled regions in Asia, was selected as a pilot-area. This programme included several different research and evaluation projects. One important component of the programme was to assess the role and prospect of increasing rural-urban linkages for the development process and planning of Yogyakarta Special Region, and beyond this monographic work which is useful for the planning of this specific region, to draw lessons and conclusions for other Indonesian and ASEAN subnational regions.

This book draws from the result of the fieldwork conducted in Yogyakarta Special Region in 1991 and 1992, with the aim of assessing the consequences of the strengthening of urban-rural linkages upon local development in five hinterland communities. Emphasis was laid on employment issues - especially with regard to diversification of the economy - and the process of urbanization in suburban communities for socioeconomic and physical changes. This work required intense effort and care during the initial fieldwork and data-processing phases, both in Indonesia and at the United Nations Centre for Regional Development (UNCRD) in Nagoya, Japan. The rural-urban linkages evaluation project was coordinated by Vincent Rotgé who designed the research objectives, organized and attended to the overall fieldwork in Indonesia, undertook the enormous task of statistical analysis, and edited the research material, a large part of which he also wrote. The Regional Planning Board (BAPPEDA) of Yogyakarta Special Region and the Ministry of Public Works of Indonesia provided their continuous support. This, together with the generous hospitality of the residents of the studied communities, enabled those involved to bring this project to a successful conclusion.

Parts of the research findings were included in a volume published in 1995 by UNCRD,[3] and were presented at workshops held in Yogyakarta in 1991 and 1992, respectively, and at the International Conference on Geography in the Asean Region, Gadjah Mada University, Yogyakarta, 31 August to 3 September 1992. Also, part of the material included in this volume was used as teaching material for a training programme which was held twice at UNCRD in 1993 and 1994 for Indonesian local government officials, as part of the Human Resource Development Program operated by the National Development Agency (BAPPENAS), Government of Indonesia.

This book builds upon these previous works and includes a new conclusion in which the findings of the study conducted in Yogyakarta are set in a wider international context. It addresses the increasing importance of rural-urban integration in Java and Monsoon Asia. It begins with an analysis of communities located in different agroecological settings, but all within a short distance of Yogyakarta, in one of the most densely populated regions of the world. It examines the effect of rural-urban linkages on regional growth, employment and rural poverty and shows the increasing interrelation between rural and urban economies. The book analyzes in particular detail the changes in agriculture and questions whether the resulting industrialization and urbanization is generally beneficial. Providing directions for future policy and research in its conclusion, the book extends its theoretical findings into a wider international context and evaluates the process of urbanization in other parts of densely populated rice-growing Asia.

Yogyakarta Special Region (D.I.Y.)

Yogyakarta Special Region (known as 'Daerah Istimewa Yogyakarta' in Bahasa Indonesia, hereinafter as D.I.Y.) is located in the centre of the southern coast of Java - Figures 1.1 and 1.2. The history of this region located near the major archaeological landmark of Borobudur, and where other important archaeological remains can be found in a large number covering a very large time span, is exceptionally rich and ancient. Agriculture and irrigation have been developed in this region over many centuries. The irrigation network has been constantly improved over time especially in the plain occupying the areas surrounding the contemporary city of Yogyakarta, leading in this latter district to very important population densities long before the outbreak of the Second World War. Also, population pressures in lowland areas as well as various historical circumstances (related to land tenure and cultivation arrangements in lowland areas) would have led to immigration movements to some upland areas in particular during the 19th century.[4] Today in some upland areas of this region population densities are relatively high though some of these areas are now experiencing net out-migration. At the same time, the D.I.Y. can be termed as an inland region for important harbours cannot be built in most areas along the southern coast of Java - apart from in Cilacap for instance - and as this region is separated from the northern coast by a volcanic mountain range. Due to such geographical characteristics and also historical circumstances (see Part I) the region and its economic base remained until recently very much agrarian in nature as well as occluded from other regions of Java where the most economic growth was taking place. As a consequence, by the late 1960s, this region seemed doomed to 'agricultural involution' and a 'Malthusian' future with a high rate of out-migration fueled by transmigration resettlement programmes to outer islands and spontaneous forms of migrations to Jakarta in particular. The case of the D.I.Y. seemed to verify the hypothesis introduced by the anthropologist Clifford Geertz in the 1960s which suggested that the paucity of nonagricultural employment alternatives, already existing high man-land ratios, and a steady natural population growth in Java would lead to worsening land fragmentation and a concomitant and general process of impoverishment of rural households. Such a hypothesis was pivotal in the theory of 'agricultural involution' developed by this author.[5] However intellectually stimulating this theory at first seemed (for it tried to cast light on the process of agricultural change in Java in a systematic way), it was to be widely revised in the following decades. For instance, referring to the D.I.Y., McDonald and Sontosudarmo[6] noted in the mid-1970s that agricultural involution could no longer describe the process of social and agricultural change occurring in this region. Instead, these authors stressed that in their opinion out-migration was, and would probably remain, the dominant existing answer to population pressures for the next decade.

Jean-Luc Maurer, in a study of the impact of the modernization programmes of rice agriculture in the 1970s upon rural communities of the D.I.Y.,[7] emphasized strong differences among villages in terms of economic basis as a function of their agroecological setting and location. In one suburban village located next to an important road among the four studied, the same author noted a more diversified economic basis and the existence of broader job opportunities being accessible to landless villagers than in the other three which lay further away from urban centres. Maurer's main conclusion was that in the studied villages, both the capacity of peasants to take advantage of existing economic opportunities and the impulse for socioeconomic change proved very strong. A further important conclusion was that locational and agroecological characteristics of rural communities played an essential role in economic development.

Above all, a major process brought considerable changes in rural Java and in particular in the D.I.Y., especially from the 1970s onwards, whose effects have contributed to transforming our perception of regional development in Java. This process of change was triggered by the programme of modernization of agriculture - one may say in reality various programmes undertaken from the mid-1960s onwards in the wake of the so-called 'Green Revolution'.[8] Since the late 1970s onwards, some authors have agreed that such programmes entailed positive effects in terms of yields as far as the rice subsector was concerned. Such programmes have brought about surpluses in the countryside and contributed to the commercialization and monetization of the rural economy in Java.

Still, some authors have noted that such success would have been met, to some extent, at the expense of the displacement of certain subsistence crops. Other less radical authors are of the opinion that modernization programmes are also necessary for crops other than rice, such as certain valuable cash crops, and that in that sense previous agricultural modernization policies would have been wrong in favouring rice too excessively over such crops. Also, a number of authors writing in the late 1970s and in the 1980s have emphasized certain negative side-effects of the programmes of agricultural modernization upon rural employment such as mechanization of some agricultural tasks and also differential access to inputs or differential capacity to take advantage of the benefits of such programmes. Larger-scale farmers, indeed, seem to have been in a better position to fully benefit from such programmes while mechanization of some agricultural tasks previously implemented manually undercut the employment basis for landless rural dwellers.[9]

At the same time, the main development experienced in the 1980s in the D.I.Y. led to the very rapid expansion of the service sector during the period, partly as a consequence of large government expenditures and of the development of tourism and of a great many educational institutions (both private and public, including several universities) that the region has been famed for especially since the late 1940s. This occurred together with a very important decrease in the labour force engaged in agricultural services over the past two decades partly as a consequence of agricultural modernization. Following such developments, one may wonder whether out-migration will continue to act in this region as the dominant factor for accommodating regional labour 'surpluses' as it has done for decades. Could, indeed, the reinforcement of communications and of the mobility of workers and capital between rural and urban areas within the D.I.Y., through broadening rural employment opportunities, be conducive to settling a larger number of rural residents thereby somewhat reducing the need for extraregional migration, while the effects of family planning are felt - as clearly shown by the results of the 1990 population census - with a reduction in the number of young workers coming of age in the next decade? In a nutshell, in the wake of the recent abovementioned developments in the D.I.Y., the main thrust of this study is to show how and to what extent a sectoral shift is occurring in the employment structure of villages of the D.I.Y. from the agricultural to the service sector. In so doing, special attention is given to the role played by increased rural-urban linkages in the course of this process. The discussion is based on empirical evidence and on quantitative data collected in a selection of five villages of the D.I.Y. in 1991 and 1992. Communities were selected as a function of agroecological and geographical characteristics (in particular, their distance to main roads and to the city of Yogyakarta and other secondary towns). The work of Maurer[10] proved very useful in the early stages in setting selection criteria for the studied communities.

This book is organized in four main parts together with a general introduction and conclusion. In Part I, the region is introduced in geographical and economic terms, and communities where fieldwork was conducted are introduced in their geographical setting. In Part II, the results of the field studies are presented for each of the studied communities. In Chapter 9, possible regional development policies geared towards encouraging the regional integration process whose emergence was pinpointed in the earlier sections of this work are introduced. In Part III, important questions and implications of increasing rural-urban linkages for urban and societal changes in Monsoon Asia are reviewed on the basis of the lessons drawn from the case studies in the D.I.Y. Special attention is given to the consequences for employment and metropolitan changes in the wake of the changes now taking place in this region of the World.

The Focus on Rural-urban Linkages

A hypothesis which is pivotal in this study is that labour displacement which occurred from agriculture together with the growth of services located in urban and suburban areas of the D.I.Y. and the improvement of communications (improvement of roads and diffusion of private and public means of transportation) may be to some extent compensated for by a general ongoing process of regional integration of rural and urban areas. In other words, in the course of this study, the question whether employment generated in rural communities of the D.I.Y. through the process of regional integration, eventually compensates to a significant extent employment which has been lost in such rural areas through agricultural modernization of the past two decades will be closely examined. The process is studied by looking at the various ways in which urban and rural areas interact in financial and demographic terms and in terms of industrial subcontracting and intraregional delocalization of economic activities. In a second stage, the means to strengthen the positive effects of increasing regional integration upon employment in rural communities are reviewed. Such an approach is consistent with that of other works which have been implemented, in particular in the past decade. Abundant literature has been produced in the preceding decade regarding how growth linkages affect regional development.[11] Such works can be mainly divided among those which focus upon the spatial dimension of linkages taking place between two geographical environments, namely urban and rural areas,[12] and those which focus upon linkages taking place among different economic sectors in a given geographical setting, such as for instance the linkages between agricultural and nonagricultural economic sectors in a given rural community.[13]

Belonging to a third category, studies of a more geographical and comprehensive nature examine the processes of change happening in communities which from 'rural' are turning 'urban'. Such communities, generally suburban or located in fast-developing transit corridors and in the middle of highly fertile, well-irrigated and densely populated alluvial plains of Southeast Asia are studied at the micro-level by Brookfield, *et al.*,[14] in suburban Kuala Lumpur, or by Manuelle Franck[15] in East Java at a more macro-level and in the perspective of the spread of urbanization throughout hinterland communities.

The present study mainly focuses upon spatial linkages which are taking place between the studied rural communities and urban areas. This is also to say that rural-urban linkages are essentially considered here from a rural point of view. Moreover, throughout the present study, 'urban' areas are mainly defined as the city of Yogyakarta but also neighbouring secondary towns of the region and also those fast-developing areas in terms of economic and demographic growth, diversification of the economy, and physical construction, which are constituted by being in the vicinity of main regional transit corridors. Still, in numerous instances, it is impossible to set a clear divide between spatial (rural-urban) and intersectoral linkages. This is true for instance when savings or remittances from an urban origin - such as the savings of a former urban dweller moving to hinterland areas or the wages of an urban commuter - are invested in either full- or part-time farm activities or spent on locally-produced and/or sold commodities in the hinterland. This is also true when a trade-off exists for rural dwellers between agricultural and nonagricultural activities whose expansion is often dependent on accessing urban markets. For all these reasons, intersectoral linkages have not been overlooked in the course of this study.

Moreover, as some of the communities studied are either suburban or located along important transit corridors where significant socioeconomic and physical transformations are taking place, this study also examines the process of *in situ* urbanization, which takes place in such communities, and draws some main policy implications. It must be acknowledged that the D.I.Y. is not located in the fastest-developing economic area of Java. Changes in hinterland communities of this region may be less impressive than in fast-developing hinterland areas of Java located in well-known corridors of urbanization, such as those in areas lying between Jakarta and Bogor. This is true in particular in terms of changes in land-use, industrial development and new physical developments which by and large are taking place at a much more moderate pace in the D.I.Y. Nevertheless, some extremely fast developments are taking place in the vicinity of the city of Yogyakarta along a so-called ring road thoroughfare which has recently been built. Also, the results of our fieldwork have shown that the contribution of nonfarm urban activities undertaken by commuters to the household income in some of the studied communities can be very high and affect a surprisingly large number of households.

In that sense, one should not underestimate the role of urban-rural linkages and of a form of 'hidden' urbanization which is taking place in many hinterland communities of the D.I.Y., especially in lowland areas surrounding the city of Yogyakarta. Though it is important, this phenomenon is nevertheless less immediately perceptible. It is also likely that the process of shift from rural to urban activities is of a gradual nature in many hinterland areas of the D.I.Y., as in many instances opportunities offered by agricultural and nonagricultural activities being alone insufficient, many households remain involved in both types of activities. If the strengthening of rural-urban linkages cannot be considered as the only cause of urbanization, it undoubtedly represents an intermediary stage before hinterland communities turn urban.

Notes

1   Except the chapter 'Background of this Work'. See following note.

2   The chapter 'Background of this Work' includes large excerpts of the foreword written by Hideki Kaji, UNCRD's former Director, to Vincent Rotgé, ed., *Rural-Urban Integration in Java, Consequences for Regional Development and Employment* (UNCRD Research Report Series no 6) (Nagoya: UNCRD, 1995).

3   Vincent Rotgé, ed., *op. cit.*

4   See Khan, 1963 and 1964; Nibbering, 1991, and; Hugenholtz, 1986.

5   See Geertz, 1963, and footnote 15, Chapter 3, Part I.

6   McDonald and Sontosudarmo, 1976.

7   Maurer, 1986.

8   *Ibid.*

9   *Ibid.*, and Manning, 1988.

10   Maurer, 1986.

11   McGee, 1987; Ginsburg, Koppel, and McGee, eds., 1991; Stokke, Yapa, and Dias, 1991; and Effendi, 1991. In his 1987 seminal paper, McGee described what he called the process of *kotadesasi* coined from the words *kota* and *desa* meaning respectively 'town' and 'village' in Bahasa Indonesia. This neologism refers to a multifaceted process of integration of urban and rural areas in regions of Asia, especially Indonesia, whereby the divide between the two milieus becomes blurred.

12   See McGee, 1987.

13   Stokke, Yapa, and Dias, 1991; and Effendi, 1991.

14   Brookfield, Hadi, and Mahmud, 1991.

15   Franck, 1993.

Acknowledgements

I am indebted to the pioneering work of Terry McGee from the University of British Columbia who provided early comments on this research work. Many thanks also go to Paul Claval from Sorbonne University in Paris, and to Mike Douglass from the University of Hawaii for their generous advice and comments. Special thanks go to Hidehiko Sazanami, former Director of UNCRD and Director of the International Research Centre for Environment and Development (IRCED) at Ritsumeikan University in Kyoto, Japan, for promoting this research during his period of office at UNCRD, and to Wilbert Gooneratne, Head of the Centre of Regional Studies in Colombo, Sri Lanka, who provided advice on this work at an initial stage when he was Senior Economist at UNCRD.

I am also grateful to Manuelle Franck, Professor, National Institute of Oriental Languages and Civilizations (INALCO), Paris University, Jean-Luc Maurer, Director of the Graduate Institute for Development Studies (IUED), Geneva, and Milan Titus, Professor, Rijksuniversiteit, Utrecht, whose encouragement and comments were very helpful.

This book could not have been completed without the support and collaboration of a very large number of people at the United Nations Centre for Regional Development (UNCRD) in Nagoya, Japan. In particular, many thanks go to James F. Goater who saw the first three parts through to their completion and to Jo Edralin who encouraged me to publish this book.

The assistance of Haruo Kuroyanagi of Aichi Gakuin University, Japan, who provided some of his own research findings and practical advice, was very helpful at the initial stage of the project. In Indonesia, the enthusiastic assistance of students from Gadjah Mada University, Yogyakarta, who interviewed villagers and filled in questionnaires also proved indispensable. The villagers should be thanked for their patience and generosity together with the host families who provided us with the kindest form of hospitality.

Moreover, I would like to express my gratitude to the Population

Studies Centre and the Faculty of Geography of Gadjah Mada University and to the Deans of these institutions for providing their assistance to the project. Also, many thanks go to T. N. Effendi from the Population Studies Centre for his kind encouragement. The support of the Ministry of Public Works of Indonesia - in particular Cipta Karya - in Jakarta and BAPPEDA - the regional planning board - in Yogyakarta which made this work possible, should be acknowledged.

I would like to thank Valerie Rose, Commissioning Editor, Regional Studies, Claire Annals, Desk Editor, and Anne Keirby, Editorial Administrator, at Ashgate Publishing Limited for their efficient assistance. Many thanks also to John Archer in Brussels, who helped me to translate the Conclusion from the original French, and to Renée Rousso, Gie Siauw, Paul-Alain Beaulieu, Upali Ananda Kumara, Houchang Chehabi, Eden Quainton and Alison Eades for their assistance and friendly support.

Last but not least, the constant support and encouragement of my wife, Yukari, and my daughters, Sayoko and Miyako were essential.

Vincent Rotgé

Part I
Regional Development
Aspects

1 Brief Historical Background

- by Vincent Rotgé -

Inland Kingdoms and Northern Coastal Cities in Java

The presence of human settlements has been established in what is today the region of Yogyakarta, which predates by far the 'Javanese agrarian-based interior' kingdom that built Borobudur (between 760 and 820 AD) and the temples complex of Prambanan (built in 900 AD). There may have been capitals between Borobudur and Prambanan during this period, whose names, however, did not survive.[1] Early in the 10th century under a specific set of historical circumstances, a shift of population occurred from Central Java (including the region of Yogyakarta) to the Brantas Basin in East Java, where Majapahit was eventually to emerge as the strongest regional kingdom in the late 13th century.[2] As trade with other Southeast-Asian kingdoms flourished across the Java Sea, the diffusion of Islam in the 15th century brought considerable changes in Java. Cities of the northern coast of Java grew in importance.[3] The Kingdom of Majapahit eventually fell into decline, being taken over by the Javanese port-cities, including Demak (located near the site of the contemporary city of Semarang) which soon emerged as the strongest of the Islamic port-cities of Java. A new shift of power occurred from Demak to Pajang - a central Javanese kingdom - and then again to Mataram which was established towards the end of the 16th century approximately at the same location as the ancient 8th century Hindu-Buddhist Kingdom, south of the Merapi volcano - at the centre of today's Yogyakarta Special Region.

Subsequently, Islam penetrated the Kingdom of Mataram from the islamized coast through the Solo and Brantas rivers at that time a main communication thoroughfare from the coast to the region. In the middle of the 18th century, the Kingdom of Mataram was divided (Treaty of Gianti, 1755) into the Sultanate of Yogyakarta and the neighbouring Principality of Surakarta. Both passed under the *de facto* domination of the Dutch United East Indies Company (V.O.C.).[4] Thus, as stressed by Hugo, *et al*,[5] in 'pre-European contact times' cities in Java mainly consisted of coastal

3

Figure 1.1   Location of Yogyakarta Special Region (D.I.Y.) in the Indonesian Archipelago

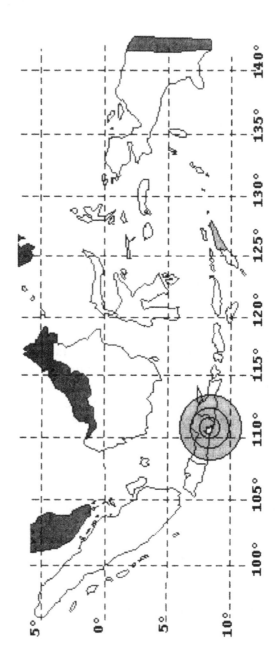

Figure 1.2 The 27 Indonesian Provinces

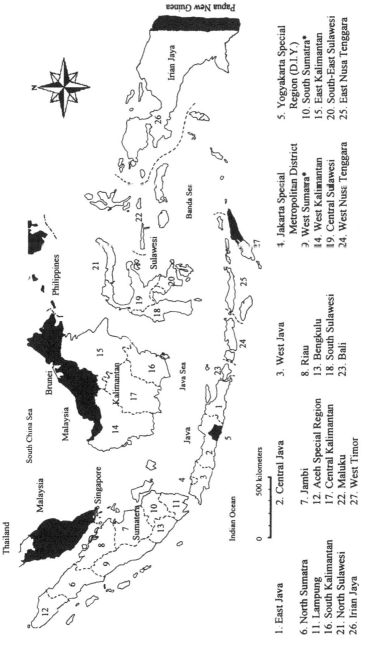

1. East Java
2. Central Java
3. West Java
4. Jakarta Special Metropolitan District
5. Yogyakarta Special Region (D.I.Y.)

6. North Sumatra
7. Jambi
8. Riau
9. West Sumatra*
10. South Sumatra*

11. Lampung
12. Aceh Special Region
13. Bengkulu
14. West Kalimantan
15. East Kalimantan

16. South Kalimantan
17. Central Kalimantan
18. South Sulawesi
19. Central Sulawesi
20. South-East Sulawesi

21. North Sulawesi
22. Maluku
23. Bali
24. West Nusa Tenggara
25. East Nusa Tenggara

26. Irian Jaya
27. West Timor

* The island of Sumatra is spelled 'Sumatera' in *Bahasa Indonesia*.

Source: UNCRD/Cipta Karya, *Regional Development of Yogyakarta*, Volume 1 (1975).

cities and the seats of inland Javanese kingdoms, including the region of today's Yogyakarta. The colonial era was to bring important changes. According to Hugo and Mantra,[6] the urban system in Indonesia was during the colonial period, indeed:

> [...] designed to expedite the production and delivery of raw materials and to subjugate the local population as cheaply and efficiently as possible. The two elements in it were a series of entrepôt cities, which were the points of contact between the colony and the home country, and a hierarchical network of generally much smaller centres, intermediaries through which the entrepôt cities' hinterlands were controlled and divested of their export crops.

Table 1.1 Population Growth of Some Major Cities in Java, 1855-1930

City	1855	1895	1905	1930	Average annual growth	
					1855-1905	1905-1930
Batavia	55,000	114,566	138,551	533,015	1.86	5.50
Surabaya	88,527	124,529	150,198	341,675	1.06	3.34
Semarang	n.a	82,962	96,660	217,796	1.64	3.30
Bandung	11,223*	46,326	47,400	166,815	2.47	5.16
Surakarta	n.a	104,589	118,378	165,484	1.25	1.35
Yogyakarta	43,000	58,299	79,569	136,649	1.24	2.19

*   1846 figure

Source: Quoted (excerpts) from G. J. Hugo, *et al.*, *The Demographic Dimension in Indonesian Development* (Singapore: Oxford University Press, 1990).

This policy contributed to the demographic and industrial growth of harbour cities of the northern coast and left the hinterland and southern coast (most parts of the southern coast in Central Java are unsuitable for the construction of ports due to physical impediments) with a very low level of urban growth, except perhaps for Bandung which partly developed as a colonial upland town. For a long time, before the first decades of this century, Surabaya remained the largest city and most important harbour and industrial centre of Indonesia, while Jakarta (formerly Batavia) with its upland extension constituted the administrative core of the Netherlands Indies.

The Region of Yogyakarta

It is likely that the region had never been fully deserted for any long period of time in the course of shifts of regional power and of population in Javanese history. Also, from the 17th century onward, the type of urban culture flourishing in areas of the region grew increasingly more sophisticated (court life in the Sultanate and its periphery, or urban culture in the ancient town of Kota Gede, which today has become merged with the city of Yogyakarta). In 1855, Yogyakarta was the fifth largest Javanese city in terms of population - Table 1.1. The city's subsequent population growth was to remain far below that of other major Javanese cities of the northern coast. In 1980, Yogyakarta ranked tenth in Indonesia for the size of its population. There is little doubt that such a *relative* loss of importance in demographic terms, as compared to the northern coastal cities, can be mostly explained by the shortage of employment alternatives either within or outside of agriculture. In this strongly agrarian-based region endowed with very fertile agricultural land in lowland areas, population densities, indeed, had already reached very high levels in lowlands. Also, since the region is surrounded by chains of mountains or high plateaus, there was probably significantly less space for the rapid expansion of the total regional irrigated area than in vaster coastal flat land of the North. Such regional employment-related problems are confirmed by the fact that the 1930 census indicated the region of Yogyakarta was a major population sending area to the north of Sumatra under a Dutch programme of population relocation (the precursor of the contemporary programme of transmigration). Further possible historical reasons for demographic stagnation may be suggested such as the imposition of heavy land taxes and duties in lowlands possibly fueling migration to uplands, etc.

Also, for centuries, the region had been connected to the northern coast by a road 'crossing the Central Javanese chain of mountains near Candi (Salatiga), leading into the Opak-Progo Basin'.[7] It is possible that the development of communications between the region and the northern coast of Java, in particular the construction of the Semarang-Surakarta-Yogyakarta railway line in 1873, may have somewhat disrupted the regional economy in a first stage, by bringing this agrarian-based society - which was also harbouring a traditional form of Javanese life-style and, as such, was probably unwittingly introverted - into even closer contact with the outer and also industrializing world. Also, it is probable that a competition between locally-produced goods and cheaper imported goods was thereby induced with the likely result of harming some regional domestic productions. For instance, side-effects of the construction of the Semarang-Surakarta-Yogyakarta railway line have been studied, showing that the import of rice from other parts of Southeast Asia at lower prices than locally-produced rice resulted in a severe drop in farmers' income in the hinterland of Semarang in the second half of the 19th century.[8] Such a process of regional development in Java has continued to evolve in the decades that followed national Independence, as patterns of industrial investment and communications further exacerbated industrial concentration in urban centres of the northern coast. The region of Yogyakarta became a 'Special Region' (*Daerah Istimewa*) after the Second World War at the time of Independence.

Conclusion

The regional economic base has largely remained dependent on agriculture and is essentially domestic in nature. As population densities are among the highest in rural Java, this situation has led to strong regional employment shortages and flows of out-migration. But at the same time, by virtue of its history, Yogyakarta Special Region occupies an unparalleled position in Java, in political, cultural, and historical terms. Such a 'dual' position casts light on the need for and, high degree of, commitment of the central state to the development of this region - which is reflected by a high level of central government's contribution to the region's budget and an important regional concentration of public administration and educational institutions.

The development path followed by the region has not prepared it for such a course of rapid industrial development, at least as far as larger-scale industry is concerned (small-scale and cottage industries are numerous), if it is ever to happen at all. Notwithstanding an agricultural sector whose employment-generation capacity is limited, for reasons discussed later in this study (though agricultural diversification is likely to bring some further room for income generation), future opportunities seem more related to the service industries such as in the educational and research sectors - where the region's prominent national position is already firmly established as reflected by the presence of a very large number of students from all over the country - and possibly also in some other service sectors, such as tourism and allied sectors, discussed later.

Hence, challenges for Yogyakarta Special Region are to solve employment problems associated with a wide dependency upon agriculture and the need to accommodate structural shifts in employment from agriculture towards an increasingly service-oriented regional economy. Such challenges must also be perceived in the context of increased national and international communications that, in turn, may contribute to bringing about changes in private investments at the national level which may ultimately benefit the region's economic base and capacity for employment and income generation in the longer or shorter terms. Some such changes can, however, already be perceived in the sectors of private education, tourism, and other allied sectors. At the intraregional level, such changes are likely to bring about the need for structural and spatial adjustments in order in particular to make employment opportunities created in service sectors which are growing accessible from rural areas. These issues will be carefully reviewed in this book.

Notes

1   Rutz, 1987.
2   *Ibid.*; Koentjaraningrat, 1985.
3   See Lombard, 1990; Reid, 1988.
4   Koentjaraningrat, *op. cit.*
5   Hugo, *et al.*, 1990.
6   Hugo and Mantra, 1983.
7   Koentjaraningrat, *op. cit.*
8   Surjo, 1986.

2 Geographical Features of the Region

- by Ryanto Rijanta and Vincent Rotgé - [1]

Introduction

Yogyakarta Special Region (*Daerah Istimewa Yogyakarta*), henceforth referred to as D.I.Y., is one of the twenty-seven Indonesian Provinces, stretching along the Indian Ocean on the south coast of Java Island Figures 1.1 and 1.2 and 2.1. It is the smallest Province of Indonesia (3,186 km² for the D.I.Y. against 132,187 km² for the whole of Java). The Special Region's Districts (Gunung Kidul, Sleman, Kulon Progo, Bantul, and the Municipality of Yogyakarta; Figure 2.2) are sharply contrasted in terms of climate, soils, physiographic configuration, and hydrology. Hence, obliterating intraregional physical characteristics would lead to a misperception of regional development trends and potentials, whereas, on the other hand, attempts at mechanistically relating levels of population density of an area to its physical characteristics, without paying respect to historical and cultural factors as well as changes in communication would prove limited.

The Importance of Monsoons' Seasonality

By and large, the climate of the region can be termed as semi-tropical and humid. Average monthly temperature ranges between 26.6 degrees Celsius to 29 degrees Celsius. Minimum monthly temperature is 19.6 degrees Celsius in July with a maximum temperature of 35.4 degrees Celsius in November. Throughout the region, annual levels of precipitation are high - Figure 2.3. A relatively wide variation of temperature between day and night for this kind of climate (partly the consequence of monsoons), and a rather constant temperature throughout the same month are recorded. However, the level of rainfall varies widely depending on the season. There is a dry season, lasting from May to October, during which there is an almost total absence of rainfall. A marked wet season follows from November through May during which 80 per cent to 90 per cent of all annual rainfall is recorded in most years. Monsoons are actually responsible for the change of seasons. Like in the eastern part of Java, the dry season coincides with an east monsoon characterized by dry winds coming from the Australian desert, and the wet season with a west monsoon characterized by wet winds blowing from the Indian Ocean. During the wet season rainfall levels range, on average, between 88 mm to 364 mm, whereas in the dry season they show a range from 8 mm to 73 mm. Intraregional variations in precipitation are noticeable. Thus, mountainous Districts such as Sleman and Kulon Progo tend to have longer wet seasons than the others. The rainy season comes earlier in these latter areas than in lowlands as wet monsoon winds release their rainfall at higher altitudes. The level of regional rainfall is also heavily influenced by both local physiographic characteristics and the influence of monsoons.[2] Thus, districts located between two ranges of mountains usually receive an annual level of precipitation of less than 2,000 mm. Such areas are characterized by a dry climate, whereas some upland areas can be classified as belonging to a wet climate zone with an annual rainfall level of more than 2,500 mm. Though receiving a relatively important amount of precipitation, the uplands located south of the District of Gunung Kidul[3] have soils which do not retain rainfall, while the groundwater lies very deep. The marked alternation of seasons in the D.I.Y. carries profound consequences for agriculture and the process of intraregional seasonal migrations, which are more accentuated in areas which, without permanent irrigation and where land is either dry or rainfed, are fully dependent upon precipitation for agriculture.

Hydrology: rivers and groundwater

Contrasting with other areas of Monsoon Asia, rivers in the D.I.Y. are not navigable and therefore are not used for transportation. On the other hand, they are used extensively for irrigation purposes. Numerous small rivers run from mountain ridges. These small rivers flow into three main rivers, namely: the Progo, Opak and Serang rivers. In turn, the latter run into the Indian Ocean. The Progo River has its catchment areas around the Sumbing, Sindoro, and Merbabu slopes. The Opak river's catchment area consists of the Merapi slopes and Gunung Kidul hills while the Menoreh hills constitute the catchment area of the Serang River in Kulon Progo.

The Progo River has the highest run-off among all regional rivers. Rivers of the region transport an important volume of sediments. By and large, these sediments have a positive effect on the agricultural performance of areas adjacent to rivers located downstream. But rivers also transport important amounts of sand that deposit in the deltas which negatively affect agricultural performances of the soils.

Groundwater in the region can be generally found at less than 10 m below the ground surface in the central plain. However, it may lie considerably deeper (often more than 100 m) in the south of Gunung Kidul which consists of a karstic area. The largest groundwater aquifers are found in the geological formation of Sleman and Yogyakarta, administratively located in Sleman District.

Effects of Merapi Volcano

As stressed by Selosoemardjan: 'It is Mount Merapi which has given the region its unusual fertile land.'[4] Volcanic materials emitted by the Merapi volcano fertilize agricultural land. This is either through the action of rivers that carry a very important volume of sediments of volcanic origin down to the lowlands, or by the spilling over of ash following an eruption. Ash-laden wind blowing southward following eruptions would have fertilized the southern part of the Merapi volcano.[5]

Relief

For the sake of simplification, one could distinguish in a rather arbitrary way six main intraregional sectors in terms of relief - Figure 2.4:

In the north of the region the slopes of the Merapi volcano that have the shape of portion of a cone (the largest part of Sleman District), soils of which are made of volcanic deposits; some higher parts of the slopes of the volcano have been terraced through puddling and leveling in order to convert them into ricefields; the top of the volcano is covered by forestland and considered as a 'major volcanic danger zone';

Lowlands circling the volcano's slopes and expanding towards the centre and the south of the D.I.Y. (south of Sleman and north of Bantul Districts), soils of which are partly made of volcanic deposits and sediments; mostly ricefields;

The Wonosari Basin, in the centre of Gunung Kidul District;

Uplands in Gunung Kidul District, peripheral to the Wonosari Basin in Gunung Kidul District, reaching about 300m and 500m in altitude in respectively the south and the north of the Wonosari Basin; barren and waterless due to limestone soils especially in the south which is a karstic area;

In the south, sandy coastal plains;

Western uplands in the western part of the District of Kulon Progo; in this District, however, there is some flat land along the Progo River, along the coast and within some valleys; flat areas are irrigated whereas slopes are usually not (*i.e.,* through canals) but only rainfed.

Land Suitability for Agricultural and Nonagricultural Activities

For Nonagricultural Activities: Construction materials are abundant in the region. Most hamlets of the central lowlands own at least one kiln where bricks and roof tiles can be locally produced. Traditional construction with organic materials (bamboo, woven fibers, thatch) is gradually being replaced by masonry.

For Agriculture: Assessing agricultural potentials of land based upon the above rapid and general analysis of soils category, climate, relief and hydrology is of course insufficient, since agricultural productivity of land results from a combination of many more factors, such as depth and moisture capacity of soils, the possibility of providing irrigation, the heritage of past generations which has created a man-made environment (such as terraced fields realized through earth puddling and leveling), the slope gradient, the application of inputs, the level of management and social organization, the level of skills and training of peasants, and the availability of credit and of technical assistance (cadres, tools and inputs and subsequently an adequate road system to transport the inputs to the site). This being acknowledged, an approximate and simplified classification of agroecological districts of the region is sketched out below.

The 'best' agricultural land for growing rice is located on the gentle slopes of Sleman District and the lower plains of Bantul District in the centre of the D.I.Y. where irrigation is easily provided from the many rivers and rivulets running through the area. Soils in this zone 'have been deposited either in form of ash or by the various rivers and streams that dissect the area';[6] they are very thick and have 'favourable moisture capacity level'.[7] Rice is extensively grown in this zone with considerable yields of more than 5 tons/hectare (*e.g.*, on average, 5.4 tons/hectare in Bantul and 5.1 tons/hectare in Sleman Districts).[8] However, the western and eastern parts of Bantul District show much lower agricultural performance. It is questionable whether current yields can be increased further in both Sleman and Bantul Districts as far as rice is concerned.

In Gunung Kidul District, some fair agricultural land is located north of the Oyo River where irrigation is provided in some areas. Less demanding crops such as cassava or maize are cultivated in this District. Gunung Kidul District produces the highest production levels of the latter crops in the D.I.Y., showing a clear specialization. Simultaneously, the highest production levels of dryland rice in the D.I.Y. are found in Gunung Kidul District. Farmers fall back upon such food crops because more nutritious or yielding crops (such as wetland rice and some types of vegetables) cannot be cultivated in many areas of this District. Also, the largest cattle and goat stock within the whole region is found in this District. The former should not prove surprising as space is far less limited in Gunung Kidul District than in other Districts of the D.I.Y. and the type of livestock that can be satisfied on poor land can be raised extensively. In contrast, in a densely populated District such as Bantul there is almost no space left for grazing or even sheltering the livestock. Gunung Kidul District shows potential for livestock-raising coupled with the introduction of new varieties of grass fodders that can resist drought and also for agroforestry (associated with the afforestation of degraded areas which is desirable from an environmental point of view). This District has the largest area of forestland of the whole region - remains of the original forest that covered the area.[9] It is possible that, in the future, new technologies will allow a better exploitation of the groundwater for human uses.

Many upland areas in Kulon Progo District cannot be permanently irrigated by canals. Also, a large part of this District is covered by soils whose agricultural performances are less favourable than those of the soils fertilized by volcanic materials of most of Sleman and Bantul Districts. Nonetheless, by and large, Kulon Progo District is better-off for its natural endowment than Gunung Kidul District.

The per-capita production of rice is much higher than in Gunung Kidul District and a large part of the rice production is grown in a wetland piedmont plain located between the foothills of the Menoreh mountain range and the Progo River in the northeast of the District. Additional food crops as in most areas of the D.I.Y., are intercropped and/or mixed with rice. Vegetables and treecrops play an important role in this District. Almost half of the total regional production of onions - a valuable commodity - comes from this District.[10] Moreover, nearly all the regional production of oranges comes from the District of Kulon Progo.[11] Nevertheless, there are within Kulon Progo District important disparities in terms of agricultural production between, on the one hand, the uplands of the Menoreh range and, on the other, the lowlands located in the northeast of the District.

Notes

[1]   The sections: 'Introduction', 'The Importance of Monsoon's Seasonality' and 'Hydrology' are by Rijanta, while the sections: 'Effects of Merapi Volcano', 'Relief' and 'Land Suitability for Agricultural and Nonagricultural Activities' are by Rotgé.

[2]   Kantor Menteri Negara Kependudukan dan Lingkungan Hidup dan Pusat Penelitian Kependudukan Universitas Gadjah Mada, 1990.

[3]   *Pegunungan Sewu* or *Gunung Sewu* means 'Thousand Mountains' in Javanese.

[4]   Selosoemardjan, 1962.

[5]   Maurer, 1986. This study is based on data collected during the 1970s.

[6]   Huisman and Stoffers, 1988.

[7]   *Ibid.*

[8]   *Daerah Istimewa Yogyakarta dalam Angka* (Yogyakarta Special Region in Figures) (Yogyakarta: Provincial Statistical Office, 1986).

[9]   See for instance: Khan, 1963, and, 1964; Nibbering, 1991.

[10]   *Daerah Istimewa Yogyakarta dalam Angka* (Yogyakarta Special Region in Figures) (Yogyakarta: Provincial Statistical Office, 1986).

[11]   *Ibid.*

Figure 2.1   Physical Map of Yogyakarta Special Region (simplified)

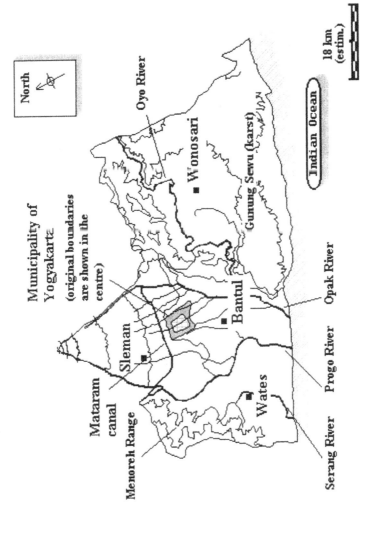

Source: Vincent Rotgé (December 1994).

Figure 2.2   **Districts** (called in *Bahasa Indonesia*: *Kabupaten* for the Regencies and *Kotamadya* for the Municipality, or Municipal District, of Yogyakarta) **and Subdistricts** (*Kecamatan*)

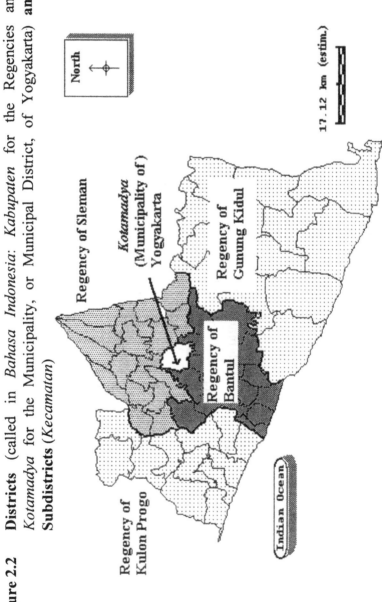

Figure 2.3   Simplified Map of the Climatic Sectors of the D.I.Y.

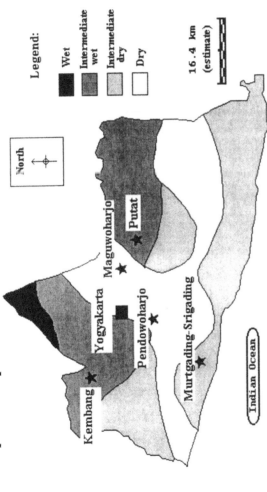

*   Stars indicate the location of villages studied in Part II.

Source: PPK-UGM and KMM-KLH (*Pusat Penelitian Kependudukan-Universitas Gadjah Mada / Kantor Menteri Negara Kependudukan dan Lingkungan Hidup*), *Faktor-faktor yang Mempengaruhi Interaksi Kependudukan dan Sumber Daya Pembangunan di Daerah Istimewa Yogyakarta* (Yogyakarta: PPK-UGM, 1990); map 1, p. 56.

Figure 2.4   Simplified Physiographic Map of the D.I.Y.

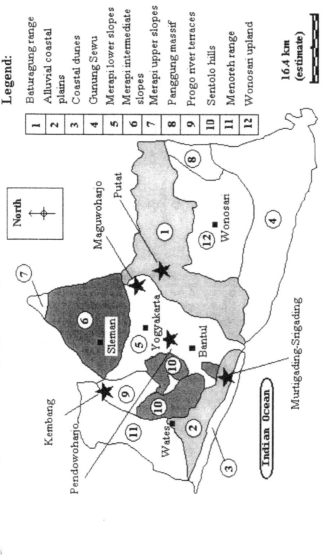

Note: Stars indicate the location of villages studied in Part II.

Source: PPK-UGM and KMM-KLH (Pusat Penelitian Kependudukan-Universitas Gadjah Mada/Kantor Menteri Negara Kependudukan dan Lingkungan Hidup), *Faktor-faktor yang Mempengaruhi Interaksi Kependudukan dan Sumber Daya Pembangunan di Daerah Istimewa Yogyakarta* (Yogyakarta: PPK-UGM, 1990); map 3, p. 59.

3   Regional Demographic Trends

- by Vincent Rotgé -

High Population Densities Coupled with a High Sectoral Share of Agriculture in Employment

The population of the D.I.Y. was about 3 million in 1990 (Java: 107,517,965).[1] Population densities in the Province are, with the exception of Jakarta the highest in the country. However, the population of the D.I.Y. grew more slowly in the 1980s than that of any other Indonesian Province - Table 3.1. This is reflected by the fact that the annual population growth rate has been the lowest among all Indonesian Provinces over the past decades (values of the population growth rate fell in between 1.07 and 1.27 in 1961-1985 for the D.I.Y. as compared with in between 2.10 and 2.15 for Indonesia and for the same period of time). But the rate of population growth in the D.I.Y. itself is not evenly distributed among Districts - Table 3.2. The two Districts of the D.I.Y., Kulon Progo and especially Gunung Kidul, are also endowed with the least fertile agricultural land, and are those having the lowest growth rates. Such a relatively low population growth rate in the D.I.Y. is the result of: a relatively strong out-migration flow from the Province to other urban centres such as Jakarta, or to the outer islands, and; a relatively low birth rate at the national level. In the aggregate, migrations play a more important role than births and deaths in the population growth of the D.I.Y. while out-migration exceeds in-migration:[2]

> [...] there is a great deal of location fluidity in the population. In a comparative sense, migration is more important than the ratio of births to deaths in understanding the growth rates of the Yogyakarta Special Region [...] Such an extremely dynamic situation illustrates the importance of migration in the aggregate sense. This is the reason why the annual rate of population growth in Yogyakarta Special Region is the lowest among Provinces in Indonesia.

An examination of time series data shows an increase in the percentage of lifetime net migrants in the D.I.Y. as a percentage of the total population. Lifetime net migrants represented the very high value of 14.4 per cent of the total population of the D.I.Y. in 1985 and 8.3 per cent in 1990 - Table 3.3.

Table 3.1   Annual Population Growth Rate, Indonesia, Selected Regions of Indonesia, and the D.I.Y.

	1961-1971	1971-1980	1980-1990
	(1)	(2)	(3)
Indonesia	2.10	2.32	1.97
Sumatra*	2.86	3.32	2.66
Nusa Tenggara	1.78	2.01	1.97
Kalimantan	2.34	2.96	3.09
Sulawesi	1.90	2.22	1.86
Maluku and Irian Jaya	2.69	2.79	3.29
Java	1.91	2.02	1.63
D.K.I. Jakarta	4.46	3.93	2.41
D.I.Y.	1.07	1.10	0.58

*   'Sumatera' in Bahasa Indonesia.

Source: Columns 1 and 2: *Statistik Indonesia* (Jakarta: Indonesian Central Bureau of Statistics, 1988) and; Column 3: Calculations from *Penduduk Indonesia, Hasil Sensus Penduduk 1990* (Series L1) (Jakarta: Indonesian Central Bureau of Statistics, 1991); (courtesy of Ida Bagoes Mantra).

Net out-migration is more severe in the poorest Districts of the D.I.Y., *i.e.* Kulon Progo and particularly Gunung Kidul, while within the same community, mobility behaviour relates to socioeconomic levels, as pointed out in a study of two villages of West Java by Tadjuddin Noer Effendi:[3]

> [...] movers from relatively developed villages are drawn from full spectrum of the socio-economic status group of households, while from the less developed villages they tend to come disproportionately from the better off households. This result suggests that the selective mechanisms of the migration process tend to be reduced as the level of development increases.

High levels of out-migration in the D.I.Y. are mainly caused by the employment shortages in the region. Employment shortages can be traced back, in turn, to the relatively low level of development of nonagricultural economic sectors in the area, as a partial result of current patterns of investments which - especially if the tourist industry is not considered - are mainly channeled into other regions: JABOTABEK (*i.e.* the large conurbation that consists of the virtually coterminous cities of Jakarta, Bogor, Tangerang and Bekasi), other important urban centres of the northern coast of Java and their periphery, or the primary resource-based industries in outlying parts of the archipelago. Second, agriculture, which is still the predominant sector of activity, is unlikely to absorb much more labour because there is no further available land in Java apart from uplands development which would cause environmental damages. Furthermore, national programmes to intensify agriculture, especially in the rice subsector, have enabled substantial increases in yields but have not necessarily led to direct job creation in the agricultural sector. On the contrary, it has been argued that they may have caused labour-displacement from agriculture.[4] But, net (direct and indirect) effects on employment are more difficult to assess because capital accumulation in the hands of the farmers who have benefited from the modernization programmes has led at the same time to the creation of job opportunities in services. This process of shift to services which is shown by the analysis of regional statistics (see 'Sectoral Share of Employment', Chapter 4), is examined at the local level in the case studies in Part II. In some parts of the D.I.Y. such as Sleman or Bantul Districts, yield levels for the rice subsector are among the highest in Java. Nonetheless, the current yield levels cannot probably be raised any further and have therefore reached a plateau as far as the rice subsector is concerned. As for the last two decades, the modernization of agriculture has placed an emphasis on the rice subsector, it has been argued that agricultural diversification might still offer some escape mechanism to absorb some of the surplus labour. While it is uncertain whether the irrigation of dry land in the poorest areas of the D.I.Y. may still offer some possibilities, diversification of agriculture might allow an increase in agricultural income in these areas, and therefore facilitate improved socioeconomic household conditions where levels of out-migration are the highest. A corollary of such a paucity of job opportunities both outside of, and within agriculture in rural areas of the D.I.Y. is the generally low level of productivity of nonagricultural and agricultural sectors, both of which tend to be labour-intensive rather than highly productive although considerable levels of land productivity are reached in the wetland areas of the central plain. Thus, it is not surprising that the rate of work participation in the D.I.Y. is high, most probably reflecting a relatively high level of underemployment associated with low rural incomes.

At the same time, population densities are rapidly increasing in Java - Table 3.5. The increase in population density in the D.I.Y. is slower than in Java in the aggregate including D.K.I. Jakarta where densities may have reached a 'ceiling'. Still, regional population density increased by 30.8 per cent between 1961 and 1985. The effects of such an increase are likely to be important because levels of population density in this region have already reached very high values and because the margin for further absorption of labour is therefore very narrow. In a region that would remain largely economically dependent on farming, such a steady increase in population densities would result into an erosion of the rural household income. Indeed, the natural increase of population leads, in the medium term, to the fragmentation of land through inheritance or landlessness. Regarding the inheritance factor, it was pointed out by Thomas Schweizer[5] that in certain rural Javanese communities:

> The laws of inheritance and ownership benefit the eldest son and prevent a long-term division of individually-owned irrigated fields under 0.5 ha [...]. Smaller areas of ownership may appear for a generation if subsidiary heirs inherit, but they have only a life interest, and their benefit reverts to the main heir and its line.

If such a mechanism can prevent an excessive fragmentation of land from happening, one may wonder what happens to the children who do not inherit. Hardjono[6] points out the consequences of a situation where the elder brothers inherit the whole property:

> The corollary would be a steadily swelling class of landless households whose members, in the absence of other forms of employment would work as labourers for their land-owing older brothers. The implication is far greater inequity in income distribution than at present prevails.

If nonfarm alternatives do not arise, such an 'involutionary'[7] process would be perverse because it is conducive to the worsening of rural underemployment, poverty, and social disparities between landowners depending on the size of their holding, and between the class of landowners as a whole and the class of landless peasants. From an economic point of view, fragmentation of land must be avoided because holdings are becoming too small 'to be economically viable'. The minimum for a family that derives its earning exclusively from land is often considered to be 0.5 ha of *sawah* (wet field). According to Hardjono:[8]

> This view appears to stem from recognition of the fact that only those with more than 0.5 ha have benefited financially from the BIMAS intensification programme.

Still, this threshold of sufficiency may vary among authors depending on the calculation methods which are used and the various characteristics of the communities which are studied - see Chapter 8. But, the increase in population densities also brings acute social and employment problems. Thus, shortage of land affects families differently depending on whether the family owns a piece of land, on the size of the parcel, or on whether villagers not having access are able to be hired as labourers. Shortage of land poses acute problems primarily because of the paucity of employment alternatives outside of the agriculture in rural areas of Java, as stressed by Hardjono:[9]

> The phenomenon of declining access to land on an ownership basis involves two separate but related trends. The first is the trend towards greater landlessness, that is, the decline in the number of households that own agricultural land. The second is the decrease in the average size of holdings. As the area held by each land-owning household becomes smaller, the proportion of marginal farmers who have to find supplementary income from non-agricultural sources increases. [...] it is incorrect to attribute the decrease in size of holdings to the inheritance system as such and it is futile to endeavour to prevent further sub-division by legislation. *Subdivision occurs because of the natural population growth in a situation where expansion of the cultivated area is impossible, where very little permanent out-migration occurs and where non-agricultural employment is limited either in availability or in return to labour.* [emphasis added]

Table 3.2   Annual Population Growth Rate in the Four
             Regencies of the D.I.Y.*, 1961-1971, 1971-1980, and
             1980-1990

District	1961-1971	1971-1980	1980-1990
	(1)	(2)	(3)
Bantul	1.32	1.21	0.94
Sleman	1.31	1.58	1.43
Gunung Kidul	0.80	0.69	- 0.13
Kulon Progo	0.96	0.30	- 0.22

*   There are five 'Districts' in the D.I.Y.: four *Kabupaten*, referred to as 'Regencies', and one *Kotamadya* which designates the Municipality (or Municipal District) of Yogyakarta.

Source: Ida Bagoes Mantra, 'Population Distribution and Population Growth in Yogyakarta Special Region', *Indonesian Journal of Geography*, 16 (December 1986); for 1980-1990: *Penduduk Indonesia, Hasil Sensus Penduduk 1990* (Series L1) (Jakarta: Indonesian Central Bureau of Statistics, 1991); (column 3: courtesy of Ida Bagoes Mantra).

Table 3.3   Lifetime Migrants Based on Province of Birth, D.I.Y.,
             1971, 1980, 1985, and 1990 (per cent of total population)

Lifetime migrants	1971 Per cent	No.	1980 Per cent	No.	1985 Per cent	No.	1990 Per cent	No.
In-migrants	5.8	101,204	6.6	180,367	7.7	229,125	9.1	266,500
Out-migrants	11.9	266,933	9.2	253,447	22.1	656,190	17.4	508,215
Net migrants	-6.1	-165,729	-2.6	-73,080	-14.4	-427,065	-8.3	-241,715

Source: Quoted from Ida Bagoes Mantra, 'Population Distribution and Population Growth in Yogyakarta Special Region', *Indonesian Journal of Geography*, 16 (December 1986); for 1990: *Penduduk Indonesia, Hasil Sensus Penduduk 1990* (Series S No. 2) (Jakarta: Indonesian Central Bureau of Statistics, 1991), (courtesy of Ida Bagoes Mantra).

Table 3.4   Basic Agricultural Data, by Districts*, D.I.Y., 1986

	Kulon Progo	Bantul	Gunung Kidul	Sleman	Kotamadya Yogyakarta (Municipality)
Surface (km²)	586	506	1.485	574	32
Population	415,699	678,884	702,710	724,613	426,342
Density	709	1,339	473	1,261	13,118
Production Wetland Paddy/capita (kg)	219	212	3.3	370	1
Yield rate Wetland Paddy (quintal/ha)	50.66	53.99	35.29	51.47	51.44
Yield rate Dryland Paddy (quintal/ha)	28.98	27.72	28.92	34.11	-
Production Dryland Paddy/capita (kg)	4.3	-	145	1.9	-

*   See note to Table 3.2.

Source: *Daerah Istimewa Yogyakarta, dalam Angka* (Yogyakarta: Provincial Statistical Office, 1986).

Table 3.5   Increase in Population (number and density) **in the D.I.Y., 1961, 1971, 1980, and 1985**

District	Area in km²	Total population			
		1961	1971	1980	1985
Municipality of Yogyakarta	35.50	306,296	340,908	380,548	442,996
Bantul	506.85	499,163 (?)	568,618	635,908	687,177
Sleman	574.82	516,653	588,304	658,647	746,793
Gunung Kidul	1,485.36	571,823	620,085	684,059	696,309
Kulon Progo	586.24	337,127	370,629	401,416	393,304
D.I.Y.	3,185.77	2,231,062	2,488,544	2,760,578	2,966,549

	Per cent increase, 1961-1985	Density per km²			
		1961	1971	1980	1985
Municipality of Yogyakarta	+ 41.5	9,622	10,512	12,689	13,630
Bantul	+ 37.5	986	1,122	1,252	1,356
Sleman	+ 43.7	904	1,023	1,178	1,299
Gunung Kidul	+ 21.8	385	418	444	469
Kulon Progo	+ 16.5	576	632	549	671
D.I.Y.	+ 32.2	704	781	863	931

Source: Ida Bagoes Mantra, 'Population Distribution and Population Growth in Yogyakarta Special Region', *Indonesian Journal of Geography*, 16 December 1986).

Table 3.6   Increase in Population Density in the D.I.Y., D.K.I. Jakarta, and Java

Population density/km²	1961	1971	1980	1985	Per cent Incr. 1961-1985
D.I.Y.	707	785	868	925	+ 30.8
D.K.I. Jakarta	5,039	7,761	11,023	13,365	+ 165.2
Java	455	532	609	652	+ 43.29

Source: *Statistik Indonesia* (Jakarta: Indonesian Central Bureau of Statistics, 1988).

Employment Creation

Hardjono summarized two main 'lines of thought' regarding changes in rural employment patterns in Java, as follows:

> The first (typified by Penny and Singarimbun 1973, White 1976a and Sajogyo 1980) argues that declining access to land and the effects of technological and institutional change have reduced employment opportunities in agriculture for the majority of the rural population. While a shift may well be occurring from agricultural to non-agricultural employment in rural areas, it involves movement into jobs with very low financial returns and hence implies lower standards of living for those affected. The opposing view (Montgomery 1975; Collier, *et al.*, 1982) also has as its starting point recognition of the fact that access to land is declining rapidly. It holds however, that on the whole rural incomes are rising and from this draws the conclusion that an expansion in relatively well-paid jobs of a non-agricultural nature is occurring. Some general indications of shifts in rural employment patterns can be gained from an examination of the impact of recent technological and institutional changes upon labour absorption in the agricultural sector. The situation in Java is similar to that throughout rural Asia where "over-all, the Green Revolution has failed to raise significantly the demand for wage labour. Often labour has been displaced and where the demand has been raised it has been absorbed by underutilised family time rather than with hired labour (ILO 1979, 14)."[10]

A Scenario with Reference to the D.I.Y.: Assumptions

It will be shown in the following section, based on regional statistics, that labour-displacements from agriculture have occurred during the past decade in the D.I.Y., while significant employment has been created in various services. Simultaneously, authors like McDonald and Sontosudarmo[11] in a study on the 'response to population pressure' in a rural community of the D.I.Y. suggested that while regional out-migration would probably continue to occur, employment shifts would be likely to take place from agriculture to services. More recently, Manning[12] stressed that economic and employment changes in rural Java that occurred in the wake of the Green Revolution programmes of the two past decades should not be viewed over-pessimistically for the increase in disparities that they may have created. Without denying that the issue of the expansion of rural employment in Java remains relatively uncertain and acknowledging that 'prospects (regarding cleavages in income and wealth and rural household economic conditions) for the immediate future are far from bright', this author suggested *at the same time* a great deal of diversity in micro-level situations and also some positive development relating to the improvement of communications for enabling rural households to participate in the urban economy, as well as the favourable impact of important government spending in rural areas made possible by the oil revenues. Finally, Maurer[13] in a study of the effects of the Green Revolution in several villages of Bantul in the D.I.Y. noted that the population of one of the villages studied by him continued to grow at a relatively high rate, in spite of high population densities, because of (a) its location on the Yogyakarta/Bantul road and (b) the existence of a nearby sugar refinery of Madukismo. The first of these two factors should attract our attention for it showed already in the 1970s the importance of the proximity to main roads in the D.I.Y. upon the economic and demographic growth of hinterland communities.

There are strong reasons to believe that such a correlation has gained in significance throughout the 1980s and 1990s. Thus, a very large number of *desa* (meaning literally 'village' - administrative units below the Subdistrict or *Kecamatan*) which are located in the lowlands of the central District (or Regency, *i.e. Kabupaten* in *Bahasa Indonesia*) of Bantul, which were considered by the Indonesian Central Bureau of Statistics as 'rural' in 1980 have been reclassified as 'urban' in 1990.[14] Figure 3.1 shows this expansion of the *desa* being reclassified as urban during the preceding decade. Most such newly 'urban *desa*' are located along important arterial roads in areas which are endowed with extremely fertile agricultural land and an excellent irrigation system - Figures 3.2, 3.3 and 3.4. 1989 regional statistical data of the District of Bantul show also that an important share of the population of Subdistricts (*Kecamatan*), which are located along the same major roads, is engaged in nonfarm activities.

By and large, the above suggests that rapid changes are actually taking place in the employment base of rural areas of the D.I.Y., simultaneously with the expansion of an 'urbanization' process. However, little is known about the nature and dynamics of such a process. Apart from basic questions regarding the process of urbanization itself, a large number of fundamental questions arise which relate to the effects of the ongoing process of employment shifts upon the levels of income and trend in socioeconomic disparities in areas which are being affected. Are, indeed, opportunities generated by such a general process of change resulting in an increase in the income of a large number of households in urban hinterland areas? Or, instead, do such opportunities result in a sort of 'urban involution'.[15] Second, what is the nature of such opportunities and are they accessible to a large segment of the native population in areas in mutation? Are they, instead, confined to segments of the local population depending on their socioeconomic origins and education. Ultimately, are employment shifts in hinterland areas of the D.I.Y. contributing to an aggravation of socioeconomic disparities, or, instead, is there an alleviation in disparities through the enablement of poor villagers to secure employment alternatives which generate sufficient income levels? Are the employment opportunities which are generated, restricted to the relatively suburban communities and lowland communities, located along main arterial roads, which are also urbanizing the fastest? More specifically, are employment opportunities - significant by their number or the income that they generate - being created in the relatively remote lowland and even more peripheral (vis-à-vis urban areas) upland communities?

Such questions will be addressed in Chapters 6 to 9, based on fieldwork carried out in five hinterland communities of the D.I.Y. These communities have been purposely selected due to their function as agroecological environments (respectively lowland, upland, and piedmont communities) and for their strategic location vis-à-vis road infrastructure and their distance from urban areas including, in particular, the city of Yogyakarta. Prior to addressing such questions, a brief general outline of the main economic activities in the D.I.Y. is provided in the following sections.

Notes

[1]   BPS, 1991.
[2]   Mantra, 1986.
[3]   Effendi, 1987.
[4]   Sinaga and Collier, 1975; World Bank, 1980.
[5]   Schweizer, 1987.
[6]   Hardjono, 1987, pp. 84-5.
[7]   See footnote 15 below.

8   Hardjono, *op. cit.*: see also pp. 247-8 for different definitions of the limit of sufficiency (*cukupan*) in land. Mantra in a further section of this Research Report cites a different definition from Singarimbun and Penny, 1976.

9   Hardjono, *op. cit.*

10   *Ibid.*; Collier, *et al.*, 'Acceleration of Rural Development of Java', *Bulletin of Indonesian Economic Studies*, 18 (3: 1982): 84-101; ILO, *Profiles of Rural Poverty* (Geneva, International Labour Office, 1979); R. Montgomery, 'Migration, Employment and Unemployment in Java: Changes from 1961-1971 with Particular Reference to the Green Revolution', *Asian Survey*, 15 (3: 1975); D.H. Penny and M. Singarimbun, *Population and Poverty in Rural Java: Some Economic Arithmetic from Sriharjo* (Ithaca, New York: Cornell International Agricultural Development Mimeograph 41, 1973); Sajogyo, 'The Basic Human Needs Approach in Development Efforts to Improve the Nutritional Status of the Poor' [Paper presented to the Third Asian Congress of Nutrition, Jakarta, October 1980]; B. White, 'Production and Reproduction in a Javanese Village', [Unpublished Ph.D. dissertation, Columbia University, 1976]. These bibliographic references are quoted from Hardjono, *op. cit.*

11   1976, pp. 86-7.

12   Manning, 1988.

13   Maurer, 1986.

14   BPS, 1980 and 1990.

15   I am grateful to Terry McGee for introducing the term 'urban involution' to me. The theory of 'agricultural involution' was introduced by the American sociologist Clifford Geertz in his study: *Agricultural Involution, The Processes of Ecological Change in Indonesia* (1963). In a nutshell, this theory states that specific historical circumstances - among which the introduction of colonial plantations - resulted in Java in the fragmentation of land holdings without any proportional increase of agricultural productivity per worker and without the creation of a manufacturing sector large enough to provide sufficient employment alternatives to the impoverished rural population. This theory has been challenged in the past two decades on the ground that programmes of intensification of agriculture (for the rice subsector), the improvement of communications, the growth of services and further factors have tranformed the premises upon which it was initially laid (see for instance Maurer, *op. cit.*). From my own understanding, the term 'urban involution' could be applied to a hypothetical process of proliferation of petty activities in urban areas, whereby existing urban economic opportunities would be shared by unskilled labour which would remain entangled in a poverty trap, because such activities would not be sufficient in number to meet the demand for jobs of urban migrants. Attempts at generalizing or drawing assumptions without the support of empirical data may prove hazardous in that respect.

Figure 3.1   **Areas Classified as 'Urban' by the Indonesian Central Bureau of Statistics in 1980 and 1990* by *Desa* (administrative villages)**

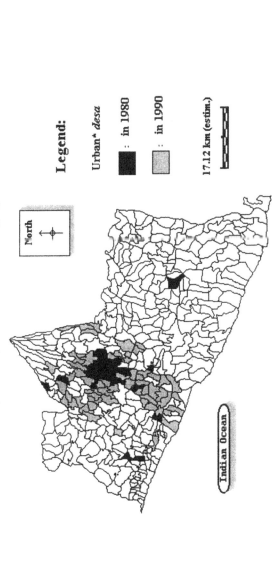

Legend:

Urban* *desa*

█ : in 1980

▒ : in 1990

17.12 km (estim.)

*   Following a definition of the Indonesian Central Bureau of Statistics (taking into account various parameters: human densities, local infrastructure, etc.).

Source: Vincent Rotgé (1994); from: *Peta Indeks Kecamatan dan Desa/Kelurahan di Propinsi Jawa Tengah dan D.I. Yogyakarta (Hasil Pemetaan Sensus Penduduk 1980* (Series 2 No. 2) (Jakarta: Indonesian Central Bureau of Statistics, 1980), and; *Peta Indeks Kecamatan per Desa/Kelurahan Propinsi Jawa Tengah dan D.I. Yogyakarta 1990* (Jakarta: Indonesian Central Bureau of Statistics, 1990).

Figure 3.2   Traffic Flow of Four-wheeled Motor Vehicles (cars, trucks and buses), **D.I.Y., 1992***

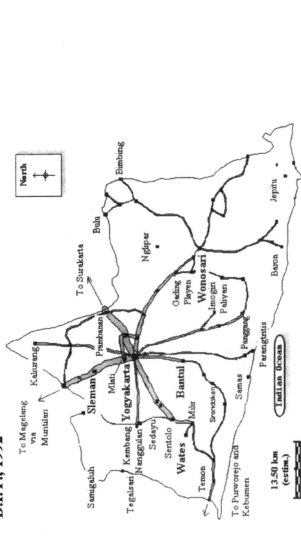

*   National and provincial roads only are included); The thickness of the lines shows the relative importance of the traffic as a function of the number of vehicles and passengers.

Source: Vincent Rotgé (1994); raw data from *Peta Jalan Nasional dan Jalan Propinsi di D.I.Y.*, and, *Interurban Road Management System Central Database, Traffic Report, Propinsi Daerah Istimewa Yogyakarta* (Jakarta: Bina Marga,1992); the numerical data were mapped by the author.

Figure 3.3 Map of Densities by *Desa* (administrative villages), D.I.Y., 1992

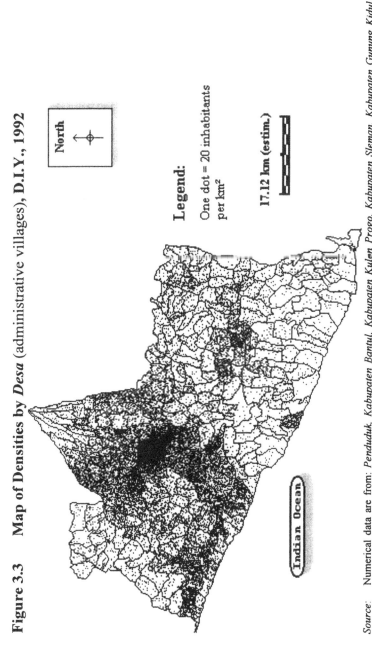

North

Legend:

One dot = 20 inhabitants
per km²

17.12 km (estim.)

Indian Ocean

Source: Numerical data are from: *Penduduk, Kabupaten Bantul, Kabupaten Kulen Progo, Kabupaten Sleman, Kabupaten Gunung Kidul, Tahun 1992*, published separately by the statistical office of each regency (*zabupaten*). These data were mapped by the author (1994). They are based on calculations from official registration acts and are less re¡iable than those of the decennial census. In this book, they are only used to give a general view of densities by *desa*.

Figure 3.4   Annual Population Growth Rate by *Desa* (administrative villages), D.I.Y.: 1980-1990, in Percentages

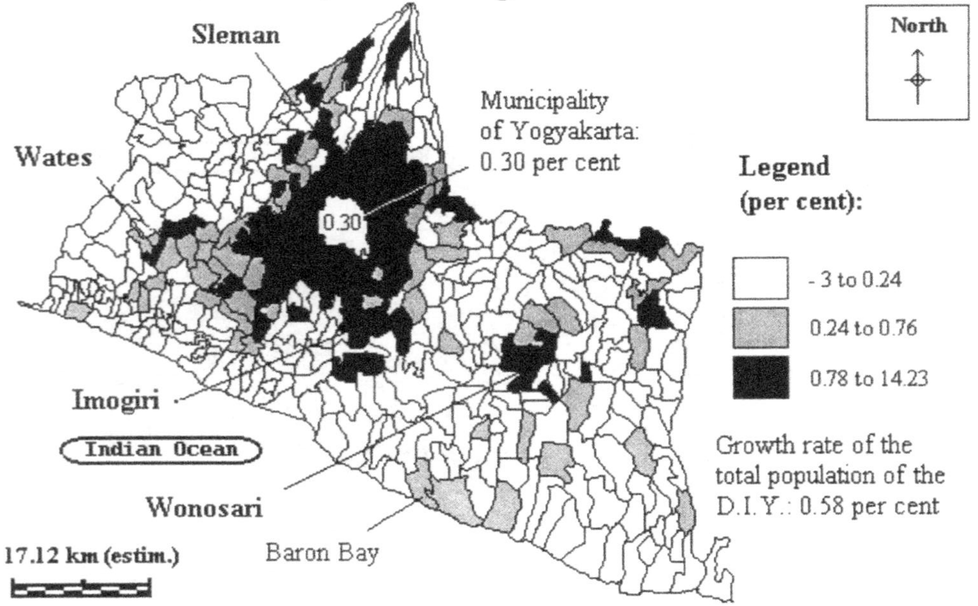

Legend
(per cent):

- 3 to 0.24

0.24 to 0.76

0.78 to 14.23

Growth rate of the
total population of the
D.I.Y.: 0.58 per cent

North

Municipality
of Yogyakarta:
0.30 per cent

Sleman

Wates

Imogiri

Indian Ocean

Wonosari

Baron Bay

17.12 km (estim.)

Source: For the numerical data: *Penduduk, Kabupaten Bantul, Hasil Sensus Penduduk 1990* (Yogyakarta: Provincial Statistical Office, February 1991 (and the same for, respectively, Kabupaten Sleman, Kabupaten Gunung Kidul, Kabupaten Kulon Progo and Koytamadya Yogyakarta); data mapped by the author (1994).

4 Outline of Economic Activities

- by Vincent Rotgé -

Economic Activities and Employment Expansion in the D.I.Y.

Increased Rate of Aggregate Gross Regional Domestic Product (GRDP)[1]

Per capita GRDP in the D.I.Y. was in 1990 slightly less than a fourth of the per capita non-oil GRDP in D.K.I. Jakarta (Rp. 653,000 in 1990 at current prices, that is about US$326 at the early 1990s exchange rate, or US$92.60 at the mid-December 1999 exchange rate). It was among the lowest in the country, being higher only than per capita non-oil GRDP of the provinces of Central Sulawesi, Lampung in Sumatra, the Nusa Tenggara Islands and Timor. Also, between 1983 and 1990 the annual rate of growth of per capita non-oil GRDP in the D.I.Y. (4.58 per cent) was lower than in the country as a whole (5.66 per cent), and lower than in the neighbouring provinces of Central and East Java (respectively 5.51 and 5.28 per cent), or Bali (7.32 per cent). However, as noted by Mubyarto, the fact that the population of the D.I.Y. was growing at a significantly slower pace (0.58 per cent annually between 1980 and 1990) than the GRDP during the same period bodes well for the future. It is also remarkable that per capita GRDP in the D.I.Y. grew faster in recent years in rural areas than in urban areas.[2]

Sectoral Share of GRDP

An examination of the sectoral distribution of activities[3] reveals that in 1986, agriculture ranked first, contributing to 29.15 per cent of the D.I.Y.'s total non-oil GRDP. Nonagricultural activities such as services (19.76 per cent) including public administration (14.33 per cent), social community services and others, were followed by trade-hotel-restaurant (19.13 per cent), by insurance-banking-business services-real estate/housing and cooperatives (8.8 per cent), by manufacturing (8.78 per cent), and lastly by transport and communication (7.53 per cent). As compared to the rest of the country, strong regional specializations in terms of non-oil GRDP appeared in livestock, real-estate and housing, public administration, defense, and particularly trade-hotel-restaurant (L.Q. Index: 200).[4] Manufacturing in the D.I.Y. was at a lower level in terms of non-oil GRDP than in the rest of Indonesia (L.Q. Index: 78.4).

Sectoral Share of Employment

An examination of the sectoral share of employment and of the distribution of increment in labour force reveals interesting findings.[5] In 1987, agriculture absorbed almost a half of the labour force (48.24 per cent), followed by services (18.6 per cent) and trade-hotel-restaurant (17.09 per cent). Manufacturing had the relatively low level of 11.59 per cent, which was however higher than in the rest of Indonesia. Thus, there was in 1987 no strong regional specialization in terms of employment as compared with the rest of Indonesia except for manufacturing (L.Q. Index as compared with Java: 113.18). The latter is surprising since in 1986 in terms of non-oil GRDP, manufacturing had the relatively low L.Q. Index of 78.4 (as compared to Java). It also suggested a lower productivity in manufacturing than in the rest of the country.

Indeed, if between 1971 and 1978, agriculture absorbed the largest share of labour in the region (as in the rest of Java and Indonesia), then between 1978 and 1987 the share of agriculture has sharply declined to such an extent that the agricultural sector actually lost labour during this period. This loss has been important (-199.6 per cent) since it has represented almost twice the total labour which has been created in the aggregate in the region for the same period in all sectors. In the meantime, the manufacturing sector also lost labour, even though of less significance than agriculture (-57.9 per cent). Thus between 1978 and 1987, trade-hotel-restaurant (+144.85 per cent) and especially other activities of the tertiary sector (+212.65 per cent) have absorbed the highest share of the total increase in labour in the D.I.Y. Nevertheless, this total increase has been very moderate, reflecting an increase of only 3.84 per cent between 1978 and 1987, whereas it has been of 19.84 per cent and of 35.96 per cent for Java and Indonesia respectively for the same period.

Figure 4.1   Sectoral Share of GRDP of the D.I.Y. in 1983 and 1990

1983

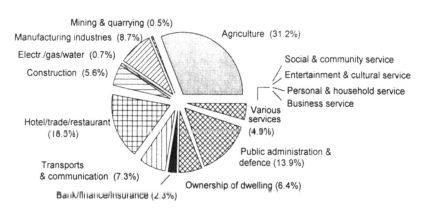

1990

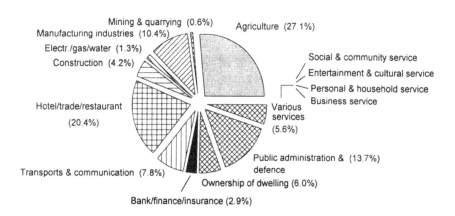

Source: Raw numerical data are from: *Pendapatan Regional Propinsi-Propinsi di Indonesia, menurut Lapangan Usaha* 1983-1990 (Jakarta: Indonesian Central Bureau of Statistics, 1992); Table 60.

Overview of the Regional Economy by Sectors

The Agricultural Sector

The Rice Subsector: The policy of modernization of agriculture in Indonesia shifted in the late 1960s from 'a policy of land redistribution to one of agricultural intensification'.[6] Also, emphasis has been given to rice-growing, and self-sufficiency in rice production has been set by the government as a main objective. At the time of its introduction, the intensification of agriculture rapidly proved successful in terms of productivity increase since, in general, it enabled in Java an increase from between 2 and 3 tons/ha to between 4 and 5 tons/ha (in D.I.Y. yields can reach today up to 6 tons/ha).[7] Throughout the 1970s and 1980s, intensification of rice-growing has been implemented through an integrated set of measures, in particular through the use of fertilizers and the establishment of credit facilities to farmers for the purchase of inputs, tools, and equipment. The intensification of cultures for rice growing has been achieved in parallel with the improvement or expansion of irrigation.

Table 4.1   Distribution of Dry and Wet Land in the D.I.Y., 1985, 1986, and 1990 (in ha)

	1985	1986	1990
Wet Land	63,458	63,766	62,234
1. Irrigated*	52,352	52,800	51,844
2. Rainfed	11,106	10,966	10,354
Dry Land	255,122	254,814	256,346

*   By means of irrigation canals.

Source: *Daerah Istimewa Yogyakarta dalam Angka* (Yogyakarta Special Region in Figures) (Yogyakarta: Provincial Statistical Office, 1986 and 1990).

However, in this region - and in the whole of Java - expansion of irrigation has proven less promising than in the preceding decades. This is mainly because irrigation in fertile lowland areas - *i.e.* in most parts of Bantul and Sleman Districts - is already good, whereas natural conditions make the expansion of irrigation difficult in Gunung Kidul and Kulon Progo, the two other Districts of the D.I.Y. (apart from Kotamadya Yogyakarta, *i.e.* the Municipal District or Municipality of Yogyakarta). As said earlier, the introduction of new technologies could, however, allow in the future better exploitation of the groundwater in the karstic part of Gunung Kidul District. Simultaneously, the objective of afforestation or reforestation in hilly and mountainous areas precludes the reclamation of some upper land for rainfed ricefields. Actually, the total area of wetland paddy (food crop) harvested in the D.I.Y. has only marginally increased in the 1980s, while the same area for dryland paddy has diminished.[8] Should we see here the effect of dry land being converted into wet land or much more likely being developed for construction especially in rapidly urbanizing areas? It is likely that, over time, the total area of wet ricefields will diminish under the effect of urban expansion and conversion of agricultural to residential, trade, or industrial uses.

Secondary Crops and Other Non-rice Subsectors[9]- Soybean and Maize: In the most fertile Districts, soybeans usually constitute an intermediary crop in between two annual rice crops. In areas where land is less fertile or where permanent irrigation cannot be provided, maize is grown. Gunung Kidul District was the main producing area of maize in the mid-1980s with almost half of the total regional production. Gunung Kidul District produces a very small share of the total regional rice output - due to the generally poor level of irrigation in that District. Maize, for instance, constitutes an alternative crop. The District of Gunung Kidul is also highly specialized in the production of soybeans.

Cassava and Peanuts: The District of Gunung Kidul produces a large share of the region's total output in cassava and peanuts.

Treecrops and Vegetables: Most vegetables grown in the D.I.Y. are potato, radish, cabbage, carrots, etc.[10] The region also produces chili, spinach, tomatoes, beans and shallots. It is most likely vegetable production could be raised in the region. The region produces, however, a large amount of papaya and a significant amount of oranges and bananas. In connection with afforestation programmes in uplands, the development of trees for fruit crops may well constitute an opportunity for the D.I.Y., particularly for the Districts of Kulon Progo and Gunung Kidul where treecrops remain relatively underdeveloped.

Cattle-raising: Except for sheep (more than 20 per cent) and goats (more than 30 per cent) which have slightly increased in number between 1950 and 1986 and pigs, which have doubled in the same period, livestock in the D.I.Y. has rather stagnated over the last decades.[11] Simultaneously, horses and buffaloes have diminished in number. The most likely explanation is that by and large, such animals as cows, buffaloes and horses require too much space in a region where densities are increasing, and where every inch has to be cultivated although this problem can be partly resolved by feeding the cattle through the 'zero-grazing' system described in Chapter 6.[12] There is very little or no grassland for grazing except in areas of the Districts of Gunung Kidul and Kulon Progo where human densities are among the lowest in the D.I.Y. This is why about half the cows and goats are raised in Gunung Kidul, with a fair share in Kulon Progo. Besides, the importance of horses and buffaloes has sharply declined since they are no longer needed for transportation. In parallel with the development of treecrops, the expansion of livestock- raising can constitute a very important alternative for the Districts of Gunung Kidul and Kulon Progo.

Gardens, Poultry-raising, Inland Fisheries: Gardens (*pekarangan*), where - apart from treecrops - bamboo, vegetables, etc., can be grown, where poultry and cattle can be raised and where fish can be bred in ponds, constitute a very important resource base. Maurer[13] has shown that in a village like Argodadi in Bantul, where soils are poor and stony, *pekarangan* can comprise a surprisingly large share of the total area of the village (half to substantially more, depending on the villages referred to by this author). The development of *pekarangan* can constitute an alternative to increase resources in villages which are located in Gunung Kidul or Kulon Progo. Alongside the development of gardens, fish-breeding can constitute another important alternative.

Sugar Cane: In principle, sugar cane plantations were dismantled after Independence to be converted into ricefields.[14] Growing sugar cane, indeed, is less profitable than growing rice for instance, even though domestic prices of sugar in Indonesia are still significantly above international prices. There is still a sugar refinery in the D.I.Y. to which lowland communities' farmers must periodically rent their land.

**Figure 4.2   The Apparent Stagnation of Husbandry in the D.I.Y.,
1950-1986: Change in Livestock** (in thousands of head, by
year)*

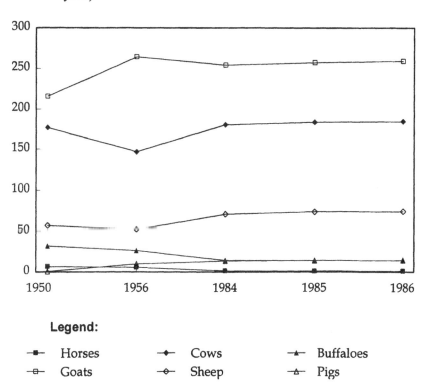

*   The degree of precision of some of the above data may be questionable.

Source: Vincent Rotgé, Septembre 1991; for 1950-1956: figures from Selosoemardjan,
Social Changes in Jogjakarta (Ithaca: Cornell University Press, 1962); for 1984-
1986: *Daerah Istimewa Yogyakarta dalam Angka* (Yogyakarta Special Region in
Figures) (Yogyakarta: Provincial Statistical Office, 1986).

Principal Nonagricultural Economic Activities

Public Sector: In 1988, civil servants represented about 3 per cent of the
population of the D.I.Y. (95,720 people). By comparison, for Indonesia the
share was about 2 per cent and for D.K.I. Jakarta 3.9 per cent.[15] Therefore
there was in the D.I.Y. a relative concentration of civil servants above the

national average. Also, Yogyakarta is a major national educational centre together with Jakarta and Bandung. Many universities and schools, public and private, are located in the capital of the region. This sector constitutes a very solid resource base for the region, as many students from all over Indonesia choose to come to study in Yogyakarta. Schools and universities, of which many are public, generate many local employment opportunities directly as well as indirectly in associated services (student housing, restaurants, trade services, etc.).

Trade/Hotel: Trade and hotel activities are growing relatively fast in the D.I.Y. These activities are benefiting from the buoyancy of tourism (both domestic and foreign) in the region. The presence of the airport and of many tourist spots, as well as the attraction of the city of Yogyakarta and the proximity of many archaeological and historic landmarks constitute a solid foundation for the tourist industry.

Manufacturing: The manufacturing base of the D.I.Y. is poor in terms of share of both national output,[16] and employment.[17] The fact that about 3 per cent of the total national labour force contributed to only a little more than one per cent of the national GDP in the second half of the 1980s, indicates a low level of productivity in manufacturing in the D.I.Y. An examination of the composition of the manufacturing sector showed at the beginning of the 1980s a very high level of concentration, in order of importance by share of value added, in the subsectors of weaving (28.3 per cent), dairy products (19.5 per cent) and sugar refining (18.35 per cent).[18] There is a need for diversification of industrial activities in the D.I.Y., in parallel with programmes for the promotion of agricultural subsectors that can provide input for agroprocessing industries.

Role of Rural-Urban Linkages in Employment Expansion in Hinterland Communities

Economic growth in the D.I.Y. has occurred relatively slowly in terms of increase of GRDP over the past decade, but on the other hand, the Special Region showed surprisingly good socioeconomic achievements in the early 1990s. For instance, child mortality has been drastically reduced and life expectancy was in 1990 the highest in the country (for both males and females). Moreover, as pointed out by Booth and Damanik,[19] the urban-rural gap in this region has narrowed in terms of various socioeconomic indicators, while it has widened in other areas of Java. In that sense, the type of development of this region in the past decade can be somewhat characterized by an important public investment in public amenities and services throughout the region, a high quality of life, but also a relatively slow rate of GRDP increase, and of industrialization as well as by a relatively moderate urbanization until the early 1980s.[20]

On the exports of the D.I.Y. to other regions of Indonesia are likely to be small. Its foreign exports account for almost nil as a percentage of GRDP.[21] By 1985, this situation had relegated the D.I.Y., together with West Nusa Tenggara, to the very lowest national position for the volume of foreign exports. In spite of a still low degree of diversification of the ooonomy and a heavy reliance on agriculture which itself still remains little diversified, two factors have shown very positive results:

- Sharp reduction in population increase through efficient family planning;
- Expansion of certain sectors of the economy such as trade and allied services, and the hotel and restaurant trade.

There are, however, clear indications that modernization of agriculture, and perhaps additional factors, have entailed strong labour displacement out of agriculture in the 1980s. Such a labour displacement has been responsible for a large share of extra-regional out-migrations. On the other hand, a positive factor is that surpluses have been created in agriculture, although those surpluses have benefited rural populations unevenly. Moreover, agriculture has been commercializing under a combination of factors. Regional economic assets such as a strong national position in the educational sector should be definitely consolidated, while attempts should be made to expand the stagnant regional industrial sector, perhaps partly by establishing linkages with its research institutions. But given the very large number of small-scale and cottage industries in the D.I.Y., options should be found to consolidate this sector - such as through subcontracting - or important labour displacement will take place from this sector also. Simultaneously, agricultural diversification should be actively pursued. Tourism, finally, can contribute to increasing the D.I.Y.'s GRDP and can impact favourably upon other sectors of the economy.

Conclusion

Whatever macroeconomic development processes for the D.I.Y. are going to be experienced, the issue of rural employment expansion must be carefully considered. A high quality of life and a narrowing rural-urban disparities gap are, indeed, remarkable assets that must also be consolidated and reinforced. In that respect, it is suggested that programmes for the regional development of Yogyakarta be developed in the context of rural-urban linkages. Rural-urban linkages, indeed, could constitute a possibility for decentralization in the region - particularly of job opportunities, either directly through commuting or subcontracting, or through jobs created in the villages by urban remittances, such as in the construction sector - and also reducing urban sprawl in the vicinity of the city of Yogyakarta. It is indeed desirable to seek the latter for environmental reasons (some of the most fertile agricultural land in the D.I.Y. is located in the vicinity of the city of Yogyakarta), and also, so as to help redistribute urban growth more evenly in the D.I.Y., *i.e.* in the secondary cities of the D.I.Y. which are mainly the capitals of Districts. A possible regional development strategy to achieve the latter would be through expanding employment in rural areas and increasing rural-urban linkages between secondary cities or small towns and their hinterland. In order to better assess ongoing changes and potentials in hinterland communities, and therefore design possible strategies, it is essential to analyse ongoing processes and collect a large set of relevant supporting data and information at the micro-level, though from a regional perspective. Towards that end, the results of fieldwork realized in five hinterland communities of the D.I.Y. are presented in Part II. In this part, the degree and nature of the interaction taking place between the studied communities and urban centres regarding employment, income generation, and broader socioeconomic changes are analysed in a regional and local context.

Notes

[1]   GRDP is the 'total market value of commodities (goods and services) produced (...)' in a region 'in a given period of time, usually a year. No allowance is made for capital consumption and depreciation; the use of market prices ensures the value of indirect taxes and subsidies are incorporated. The value of intermediate goods used in the

production of other goods is excluded, being incorporated in the market price of the final goods' (Clark, 1985). It must be further noted that GRDP includes 'all government expenditures on goods and services', see Samuelson and Nordhaus, 1989. GRDP can be expressed as a function of GRP (gross regional product) as follows: GRP - (Income derived from development outside the region) + (Profits generated by production within the region but due to extra-regional sources).

GRDP is very useful to assess sectoral shares in economic activities in Yogyakarta Special Region. On the other hand, the use of GRDP may lead to obliterating or underestimating an important aspect of the Special Region's economy, *i.e.* (1) the informal sector activities, and; (2) the remittances sent back to their family home by the out-migrants.

Considering the particular importance of the informal sector (self-consumed produce of the garden, mutifarious part-time activities, etc.) as well as the high level of extra-regional out-migration, it is therefore probable that income levels are not exactly reflected in GRDP figures. On the other hand, GRDP is a very useful indicator for showing trends for tradable goods and commodities of the so-called formal sector. Also, some studies show that services, formerly exchanged on a mutual assistance base (*gotong royong*) or paid in food, are now increasingly paid in cash - see Huisman and Stoffers, 1988.

2   BPS, 1992, Tables 3 and 4. See Mubyarto, 1993.

3   These data come from an unpublished UNCRD internal document compiled by Mike Douglass (1989) from various data published by the Indonesian Central Bureau of Statistics.

4   L.Q. (location quotient) index = an indicator of concentration which gives, as a percentage, the level of concentration within a district as compared to a district of reference. A value higher than 100 per cent means a concentration that is above that of the district of reference, while a value lower than 100 per cent means a lower concentration than in the district of reference.

5   *Statistik Indonesia 1988* (Jakarta: Indonesian Central Bureau of Statistics), Table 3.2.6.; *Statistik Indonesia 1980-81*, Table III.2.3.; *Statistik Indonesia 1975*, Table IV.2.1.; and calculations by Rotgé (1990).

6   Hardjono, 1987, p. 9.

7   In 1971; see Maurer, 1986.

8   *Daerah Istimewa Yogyakarta dalam Angka* (Yogyakarta Special Region in Figures) (Yogyakarta: Provincial Statistical Office, 1986), Table 5.2.1. (until 1986), and *Statistik Indonesia 1988* (Jakarta: Central Bureau of Statistics), Tables 5.1.3., 5.1.4. and 5.1.5. (for 1987-88) and 5.1.6.(for production in 1984-88). There are however very slight differences between regional and national statistics, and within national statistics themselves, for the totals which are not exactly the sum of the two parts. Totals here are obtained by adding the two parts (1982-86) or are taken from the abovementioned table 5.1.3.

9   *Daerah Istimewa Yogyakarta dalam Angka* (Yogyakarta Special Region in Figures) (Yogyakarta: Provincial Statistical Office, 1986), Tables 5.2.1. and 5.2.3. Attention:

national statistical data differ substantially from regional ones, see Tables 5.1.12. to 5.1.16. in *Statistik Indonesia* (Jakarta: Indonesian Central Bureau of Statistics, 1988).

10 Based on an unpublished compilation of data from BPS (Indonesian Central Bureau of Statistics) prepared by Mike Douglass (UNCRD, 1989).

11 Figures in Selosoemardjan, 1962, and in *Daerah Istimewa Yogyakarta dalam Angka* (Yogyakarta Special Region in Figures) (Yogyakarta: Provincial Statistical Office, 1986), various tables.

12 Selosoemardjan, *op. cit.*, p. 242.

13 On the village of Argodadi, see Maurer, *op. cit.*

14 See Selosoemardjan, *op. cit.*

15 Based on various statistical sources.

16 0.7 per cent of total manufacturing value added between 1975 and 1983 according to Hill, 1987, based on Indonesian Central Bureau of Statistics (1986); or 1.06 per cent of total G.D.P. in 1986 based on Indonesian Central Bureau of Statistics (1988).

17 3.01 per cent of the national labour force engaged in manufacturing; *ibid.*

18 Figures in Hill, *op. cit.*

19 In Hill (editor), 1989.

20 On quality of life, see UNESCO, 1983.

21 Central Bureau of Statistics, *Ekspor* (Jakarta, 1977 to 1985), cited in Hill, editor, *op. cit.*, p. 38.

Part II
Case Studies

5 The Communities in their Regional Context

- by Ryanto Rijanta -

Introduction

The studied communities have been purposely selected for their different agroecological settings, and in different locations with respect to their accessibility from and to urban centres - *viz.* the Municipality of Yogyakarta and capitals of Districts - Figure 5.1.

Pendowoharjo, Murtigading-Srigading (actually two villages whose territories are contiguous), and Maguwoharjo are situated in similar agroecological environments but at different distances from the city of Yogyakarta. Pendowoharjo and Murtigading-Srigading are located upon the lower slopes of Merapi Volcano in the District of Bantul, characterized by their extremely fertile wetland. Maguwoharjo in the District of Sleman, the most densely populated village among the five villages which were studied, is included in a suburb of Yogyakarta characterized by very fertile agricultural land and a well-developed irrigation network. Agricultural land in Putat - a village located in the District of Gunung Kidul - is much less fertile on average, due to unfavourable soil characteristics and limited irrigation especially on slopes.

Kembang is located in an intermediary piedmont plain west of the Progo River, between the lower slopes of the Merapi volcano and the Menoreh mountain range in the District of Kulon Progo.

Figure 5.1   Location of the Five Case Study Villages

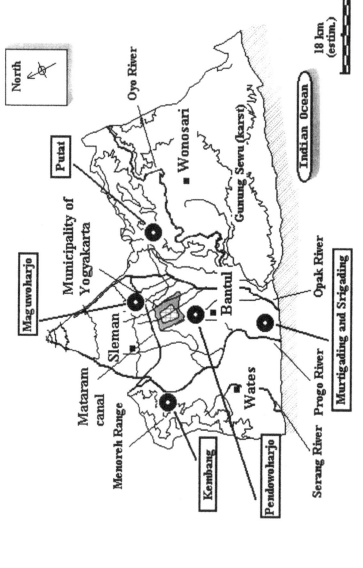

Source: Vincent Rotgé (December 1994).

The Villages of Murtigading-Srigading and Pendowoharjo in the Plain of Bantul

The villages of Murtigading-Srigading and Pendowoharjo lie in the central Plain of Bantul characterized by its highly fertile agricultural land and its excellent irrigation network. Murtigading-Srigading is located on the southern coast of Java, about 27 km away from Yogyakarta (road distance). Pendowoharjo lies 3 km north of the town of Bantul, and 15 km away from the centre of Yogyakarta to the south (10 km away from Yogyakarta's southern outskirts). All these lowland communities are, by and large, endowed with fertile agricultural land resources, but are also characterized by very high man-land ratios (especially in the case of the rather suburban village of Pendowoharjo) which have stimulated rural employment diversification.

In Pendowoharjo, improved connections to Yogyakarta have encouraged non-permanent population movements for a variety of social, economic, and educational purposes. Still, Murtigading-Srigading has benefited less from the increasing regional integration and rising rural-urban linkages than Pendowoharjo. Murtigading-Srigading, indeed, lies far away from Yogyakarta thereby prohibiting daily movement to the capital of the Province by means of bicycles. In comparison, economic activities carried out in Pendowoharjo are far more diversified, covering a wide spectrum of urban service activities.[1] Meanwhile, Murtigading-Srigading remains a very agrarian community in terms of dependency on agriculture for income and employment, land-use and patterns of human settlement.

The Suburban Community of Maguwoharjo

A steady trend for converting fertile agricultural land into other types of uses can be noticed near Maguwoharjo, following the construction of a ring road circling the city of Yogyakarta and passing through Maguwoharjo. Besides, Maguwoharjo is located near Yogyakarta airport. A number of private universities, companies of various size, hotels, and trading activities compete for land within the village and in its vicinity. A part of the village of Maguwoharjo was recently developed as a residential area accommodating the middle and upper class of white collar migrants working in urban areas, and competition for land has led to increasing land prices. It should be mentioned that some of the Maguwoharjo's agricultural land which is situated at a higher elevation must rely on rainfed irrigation during the dry season (May to October) as the water level of the main irrigation canal is lower than the land surface and as no pumping device is available. Naturally, the amount of rainfall during this period is also limited. When the wet season comes (November to May) the level of the main irrigation canal rises, and this land can be used for wetland farming.

The Piedmont and Upland Communities of Kembang and Putat

Kembang village is situated on a piedmont plain about 17 km west of Yogyakarta. Irrigation has been developed in the village in the past decades, through harnessing the water of the Progo River. Since 1990, a bridge connecting the village to Yogyakarta has been operating, enabling villagers to commute to Yogyakarta by bicycles or public buses. This has given a boost to local private companies in services and trade.

Putat is located about 15 km east of Yogyakarta and 15 km west of Wonosari. By and large, soils in Putat have both low water-retaining capacity and fertility. Irrigation is provided only in the lower parts of the village, in a strip of land located in the valley where spring water is available. Still, the introduction of various treecrops which were not indigenous to the region, and new farming knowledge have considerably improved farming activities and living conditions. A further factor contributing to poverty alleviation in this District is the long-established system of non-permanent migration (locally known as *beboro*), to secure urban employment. This system gains in momentum in the context of increasing inter- and intraregional integration as the local youth show a preference for white-collar urban jobs.

Table 5.1 Main Demographic Characteristics of the Studied Villages

	1	2	3		4	5	6
Village name	Size of the village's total population in 1990 and 1992	Size of sampled population in village	1980-1990 annual rate of population growth, in percentages		Total area of village in km² (1992)	Village density in inhabitants per km², in 1990 and 1992	Village male / female ratio in 1990
			Sub-district	Village			
Murtigading	a. 6,992			- 0.55	4.39	1,592	95.14
	b. 8,432	378 people	- 0.39			1,920	
Srigading	a. 8,212			- 0.34	7.57	1,084	95.01
	b. 9,437					1,246	
Pendowoharjo	a. 14,948	695 people	1.88	1.35	6.98	2,141	94.81
	b. 15,573					2,231	
Maguwoharjo	a. 21,491	703 people	4.50	3.54	15.01	1,431	101.79
	b. 19,482					1,298	
Putat	a. 3,131	519 people	- 0.02	0.70	7.17	436	98.16
	b. -					435	
Kembang	a. 4,119	521 people	0.12	- 0.18	5.11	806	92.84
	b. 4,932					965	

Annual rate of population growth in Indonesia (1980-1990): 1.97 per cent.

Table 5.1 (continued)

Notes:

- Murtigading-Srigading, Pendowoharjo, Maguwoharjo, Putat, and Kembang villages belong respectively to the Subdistricts of Sanden and Sewon (both are located in Bantul District), Dėpok (Sleman District), Patuk (Gunung Kidul District), and Nanggulan (Kulon Progo District).
- A total of 2,816 individuals was sampled in the aggregate.
- 'Male/female ratio': number of males divided by the number of females, calculated here for every one hundred females in the population.

Source: Table compiled by Vincent Rotgé. Data in Column 1: two types of figures are shown; figures on line (a) come from *Penduduk Kapubaten Bantul, Sleman, Gunung Kidul* and *Kulon Progo, Hasil Sensus Penduduk 1990* (Yogyakarta: Provincial Statistical Office, 1990), *i.e.* from the 1990 census. Figures on line (b) come from *Penduduk Kabupaten Bantul*, etc., *Tahun 1992* (Bantul, Sleman, Wonosari, Wates: Statistical Offices of each District, 1992); data from the decennial censuses are usually considered as more reliable than the annual series which are released by each District's statistical office. This is because the latter are based on individual registrations of residents with local offices, whereas census takers visit households at the occasion of decennial censuses. This explains discrepancies between these two types of figures which are shown here side by side; Column 2: primary data; Column 3: *Penduduk Kapubaten Bantul, Sleman, Gunung Kidul* and *Kulon Progo, Hasil Sensus Penduduk 1990*; Column 4: *Penduduk Kabupaten Bantul*, etc., *Tahun 1992*; Column 5: figures on line (a) were calculated by dividing the corresponding line (a) of Column 1 by the area given in Column 4. Figures on line (b) are calculated by taking line (b) of Column 1 instead, and come from *Penduduk Kabupaten Bantul*, etc., *Tahun 1992*; Column 6: *Penduduk Kapubaten Bantul, Sleman, Gunung Kidul* and *Kulon Progo, Hasil Sensus Penduduk 1990*; For the annual rate of population growth in Indonesia: calculations from *Penduduk Indonesia, Hasil Sensus Penduduk 1990* (Series L1) (Jakarta: Indonesian Central Bureau of Statistics, 1991) (courtesy of Ida Bagoes Mantra).

Growing Regional Integration

Growing regional integration, in particular in the D.I.Y., bears a considerable impact on rural development at the local level. This is remarkable in the employment patterns of the rural areas, agricultural production orientation and farming systems, as well as consumption patterns and life-style. For residents of communities located near Yogyakarta, the most common population movement is commuting, whereas circular and permanent migrations[2] are mostly undertaken by residents of communities located farther away. Migrations are common among the younger and more educated rural dwellers who show their preference for urban and white-collar employment. In turn, improvements in communications have made some rural communities more attractive for certain types of new settlers. Government employees are now more willing to accept posts in certain rural communities which, prior to the development of communications were very much isolated. This process has contributed to the socioeconomic development of rural communities.

Many villagers from the studied communities undertake nonfarm activities. Among them are activities related to the processing of local materials to be sold on the urban market as well as trading urban-produced goods. These latter activities are facilitated by improved regional transportation. Traders also benefit from improvements in communication since they use available public transportation to carry their goods. Such traders not infrequently play a dual role, selling as retailers urban goods in rural areas, and purchasing urban-made goods after selling the agricultural products.

Some of the studied communities are strongly linked to the urban areas, not only in terms of flow of labour but also of commodities. Traders of Kembang, for instance, sell agricultural products such as bananas, banana leaves, jack fruit, coconuts, and cassava to Yogyakarta regularly. Pick-ups rented by these traders regularly enter Yogyakarta in the evening so as to avoid traffic congestion. These products are sold in the market directly to the urban consumers or to retail traders. The recent construction of a bridge connecting Kembang directly to Yogyakarta has been favourable for such activities, resulting in cheaper transportation costs and also reducing the possibility of loss due to delays in accessing the urban market as some agricultural products, especially some fruits, are very vulnerable to delays in marketing.

Putat and Pendowoharjo are characterized by the importance of small-scale industry products to sell in Yogyakarta, and Wonosari and Bantul towns. In Putat where wood is produced, a number of small-scale industries are related to wood crafts and charcoal-making. These products are brought to Yogyakarta regularly by local traders. Traders from the urban areas will come to pick up such products as wooden masks and other types of wood crafts. Putat did not establish trading relations only with Yogyakarta, but also, for instance, with the town of Klaten (located east of the D.I.Y. in the Province of Central Java) and Jakarta. Traders from this village regularly send cattle at least once every two months to Jakarta's markets. In Pendowoharjo, as in other communities of the Plain of Bantul, perishable products are produced by small-scale industries, including mainly processed food catering for local as well as urban markets. Products from lowland communitites marketed in Yogyakarta are mainly *tempe* (fermented soybean cakes) and tofu (*tahu*), rice chips and *emping melinjo* chips (made out of the ground fruits of a tree which is common in the Javanese gardens). These small-scale industries are labour-intensive and utilize female rather than male labour.

Conclusion

The studied communities have experienced important physical and socioeconomic transformations. Easy access from urban to rural areas (and *vice-versa*) have played an essential role in this process as well as in local socioeconomic development. Among the most important such changes are the diversification of rural economic structures towards the increased rate of non-agricultural employment and income (both *in situ* and outside the area); the abandonment of traditional labour relations;[3] the diversification of agriculture which, increasingly, includes non-staple and urban-oriented crops; improved regional communications; and a shift in the consumption pattern towards an increased consumption of goods of an urban origin. This, with the improvement of communications, has enhanced the role played by rural-urban linkages in the process of regional integration.

Notes

1   See the study of the communities of the Plain of Bantul by Vincent Rotgé – Chapter 6.

2   Editor's note: A 'commuting' refers to an absence from home for more than six hours but less than twenty-four hours (commuters do not sleep at their destination). 'Circular migration' refers to an absence of at least twenty-four hours from home for an indefinite duration but with the intention of returning in the future. 'Permanent migration' refers to an absence with the intention of never coming back except for short-term visits such as on the occasion of holidays (*Lebaran*, for instance). Other definitions exist, but they are not used in this study.

3   Changes in the orientations of agricultural production and in farming systems taking place in the studied communities can be detected in particular through changing labour relations. Traditional labour relations were established on the basis of a system of mutual-help and reciprocation of labour among groups of farmers, whereby each farmer assisted other farmers of the same group, receiving some food allowance. This system - called *sambat-sinambat* - has been widely replaced in the studied communities by a new one, whereby a contractual system involving two parties placed on an unequal footing - employees versus employers - and whereby the provision of services is paid in cash.

6 Lowland Communities of the Plain of Bantul

- by Vincent Rotgé -

Introduction

The purpose of these case studies is to assess the nature and level of rural-urban linkages in hinterland villages of the D.I.Y. and how such linkages may offer employment alternatives and additional sources of income to local residents. Two main case study areas were selected. Both are located in the central lowland area of the Plain of Bantul where rice constitutes the main crop - Figure 5.1. Land in this plain is particularly fertile since rice yields are usually above five tons per hectare in irrigated areas (5.4 and 5.9 tons per hectare and per crop in 1986 and 1990 respectively, for the whole District of Bantul).

Included in Pendowoharjo village, the hamlet of Bandung was selected, a short distance from the centre of Yogyakarta (15 km) in the south, and 3 km north of the town of Bantul. Included in the second case study area (Murtigading-Srigading), a second hamlet, Piring was chosen further south from the first research village, near the coast and 27 km away from Yogyakarta - Figure 6.1. Both hamlets are located near, but not along, the Yogyakarta-Bantul-Samas Beach road.

Moreover, in both Murtigading-Srigading and Pendowoharjo villages, an additional sample of households was selected along the main road and located a few kilometres away from the main case study area - Figures 6.2 and 6.3. The purpose of this was to compare socioeconomic characteristics of the population in areas located within the transit corridor with those of the population living within the hinterland a few kilometres away from the transit corridor. Additional samples located within transit corridors were the hamlet of Celep located near the inland hamlet of Piring in Murtigading-Srigading, and the hamlet of Karanggondang-Cepit (actually two contiguous hamlets) located near the inland hamlet of Bandung in Pendowoharjo - Figures 6.2 and 6.3. Both Karanggondang-Cepit and Celep are located along the road linking Yogyakarta to Samas Beach via the town of Bantul, but at different distances from Yogyakarta.

In all studied communities of the Plain of Bantul, households were sampled areawise. Total sample was two hundred and thirty-eight households or about one thousand and eighty-two individuals. Main samples were chosen in hinterland communities, *i.e.* Piring (seventy-eight households) and Bandung (one hundred and nineteen households). Furthermore, smaller samples were chosen along the Yogyakarta-Samas Beach road in Celep (sixteen households) and Karanggondang-Cepit (twenty-five households). The purpose of including samples along the Yogyakarta-Samas Beach road was to make comparisons possible with the corresponding hinterland samples in terms of the communities' socioeconomic characteristics and structure of employment. The size of the latter sample is rather small, but it comprises most of the households which are located along the road in, respectively, Celep and Karanggondang-Cepit.

Throughout Chapter 6, the emphasis is laid on the villages of the Plain of Bantul, *i.e.* Murtigading-Srigading and Pendowoharjo. But Maguwoharjo village is often referred to. Though the latter is not located in the Plain of Bantul (but in the neighbouring Sleman District), it is also a lowland community. Besides, Maguwoharjo lies in a rapidly urbanizing transit corridor near Yogyakarta. Therefore, Maguwoharjo shares commonalities with Murtigading-Srigading and Pendowoharjo, and it is useful to make cross-comparisons. However, Maguwoharjo could not be studied in as much depth as the other communities analysed in this book. That is why many remarks regarding Maguwoharjo are drawn from field observations. See Figure 6.4 for hamlets studied.

Figure 6.1   Location of the Villages of Pendowoharjo, Murtigading-Srigading in the Plain of Bantul, and of Maguwoharjo

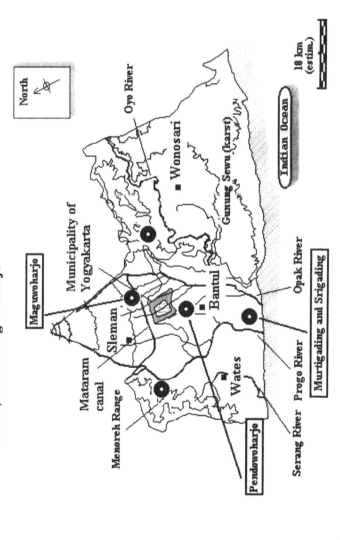

Note: Maguwoharjo is located in Sleman Regency.

Source: Vincent Rotgé (December 1994).

Figure 6.2   Map of the Area Covered by the Study in Murtigading-Srigading (hamlets of Piring and Celep)

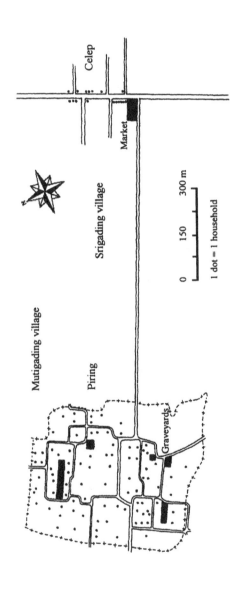

Notes: - The layout of the road running from Piring to Celep is approximate.
    - Murtigading and Srigading are two villages whose territories touch each other. The studied area spreads over the two villages.
    - The boundaries of Murtigading and Srigading villages and of Celep hamlet are not shown on this map.

Source: Vincent Rotgé (1992; based on the village map: the map of Piring hamlet, courtesy of Haruo Kuroyanagi; and; field survey).

Figure 6.3 **Map of the Area Covered by the Study in the Village of Pendowoharjo** (hamlets of Bandung and Karanggondang-Cepit)

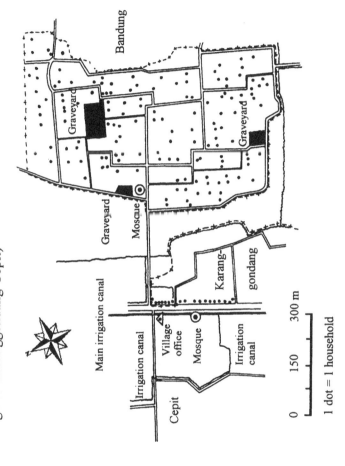

Source: Vincent Rotgé (1992; based on Bandung map and field survey).

Figure 6.4   Map of the Area Covered by the Study in the Village of Maguwoharjo
(hamlets of Ringinsari, Nanggulan, Kradenan and Gondangan)

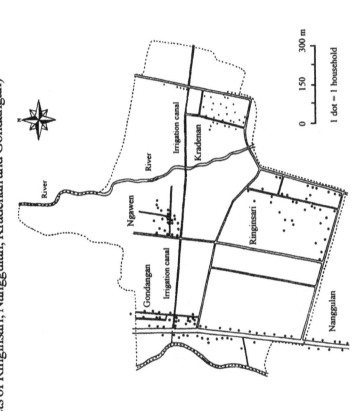

Source: Laboratory of Cartography, Faculty of Geography, Gadjah Mada University; adapted by Vincent Rotgé (1992).

Basic Differences among the Studied Communities

Important differences exist in terms of geographical and locational characteristics between Murtigading-Srigading and Pendowoharjo which can be summarized as follows.

(1) *Access to the city of Yogyakarta*: Pendowoharjo and Murtigading-Srigading are, respectively, about 20 and 40 minutes by bus from Yogyakarta's southern outskirts.

(2) *Different strategic locations along the Yogyakarta-Samas Beach road*: The section of the road located between Pendowoharjo and Bantul is busier in terms of traffic than the section located between Bantul and Murtigading-Srigading. The bulk of the traffic originating from Yogyakarta, indeed, diverges in the town of Bantul towards Wates and beyond, towards the southwestern coast of Java - Figure 3.2, where, however, the road connecting the town of Bantul to Samas Beach through the village of Murtigading-Srigading is not shown.

(3) *Differences in land-use and population densities*: As a matter of fact, although both Murtigading-Srigading and Pendowoharjo villages were still considered rural by the criteria set by the Indonesian Central Bureau of Statistics in 1980, they were both reclassified urban in 1990 - Figure 3.1. However, strong contrasts exist between the villages in terms of average farmland size.

Types of Land-use and Tenure, and of Sharecropping Arrangements

In the studied communities of the Plain of Bantul, the most common cultivation pattern is three crops a year including two rice crops and one intermediary crop or *palawija:* usually soybeans, or maize for lower quality soils or irrigation. Other main crops are treecrops grown in the home-compound or *pekarangan* (garden). Maurer's study[1] of four villages of the D.I.Y. based on fieldwork implemented in the 1970s showed that the economy of the villages which are located in certain areas peripheral to the best irrigated and most fertile lowland areas rely more on the products of the *pekarangan*. This observation holds true in the case of the hamlets of Bandung and Piring in the Plain of Bantul. While most households supplement their income by selling fruits of the *pekarangan* in Piring, very few actually do so in Bandung. Accordingly, average size of *sawah* (ricefield irrigated by canals or wet field as opposed to rainfed ricefield or dry land) in Pendowoharjo is much lower than in Murtigading-Srigading while the opposite observation can be drawn for *pekarangan*. Moreover, the average size of household-owned and -operated *sawah* in Bandung is only 0.0975 ha against 0.2316 ha in Piring - Table 6.1, d. and b. Population densities are higher in Bandung as can be expected from a more suburban community. At the same time, the average size of wet fields (*sawah*) which are owner-cultivated, is about twice as large in Piring as in Bantul, while especially in Bandung, a large percentage of households have no access to land – *ibid.* and Figure 6.5. Nevertheless, in the two villages, an important share of cultivated land is not owner-operated but rented out (average size of plots is 0.45 ha), or sharecropped (average size of plot is about 0.19 ha).

By far the most common system of sharecropping is the so-called *maro* system, whereby the cultivator and the landlord receive half of the crop and pay half of the costs each. This system has been traditionally in use in wetland areas of the D.I.Y. In contrast, the so-called *mertelu* sharecropping arrangement, whereby a third of the harvest goes to the cultivator and the rest to the landlord and the 'cultivator pays all costs',[2] is virtually absent from these wetland communities.[3] Permanent irrigation is widely available in Pendowoharjo and Murtigading-Srigading, though some slight differences exist in terms of quantity of water accessible to paddy fields which relate to their distance from main irrigation canals. Such differences are reflected by differentials in land price: the closer a wet field (*sawah*) to the main irrigation canals, the more expensive it is. Also, as a consequence of the widespread availaility of permanent irrigation, virtually no dry land (*tegal*), apart from the gardens, is cultivated in these lowland villages.

Some villagers raise poultry or fish in fishponds and also raise cattle. In the latter case, shortage of space for grazing is bypassed by practicing 'zero-grazing' whereby the fodder is collected from the surrounding areas. Nevertheless, the severe shortage of capital available to local farmers is responsible for the low development of cattle-raising in Piring as compared with Bandung, in spite of a higher space availability in Piring where home-compounds are less densely built. In all of these communities, vegetable growing was still very poorly developed at the time of the fieldwork in the early 1990s. Worth noting is that though a majority of residents in the communities lying within the transit corridor are not engaged in farming as a primary activity, some households own wet fields whose sizes are far above average even for wet fields located in the hinterland (see the case of Karanggondang-Cepit - Table 6.1e). This

Figure 6.5 **Households with Access to *Sawah*,
i.e. Irrigated Land, Including All Types of Land
Tenure and of Sharecropping Arrangements,*
by Studied Communities of the Plain
of Bantul** (percentages)

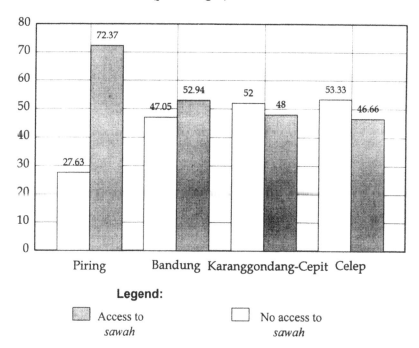

* All types of land tenure and of sharecropping arrangements through which access
to land is possible are included in this table. Refer to Table 6.1 and to glossary for
types of land tenure and of sharecropping arrangements.

Source: Primary data processed by Vincent Rotgé using SAS (fieldwork implemented in
1991).

suggests that the probability that the more suburban and high-density the
community, the more fragmented is the agricultural land, does not preclude
the existence of some very large landowners in communities lying within
the transit corridors. Also, landownership as a factor of social disparities
does not vanish in some urbanizing areas where fast sectoral shifts are
taking place in the employment structure. Some of the large landowners
rent out some or all of their land or have it sharecropped, while
simultaneously undertaking some nonfarm[4] activity.

Sectoral Share of Employment

For the purpose of this study, the economic activities of all household members in selected communities were recorded, being divided among primary, secondary, and tertiary activities that were ranked on the basis of their respective annual levels of return. An examination of the sectoral share of employment for primary activities shows the following - Figure 6.6.

(1) Slightly more than half of the work force above 15-years-old undertakes primary activity in the agricultural sector in Piring (54 per cent). The share of agriculture drops significantly in Karanggondang-Cepit (9.8 per cent), Celep (14.7 per cent), followed by Bandung (23 per cent). However, some individuals undertaking primary activities outside agriculture in urban areas, may possibly cultivate land in the evenings, frequently as a subsistence activity.

(2) As the share of agriculture in employment decreases in more suburban or transit-corridor communities, the share of services and trade, and then of clerical and educational employment rises. The role of the construction subsector is especially significant. Only in Piring (a nonsuburban and non-transit-corridor community), the share of settled services and trade remains very low being less than the share of petty nonfarm jobs undertaken on a daily basis (10.8 per cent); intermediate and upper clerical workers-teachers-managers (10.1 per cent); and peddling services and trade (8.6 per cent).

(3) The employment shift from agriculture to trade and services is much more accentuated in the transit-corridor than in hinterland communities even when the former are located a short distance from the latter. Settled trade and services are especially well-represented in Celep which is a local trade centre where a market is held once every Javanese week (comprising of five days).

(4) In none of the communities does industry absorb more than 10 per cent of the work force, as far as primary activities are concerned. However, it appears that the share of industry increases as the distance from Yogyakarta (subsequently the main road) decreases.

In short, three main points need emphasizing:

(1) In all communities there are considerable and varied nonfarm activities for primary employment. Only in Piring which is located in a sort of *cul-de-sac* and relatively far from Yogyakarta does agriculture remain the dominant sector of primary activity.
(2) There is a clear relationship between locational characteristics and the level of importance of nonfarm activities for primary employment.
(3) There is a high level of development of trade and services and a relatively low level of development of industry for primary employment among all studied communities of the Plain of Bantul.

A further important observation is that, though a very high share of nonfarm primary employment can be found in some communities, it does not mean that agricultural activities have virtually disappeared from the rural dwellers' choice. In reality, a large number of residents have no access to land, and some residents, who do have access to land, are engaged in agriculture as a secondary activity.

Table 6.1   Wetland Farming (wet fields or *sawah*): Size of Land in m² Tenanted by Households, by Types of Land Tenure and Sharecropping Arrangements

a. All Studied Communities of the Plain of Bantul

	Number of occurrences	Minimum size (in m²)	Maximum size (in m²)	Average (in m²)	Standard deviation
The household owns the land which is sharecropped:					
Sharecropping system *maro**	18	200	7,000	1,899	1,862
*mertelu**	2	1,100	70,000	35,500	48,720
The household owns the land which is not sharecropped:					
The household operates the land:	78	100	32,900	1,790	3,920
The household rents out the land:	14	3	10,000	4,547	4,322
The land is mortgaged by the household:					
The mortgagee operates the land:	1	2,800	2,800	2,800	.
The household operates the land:	1	770	770	770	.
The household does not own, but operates, the land which is sharecropped:					
Sharecropping system *maro**	19	500	3,000	1,101	595
The household leases the land:	16	150	3,000	784	651
The land is mortgaged to the household:					
The household operates the land:	2	10,000	10,000	10,000	.
Other land tenure system:	13	500	10,500	4,740	4,455

Table 6.1 (continued)

b. Piring

	Number of occurrences	Minimum size (in m²)	Maximum size (in m²)	Average (in m²)	Standard deviation
The household owns the land which is sharecropped: Sharecropping system: *maro**	7	235	7,000	2,534	2,424
The household owns the land which is not sharecropped: The household operates the land:	33	23	32,900	2,316	5,671
The household rents out the land:	4	1,260	10,000	3,753	4,178
The land is mortgaged by the household: The mortgagee operates the land:	1	2,800	2,800	2,800	.
The household operates the land:	1	770	770	770	.
The household does not own, but operates, the land which is sharecropped: Sharecropping system: *maro**	9	700	1,820	1,213	408
The household leases the land: The household operates the land:	10	150	1,400	624	342
The land is mortgaged to the household: The household operates the land:	1	10,000	10,000	10,000	.
Other land tenure system:	5	630	10,000	4,864	4,679

Table 6.1 (continued)

c. Celep

	Number of occurences	Minimum size (in m²)	Maximum size (in m²)	Average (in m²)	Standard deviation
The household owns the land which is sharecropped:					
Sharecropping system: *maro**	1	1,000	1,000	1,000	.
The household owns the land which is not sharecropped:					
The household operates the land:	4	980	9,800	3,570	4,179
The household rents out the land:	2	4,200	10,000	7,100	4,101
The household leases the land:					
The household operates the land:	1	700	700	700	.
Other land tenure system:	1	10,000	10,000	10,000	.

Table 6.1 (continued)

d. Bandung

	Number of occurrences	Minimum size (in m²)	Maximum size (in m²)	Average (in m²)	Standard deviation
The household owns the land which is sharecropped: Sharecropping system:					
maro*	5	350	5,000	1,830	1,829
mertelu*	1	70,000	70,000	70,000	
The household owns the land which is not sharecropped: The household operates the land:	37	100	5,000	975	850
The household rents out the land:	7	3	10,000	3,493	4,482
The household does not own, but operates, the land which is sharecropped: Sharecropping system: maro*	10	500	3,000	1,000	732
The household leases the land: The household operates the land:	4	500	800	650	129
Other land tenure system:	7	500	10,500	3,900	4,433

Table 6.1 (continued)

e. Karanggondang–Cepit

	Number of occurrences	Minimum size (in m²)	Maximum size (in m²)	Average (in m²)	Standard deviation
Sharecropping system:					
*maro**	5	200	3,000	1,260	1,076
*mertelu**	1	1,100	1,100	1,100	.
The household owns the land which is sharecropped:					
The household operates the land:	4	670	6,000	3,143	2,754
The household rents out the land:	1	10,000	10,000	10,000	.
The household owns the land which is not sharecropped:					
The household leases the land:	1	3,000	3,000	3,000	.
The land is mortgaged to the household:					
The household operates the land:	1	10,000	10,000	10,000	.

*   See glossary

Source: Primary data processed by Vincent Rotgé using SAS (fieldwork implemented in 1991).

Figure 6.6   **Per Cent of Workers Engaged in a Primary Activity, by Sector and Community of Origin, for Workers above 15 Years of Age; All Communities of the Plain of Bantul***

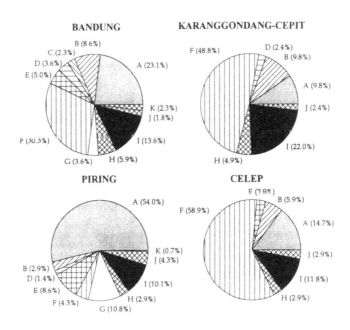

Legend:

A: Agriculture

B: Cottage/Small-scale industry**
C: Medium/Intermediate/Large industry***
D: Transport
E: Peddling services and trade
F: Non-peddling services and trade****

G: Daily workers outside
   agriculture/Scavengers
H: Lower clericals
I: Administrators/Managers
J: Other non-trade services
K: Domestic servants

*   Figures in parentheses represent number of occurrences.

**   Cottage/household industry = labour-force of up to 5 workers; and small-scale industry = labour-force of 5 to 19 workers.

***   Medium-scale industry = labour-force of 20 to 49 workers; intermediate large industry = labour-force of 50 to 100 workers; and Large industry = labour-force of more than 100 workers.

**** Including construction workers.

Source: Primary data processed by Vincent Rotgé using SAS (fieldwork implemented in 1991); M. Takahashi assisted for the graphic display of data.

Levels of Household Income by Communities

Total income of a household of n working members (Yhh) was constructed thus:

$$Yhh = \sum_{i=1}^{n} (Y1i + Y2i + Y3i) + \sum_{j=4}^{10} Yj$$

where,

$Y1i$ = net annual return from primary activity of household member i (including cash equivalent of rice allowance to civil servants),

$Y2i$ = net annual return from secondary activity of household member i (including cash equivalent of rice allowance to civil servants),

$Y3i$ = net annual return from tertiary activity of household member i (including cash equivalent of rice allowance to civil servants),

$Y4$ = net annual return from renting household-owned land (except land rented out to sugar cane factory),

$Y5$ = annual amount of remittances received by the household,

$Y6$ = net annual return from treecrops,

$Y7$ = net annual return from livestock products (including fish, cattle, poultry); when primary, secondary or tertiary activity of one household member are related to livestock raising, $Y7$ is adjusted in order to prevent double-counting,

$Y8$ = net annual return from renting land to sugar cane factory,

$Y9$ = annual cash equivalent of rice used for home consumption (food) which is grown by the household; $Y9$ is adjusted in order to prevent double-counting,

$Y10$ = other household non-agricultural income (net).

Per capita income was then calculated as the total household income divided by the number of members within the household. In other words, it is the household income calculated for each household as shown above, then weighted by the number of members that each household comprises. Taxes not being taken into account, the formula was constructed before taxes. Average per capita income was calculated for each community. The highest average was found to be in the transit-corridor community which lies the closest to Yogyakarta (Karanggondang-Cepit), the second highest in the transit-corridor community situated further away from Yogyakarta (Celep), the third highest in the hinterland community which is the closest to Yogyakarta (Bandung). The lowest average was found in Piring which is the hinterland community that is the farthest from Yogyakarta - Table 6.2 and Figure 6.7. In short, the more suburban and the closer to a transit corridor the community, the higher the aggregate average household income.

Figure 6.7   **Average Level of Annual Per Capita Income,* by Studied Communities of the Plain of Bantul** (in million of *rupiah*)

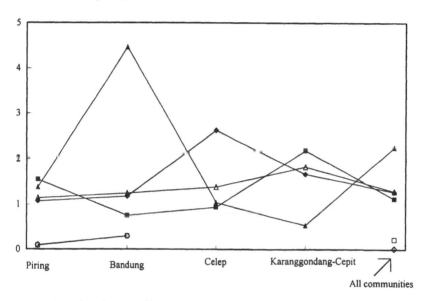

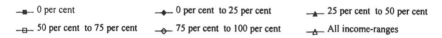

Legend: **Per cent of income derived from agriculture**

—■— 0 per cent   —♦— 0 per cent to 25 per cent   —▲— 25 per cent to 50 per cent

—□— 50 per cent to 75 per cent   —◇— 75 per cent to 100 per cent   —△— All income-ranges

*   Per capita income is defined here as the total household income weighted by the number of members within each household.

Source: Primary data processed by Vincent Rotgé using SAS (fieldwork implemented in 1991); M. Takahashi assisted for the graphic display of data.

Share of Household Income Derived from Agriculture

Furthermore, households were categorized according to the degree to which their income was derived from agriculture - Table 6.2 and Figure 6.8.[5] This showed that a very high percentage of households in transit-corridor communities are fully independent of the agricultural sector for their income (40 per cent of all households in Karanggondang-Cepit and

56 per cent in Celep derive no income at all from agriculture). Such a figure is also high in Bandung (37 per cent).

Though about one out of five households earns nothing from agriculture in Piring, a very large share of households have diversified their income such that they derive income from both agricultural and nonfarm activities undertaken simultaneously. In that sense, in many cases agriculture has become a part-time activity whose purpose is to secure food products for subsistence. It is not infrequent in the case of such households that a small wet field is cultivated by an elderly person or by the head of household in the evenings after having completed a primary wage-earning activity. In fact, about 68 per cent of all households in Piring derive up to 50 per cent of their total income from agriculture. It is interesting that those households in Piring which derive no income from agriculture have a higher income than other households. This is not surprising as those few households probably include a large share of civil servants who are urban commuters. Also, one can observe that in all communities those households that are still the most dependent on agriculture for their incomes are among the poorest. Hence, it can be said that those households which are better off are those which have succeeded in diversifying their income sources to include nonfarm activities. Such an observation, however, only holds true in the aggregate. In reality, large disparities exist among nonfarm activities in terms of return levels that cannot be further studied here for lack of space.

To sum up, diversification of income and of primary employment, and the level of average household income are higher in communities which are closer to Yogyakarta and to transit corridors bordering regional or national roads. Nevertheless, it should be mentioned that the studied communities of the Plain of Bantul had been selected for sugar cane cultivation the year preceding the implementation of the fieldwork. This occurs once every five years. During such periods, wet fields are rented out by the Madukismo sugar company which carries out the cultivation work. As a result, household members probably have to find alternative employment while household income might be below its normal average when rice is cultivated. It is therefore possible that the abovementioned figures indicate levels of involvement in and return from agriculture which would be somewhat lower than under normal circumstances when sugar cane is not being grown.

Table 6.2   **Income Groups* by Per Cent of Total Household Income Derived from Agriculture, by Studied Communities of the Plain of Bantul**

	0 per cent from agriculture			0^+ to 25^- per cent from agriculture			25^+ to 50^- per cent from agriculture		
	No. of cases	Row per cent	Annual average income (*Rupiah*)	No. of cases	Row per cent	Annual average income (*Rupiah*)	No. of cases	Row per cent	Annual average income (*Rupiah*)
Piring	15	20.83	1,543,350	30	41.67	1,072,660	19	26.39	1,379,570
Celep	9	56.25	942,370	4	25	2,626,500	3	18.75	1,042,890
Bandung	42	37.17	757,390	52	46.02	1,178,960	10	8.85	4,467,640
Karang-gondang - Cepit	10	40	2,188,020	14	56	1,665,540	1	4	547,120
All	76	33.63	1,123,060	100	44.25	1,273,100	33	14.60	2,259,520

	50^+ to 75^- per cent from agriculture			75^+ to 100^- per cent from agriculture			All households		
	No. of Cases	Row per cent	Annual average income (*Rupiah*)	No. of cases	Row per cent	Annual average income (*Rupiah*)	No. of cases	Row per cent	Annual average income (*Rupiah*)
Piring	1	1.39	8,750	7	9.72	100,010	72	# 100	1,142,790
Celep	-	-	-	-	-	-	16	# 100	1,382,250
Bandung	3	2.65	297,290	6	5.31	296,880	113	# 100	1,243,060
Karang-gondang - Cepit -	-	-	-	-	-	-	25	# 100	1,829,800
All	4	1.77	225,150	13	5,75	190,880	226	# 100	1,285,880

*   Total household income weighted by the number of members within household, as defined above.

Source: Primary data processed by Vincent Rotgé using SAS (fieldwork implemented in 1992).

Figure 6.8   **Income Groups by Per Cent of Total Household Income[6] Derived from Agriculture, by Studied Communities of the Plain of Bantul**

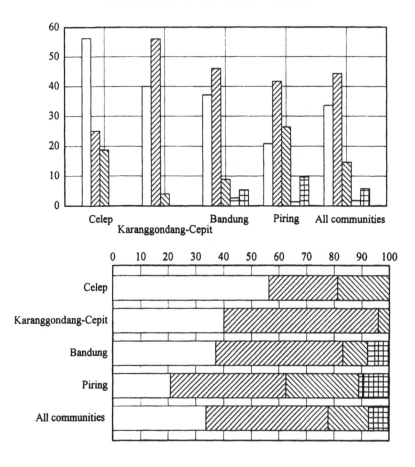

Legend: **Per cent of income derived from agriculture**

☐ 0 per cent from agriculture   ▨ 0 per cent to 25 per cent from agric.

▧ 25 per cent to 50 per cent from agric.   ▤ 50 per cent to 75 per cent from agric.

▦ 75 per cent to 100 per cent from agric.

Source: Primary data processed by Vincent Rotgé using SAS (fieldwork implemented in 1991); M. Takahashi assisted for the graphic display of data.

The Role of Commuting[7] in Employment Diversification

Though, as shown above, a substantial share of the work force is primarily employed in nonfarm activities and also a substantial share of total income generated in the studied areas is derived from nonfarm activities, the development level of locally-based nonfarm activities which are not retail trading, remains conspicuously low in all studied communities. As a result, many villagers who are involved in nonfarm activities, must commute to urban areas for work. Thus, about 28 per cent of all workers above 15 years old in Bandung, but only 5 per cent in Piring, commute in direct relation to their primary activity to Yogyakarta, the town of Bantul or other nearby communities. A very small number of commuters work in the city of Purworejo in Central Java. The most common destination for 'rural-urban' commuters from all communities remains Yogyakarta though the town of Bantul actually lies closer to all the studied communities. In all communities, commuters are mostly engaged in the following primary activities - Figure 6.9.

- non-peddling services and trades (including construction);
- administration (including the civil service), management;
- lower-level clerical positions, and;
- other services.

Varying Degrees of Out-migration among Communities

An examination of the ratios of permanent migrants[8] to local population reveals that relatively more out-migrants have left Piring than Bandung, especially in the previous decade. An important share of permanent out-migrants migrate within the D.I.Y. (34.71 per cent in Piring and 43.80 per cent in Bandung). It is likely that many among the latter move to homes of their husband/wife after marrying. Remarkably few among these intraregional out-migrants went to Yogyakarta. But, a large share of out-migrants from the studied communities of the Plain of Bantul went to D.K.I. Jakarta and other large urban centres of the northern coast of Java or other in-migration regions such as Riau or Lampung Provinces in Sumatra - Table 6.4. Also, an important share of out-migrants migrated within the D.I.Y., usually within the Regency of Bantul where they were born. When relatives of permanent out-migrants were interviewed about their motives for outmigrating, the usual answer was 'searching for a job

Figure 6.9   Per Cent of Commuters in Primary Activity, by Sector of Primary Activity and Community of Residence, for Commuters above 15 Years of Age*

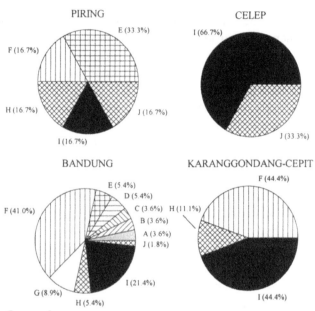

Legend:

A: Agriculture

B: Cottage/Small-scale industry**
C: Medium/Intermediate/Large industry***
D: Transport
E: Peddling services and trade
F: Non-peddling services and trade****

G: Daily workers outside agriculture/Scavengers
H: Lower clericals
I: Administrators/Managers
J: Other non-trade services
K: Domestic servants

Notes:

*   Figures in parentheses represent number of occurrences
**   Cottage/household industry = labour-force of up to 5 workers; and small-scale industry = labour-force of 5 to 19 workers
***   Medium-scale industry = labour-force of 20 to 49 workers; intermediate large industry = labour-force of 50 to 100 workers; and Large industry = labour-force of more than 100 workers
****   Including construction workers

Source: Primary data processed by Vincent Rotgé using SAS (fieldwork implemented in 1991); M. Takahashi assisted for the graphic display of data.

Table 6.3 **Per Cent of Permanent Migrants from the Villages of Murtigading-Srigading and Pendowoharjo, by Year of Departure, 1971-1991**

```
71|*************
72|********************
73|************************
74|****************************
75|**************************************
76|***********************
77|*********
78|*****************************************
79|****
80|********************************************************
81|*******************************************
82|**************************************************
83|*********************
84|***********************************
85|*******************************************************
86|************************************
87|***************************************************
88|*******************************************************************************
89|************************************************************
90|***********************************************
91|****

   ----+----+----+----+----+----+----+----+----+----+----+
       1    2    3    4    5    6    7    8    9    10   11

                          PERCENTAGE
```

Source: Primary data processed by Vincent Rotgé using SAS (fieldwork implemented in 1991).

Table 6.4   **Province of Current Residence of Permanent Out-migrants, by Community of Origin**

Province   **Community of Origin**

	Piring		Celep		Bandung		Karang-gondang – Cepit		All locations	
	Per cent		Per cent		Per cent		Per cent		Per cent	
East Java	2.48	(3)	.		2.48	(3)	.		2.24	(6)
Central Java	9.92	(12)	11	(2)	5.78	(7)	12.5	(1)	8.21	(22)
West Java	11.57	(14)	.		0.83	(1)	.		5.6	(15)
DKI Jakarta	24.79	(30)	16.66	(3)	9.92	(12)	.		16.79	(45)
North Sumatra	.		11	(2)	.		.		0.75	(2)
Jambi	0.83	(1)	.		.		.		0.37	(1)
Riau	4.96	(6)	.		2.48	(3)	.		3.36	(9)
West Sumatra	0.83	(1)	.		0.83	(1)	.		0.75	(2)
South Sumatra	0.83	(1)	.		4.96	(6)	.		2.61	(7)
Lampung	1.65	(2)	.		4.13	(5)	.		2.61	(7)
Aceh	.		.		0.83	(1)	.		0.37	(1)
Bengkulu	.		5.55	(1)	1.65	(2)	.		1.12	(3)
West	.		.		0.83	(1)	.		0.37	(1)
East	0.83	(1)	.		.		.		0.37	(1)
Central	.		.		0.83	(1)	.		0.37	(1)
Maluku	0.83	(1)	.		1.65	(2)	.		1.12	(3)
Bali	.		5.55	(1)	.		.		0.37	(1)
West Nusa Tenggara	0.83	(1)	.		.		.		0.37	(1)
East Nusa Tenggara	2.48	(3)	.		.		.		1.12	(3)
Yogyakarta Special Region	34.71	(42)	44.44	(8)	43.80	(53)	75	(6)	40.67	(109)
Not available	2.48	(3)	5.55	(1)	19.01	(23)	12.5	(1)	10.45	(28)
All locations	100 (121)		100 (18)		100 (121)		100 (8)		(268)	

*   Figures in parentheses represent the number of migrants.

Source: Primary data processed by Vincent Rotgé using SAS (fieldwork implemented in 1991).

outside the D.I.Y.'. It was reported also that a significant share of permanent out-migrants left in order to try their luck and search for a job without having, at the time of departure, any definite job prospect in the intended destination. Nevertheless, a significant percentage of out-migrants did have a job offer at the intended destination at the time of departure. This must be related to the frequent phenomenon of chain migrations when an elder brother or other relative finds a job for his younger relatives at home. Chain migration is probably responsible for the appearance of specialized networks among relatives and friends originating from the same community. For instance, a number of out-migrants from the Piring area now hold a variety of positions in a small private clinic in Bekasi near Jakarta which is owned by a native doctor. The latter example is particularly significant for the size of employment that it generated for native workers and the relatively high level of some of the latter's skill and specialization in the health sector. As an example of chain migration it should not be regarded as exceptional.

Strong out-migration levels should be related to employment shift that occurred in the past two decades and the paucity of full-time employment in the regional agricultural sector (the latter is reflected by regional labour statistics in the past two decades). Such levels of permanent out-migration translate into male population deficits in the age groups between 20 and 39 years-old, as can be seen in age pyramids and the low male/female ratios in the 25-34 years-old age group. This pattern is more accentuated in Piring than in Bandung. At the same time, the percentage of commuters as a share of the total population is higher in Bandung than in Piring. Nonetheless, demographic deficits in the male population belonging to the 20-29 years-old age groups were clearly less acute in transit-corridor communities. This should be related to the broader diversification of locally-based economic activities in such communities.

In short, this study shows clearly that permanent out-migration levels are lower, particularly among young adult males, when employment opportunities generated by the urban sector but also other activities which are related to urbanization of neighbouring rural areas (such as the construction subsector and the service sector) can be found at shorter rural-urban commuting distances from the place of residence. In Piring, which is neither situated at a short commuting distance from Yogyakarta nor close to fast urbanizing areas, where the service sector and a booming construction subsector are rapidly expanding, permanent migration constitutes one among the few alternatives left for young people entering the labour market. A primary reason for a very significant share of permanent migrants to leave Piring relates to securing a position at the place of destination, while in Bandung a majority of permanent migrants migrate after marrying a non-resident whose place of residence they will move to. At the same time, it does not seem that the lower population densities in Piring, compared to more suburban communities, is sufficient in the current situation of low agricultural diversification to alleviate such a trend towards out-migration. But the paucity of local employment opportunities that causes out-migration does not necessarily mean that all potential for expanding locally-based activities has been exhausted. The latter is true for agricultural diversification which remained at a conspicuously low level when the fieldwork was implemented (1991-1992).

Concomitant In-migration Movements in Urbanizing Corridors: Are Transit Corridors a Frontier?

Varying degrees of rural out-migration among villages located in different agroecological areas and geographical locations should not obliterate the fact that smaller in-migration movements are simultaneously taking place in transit-corridor communities. One could expect to find in transit corridors native rural farmers or their children who have shifted their main activity from agriculture to locally-based nonfarm activities. On the contrary, a significant number of residents of transit corridors can be found who are not native rural residents, but recently-settled residents who are in their 30s and who often originate from Yogyakarta. It is probable that the lower demographic deficit for young male adults, noticeable in age pyramids of transit-corridor communities, is to some extent related to the latter phenomenon. Similar studies undertaken by us in 1992 in Maguwoharjo village near Yogyakarta airport where the recent building of a new ring-road circling Yogyakarta has triggered important development changes, tend to show that recent settlers of urban origin would not be unusual in suburban transit-corridor communities which have recently been affected by the development of communications. Main reported reasons for settlers from urban areas moving into transit corridors in Maguwoharjo and, to a lesser extent, in Pendowoharjo and Murtigading-Srigading, may be summarized thus:

Table 6.5 Age Pyramids of the Studied Communities of the Plain of Bantul

a. All Studied Communities of the Plain of Bantul - including transit-corridor and hinterland communities of Murtigading-Srigading and Pendowoharjo villages

MALES				Age	FEMALES			
(1)	(2)	(3)	(4)		(1)	(2)	(3)	(4)
17	17	3.24	3.24	75-	16	16	2.88	2.88
14	31	2.67	5.92	70-74	15	31	2.70	5.59
16	47	3.05	8.97	65-69	12	43	2.16	7.75
28	75	5.34	14.31	60-64	19	62	3.42	11.17
18	93	3.44	17.75	55-59	20	82	3.60	14.77
23	116	4.39	22.14	50-54	25	107	4.50	19.28
26	142	4.96	27.10	45-49	24	131	4.32	23.60
32	174	6.11	33.21	40-44	31	162	5.59	29.19
39	213	7.44	40.65	35-39	32	194	5.77	34.95
28	241	5.34	45.99	30-34	51	245	9.19	44.14
41	282	7.82	53.82	25-29	51	296	9.19	53.33
49	331	9.35	63.17	20-24	50	346	9.01	62.34
58	389	11.07	74.24	15-19	63	409	11.35	73.69
56	445	10.69	84.92	10-14	62	471	11.17	84.86
54	499	10.31	95.23	05-09	49	520	8.83	93.69
25	524	4.77	100.00	00-04	35	555	6.31	100.00

Males Percentage axis: 18 14 11 7 4

Females Percentage axis: 4 7 11 14

Note: Column (1): Number of cases; Column (2): Cumulative number of cases; Column (3): Per cent of the total population; Column (4): Cumulative per cent of the total population.

Source: Primary data processed by Vincent Rotgé using SAS (fieldwork implemented in 1991).

Table 6.5 (continued)

b. Piring: non-transit-corridor community far from Yogyakarta

	MALES			Age	FEMALES			
(1)	(2)	(3)	(4)		(1)	(2)	(3)	(4)
0	0	0.00	0.00	95–	2	2	1.12	1.12
1	1	0.72	0.72	90–94	1	3	0.56	1.69
1	2	0.72	1.45	85–89	1	4	0.56	2.25
2	4	1.45	2.90	80–84	4	8	2.25	4.49
2	6	1.45	4.35	75–79	2	10	1.12	5.62
3	9	2.17	6.52	70–74	3	13	1.69	7.30
4	13	2.90	9.42	65–69	5	18	2.81	10.11
10	23	7.25	16.67	60–64	5	23	2.81	12.92
9	32	6.52	23.19	55–59	8	31	4.49	17.42
8	40	5.80	28.99	50–54	7	38	3.93	21.35
8	48	5.80	34.78	45–49	12	50	6.74	28.09
13	61	9.42	44.20	40–44	13	63	7.30	35.39
8	69	5.80	50.00	35–39	9	72	5.06	40.45
7	76	5.07	55.07	30–34	10	82	5.62	46.07
6	82	4.35	59.42	25–29	12	94	6.74	52.81
11	93	7.97	67.39	20–24	13	107	7.30	60.11
16	109	11.59	78.99	15–19	20	127	11.24	71.35
21	130	15.22	94.20	10–14	21	148	11.80	83.15
6	136	4.35	98.55	05–09	21	169	11.80	94.94
2	138	1.45	100.00	00–04	9	178	5.06	100.00

Percentage — 14 11 7 4 ‖ 4 7 11 14 — Percentage

Note: Column (1): Number of cases; Column (2): Cumulative number of cases; Column (3): Per cent of the total population; Column (4): Cumulative per cent of the total population.

Source: Primary data processed by Vincent Rotgé using SAS (fieldwork implemented in 1991).

Table 6.5 (continued)

c.   Celep: transit-corridor community far from Yogyakarta and close to Piring

Population pyramid (MALES left, FEMALES right) by Age and Percentage.

MALES (1)	(2)	(3)	(4)	Age	FEMALES (1)	(2)	(3)	(4)
1	1	3.33	3.33	70-74	2	2	6.06	6.06
1	2	3.33	6.67	65-69	2	4	6.06	12.12
3	5	10.00	16.67	60-64	3	7	9.09	21.21
1	6	3.33	20.00	55-59	0	7	0.00	21.21
0	6	0.00	20.00	50-54	1	8	3.03	24.24
1	7	3.33	23.33	45-49	0	8	0.00	24.24
2	9	6.67	30.00	40-44	2	10	6.06	30.30
1	10	3.33	33.33	35-39	0	10	0.00	30.30
4	14	13.33	46.67	30-34	5	15	15.15	45.45
4	18	13.33	60.00	25-29	6	21	18.18	63.64
3	21	10.00	70.00	20-24	3	24	9.09	72.73
2	23	6.67	76.67	15-19	1	25	3.03	75.76
1	24	3.33	80.00	10-14	1	26	3.03	78.79
5	29	16.67	96.67	05-09	2	28	6.06	84.85
1	30	3.33	100.00	00-04	5	33	15.15	100.00

Percentage (Males): 18 14 11 7 4
Percentage (Females): 4 7 11 14 18

Note: Column (1): Number of cases; Column (2): Cumulative number of cases; Column (3): Per cent of the total population; Column (4): Cumulative per cent of the total population.

Source: Primary data processed by Vincent Rotgé using SAS (fieldwork implemented in 1991).

Table 6.5 (continued)

d. Bandung: non-transit-corridor community at a short commuting distance from Yogyakarta

	MALES			Age	FEMALES			
(1)	(2)	(3)	(4)		(1)	(2)	(3)	(4)
1	1	0.34	0.34	90-94	1	1	0.38	0.38
2	3	0.67	1.01	85-89	0	1	0.00	0.38
6	9	2.02	3.03	80-84	1	2	0.38	0.75
2	11	0.67	3.70	75-79	4	6	1.51	2.26
10	21	3.37	7.07	70-74	9	15	3.40	5.66
9	30	3.03	10.10	65-69	5	20	1.89	7.55
15	45	5.05	15.15	60-64	8	28	3.02	10.57
7	52	2.36	17.51	55-59	11	39	4.15	14.72
12	64	4.04	21.55	50-54	15	54	5.66	20.38
13	77	4.38	25.93	45-49	5	59	1.89	22.26
15	92	5.05	30.98	40-44	14	73	5.28	27.55
26	118	8.75	39.73	35-39	19	92	7.17	34.72
14	132	4.71	44.44	30-34	30	122	11.32	46.04
24	156	8.08	52.53	25-29	24	146	9.06	55.09
25	181	8.42	60.94	20-24	25	171	9.43	64.53
29	210	9.76	70.71	15-19	23	194	8.68	73.21
28	238	9.43	80.13	10-14	34	228	12.83	86.04
38	276	12.79	92.93	05-09	21	249	7.92	93.96
21	297	7.07	100.00	00-04	16	265	6.04	100.00

MALES Percentage: 14 11 7 4   18   FEMALES Percentage: 4 7 11 14

Note: Column (1): Number of cases; Column (2): Cumulative number of cases; Column (3): Per cent of the total population; Column (4): Cumulative per cent of the total population.

Source: Primary data processed by Vincent Rotgé using SAS (fieldwork implemented in 1991).

Table 6.5 (continued)

e. Karanggondang-Cepit: transit-corridor community at a short commuting distance from Yogyakarta and close to Bandung

	MALES			Age		FEMALES		
(1)	(2)	(3)	(4)		(1)	(2)	(3)	(4)
0	0	0.00	0.00	70-74	1	1	1.27	1.27
2	2	3.39	3.39	65-69	0	1	0.00	1.27
0	2	0.00	3.39	60-64	3	4	3.80	5.06
1	3	1.69	5.08	55-59	1	5	1.27	6.33
3	6	5.08	10.17	50-54	2	7	2.53	8.86
4	10	6.78	16.95	45-49	7	14	8.86	17.72
2	12	3.39	20.34	40-44	2	16	2.53	20.25
4	16	6.78	27.12	35-39	4	20	5.06	25.32
3	19	5.08	32.20	30-34	6	26	7.59	32.91
7	26	11.86	44.07	25-29	9	35	11.39	44.30
10	36	16.95	61.02	20-24	9	44	11.39	55.70
11	47	18.64	79.66	15-19	19	63	24.05	79.75
6	53	10.17	89.83	10-14	6	69	7.59	87.34
5	58	8.47	98.31	05-09	5	74	6.33	93.67
1	59	1.69	100.00	00-04	5	79	6.33	100.00

Note: Column (1): Number of cases; Column (2): Cumulative number of cases; Column (3): Per cent of the total population; Column (4): Cumulative per cent of the total population.

Source: Primary data processed by Vincent Rotgé using SAS (fieldwork implemented in 1991).

Push factors:
- increasing urban competition in the retailing (in the case of retail sellers or even hawkers such as ambulant sellers of a soup called *bakso*);
- rise in urban land prices while suburban land is still relatively cheap;

Pull factors:
- improvement of regional transportation reducing former locational disadvantages of suburban communities for the setting up of trade or small- and medium-scale industries; the latter is especially true along main roads including the newly-built ring road where the urbanization process has been boosted.

Even more fundamental reasons relate to the growth of a locally-based market in retailing activity and the building up of easier regional road connections that enable large urban wholesale traders to deliver commodities to remote retailers. Additional economic opportunities (furniture-making and certain agroprocessing activities) are generated by the development of a regional demand and market and by the simultaneous appearance of a set of positive factors such as increasing price differentials in land prices between urban and rural areas, reduced transportation costs and time (due to better road connections and the competition in public transport), as well as the establishment of more basic infrastructure such as telephone lines needed by the few enterprises which are more competitive. All in all, trade-off advantages are responsible for young entrepreneurs settling down in the transit corridors of Pendowoharjo or Maguwoharjo (this latter village located near Yogyakarta and Yogyakarta airport was studied less in depth and more qualitatively than the others).

Lastly, differences exist in the nature of activities being undertaken in transit corridors as a function of location which can be differentiated among consumption-oriented and production-oriented ones. Thus, industries are more scarce in Celep or even Karanggondang-Cepit, which are more remote from existing urban centres and where the largest share of nonfarm activities is comprised of retailing activity. Celep, for instance, which is remote from existing urban centres, typically functions as a small retail centre catering for local residents' consumption needs. In contrast, transit corridors which are more easily accessible from Yogyakarta, are more prone to welcome services and industries which are outwardly oriented, and more widely integrated in the array of backward and forward linkages making up the regional economy. In the village of Maguwoharjo which is attractively located along the newly-built ring road, subbranches of companies, which have main branches located either in Yogyakarta or in its close suburbs, have blossomed over the past few years.

Uneven Competition between Newcomers and Native Residents?

A fundamental question remains which relates to the capacity of native rural dwellers (*penduduk asli*, *i.e.* the original population) to compete with new settlers (*pendatang*, *i.e.* the 'newcomers') on an equal footing in seizing new economic opportunities, especially in transit corridors where the shift to nonfarm activities is the most rapid. One can indeed question the extent to which the *in situ* sectoral shift in such areas is accompanied by a commensurate shift in the activities of native residents from agriculture to nonfarm activities. In particular, the noticeably important share of non-native settlers of urban origin in the Karanggondang-Cepit and Celep transit-corridor communities should lead us to assume that native rural residents may be somewhat in a less favourable position than new urban settlers to seize new economic nonfarm opportunities. Furthermore, it appears from interviews that a noticeable share of small-scale industries in Magowoharjo's transit corridor are operated by the children of owners of similar enterprises located somewhere else in the D.I.Y., usually in urban or even more suburban communities. The former often established their enterprise with the initial financial assistance of their parents without which their project would probably not have been realizable. The possibility of uneven access to newly emerging economic opportunities, between natives and new settlers, raises important implications.

Such a process could, indeed, lead to a situation whereby native rural residents find themselves losing the competition for emerging markets to newcomers, and as a result, possibly become restricted to poorer productive economic activities. They may even be obliged to leave their community of residence through the process of land resale. Should the following fact recorded in Karanggondang-Cepit be considered a precursor? A few farmers owning land along the road in this community sell it and use the profit thereby generated to purchase a larger plot of land in an area more distant from the road where land prices are lower.

This question definitely needs to be further addressed. Thus far, one can hypothesize from observations that lack of capital on the part of native rural residents plays a very important role in preventing them from taking advantage of rising economic opportunities in transit corridors.

A cultural factor is also probably responsible for inhibiting native rural residents from taking out bank loans as to do so would usually mean their using land certificates as collateral with the risk of losing it if the venture fails. Land is traditionally too important in an agrarian cultural context for farmers to take such a risk, while native residents usually lack a sufficient degree of knowledge about emerging opportunities, management practices, technology, supply sources, and marketing opportunities that can be expected from urban entrepreneurs who not infrequently are already experienced and are sometimes expanding their main activity through opening up suburban branches.

Lastly, a few recent settlers were identified in Pendowoharjo and especially Maguwoharjo who can be identified as 'suburbanites'. They do not necessarily settle in the transit corridors. They are urban workers who took the decision to move to suburban communities where they established their home. Such a phenomenon, which again needs to be further studied is probably still at an early stage in communities such as Bandung and Maguwoharjo and apparently includes only a few households. However, it is particularly remarkable as it could be interpreted as the start of a possible process of suburbanization with possible considerable longer-term implications upon rural socioeconomic change. Some such possible changes are described below in the more limited context of changing transportation costs:[9]

> [...An] impact of reduced transportation costs is upon local residents in an isolated rural area. The effects of the changing transport costs on individuals employed in rural locations is not so clear. Some of the rural labor force will now find it to their advantage to commute to the urban center because of the reduced transport cost. If we assume that the cost of living in rural compared to urban areas is lower, then we might expect lower wage rates for rural workers. *If we assume that the net effects of changing transportation cost is a movement of urban dwellers to rural areas, then the new urban settlers will bid away the land and residential homes from the local inhabitants, forcing them to move further away from the newly formed transit routes.* [emphasis added]

But reasons for newcomers to settle in suburban communities should not be related only to economic factors such as trade-off advantages integrating land prices and reduced transportation costs and time. Considering the adequate level of local infrastructural development of the studied communities (in terms of health, *puskesmas*, *i.e.* local dispensaries, primary education, and other more basic facilities), for some young couples with a combined income and education level usually above the local average, a suburban residence may offer a better living environment where children can be more easily raised. This is especially true when the husband, usually working in the tertiary sector, owns a motor vehicle and therefore, does not need to resort to tedious and time-consuming commuting by public transport which often necessitates transfers. This process should be perceived as a side-effect of the emergence of an urban middle-class whose aspects of life-style, such as income sources, working schedule, housing, consumption patterns, and perhaps time availability for social events, etc., diverge to some extent from those of native residents. In that sense, it means the intermingling of the hinterland's native residents who are increasingly influenced by urbanization through commuting, television as well as *in situ* changes, with former urban dwellers now moving to the suburbs.

Nature of Rural-urban Linkages in the Communities of the Plain of Bantul

Macro-scale Differences among Studied Communities as a Function of their Distance from Yogyakarta

Differences were found between the hamlets of Piring and Bandung, which relate to their different levels of proximity to Yogyakarta, which themselves translate into different levels of rural-urban linkages. Overall size of agricultural plots is significantly higher in Piring which is further away from Yogyakarta, than in Bandung which is located only 15 km away from the city's centre (road distance; see Tables 6.1b and 6.1d). This can be explained by lower man-land ratios in the area for both geographical and historical reasons. Piring is located near the coast in a sort of *cul-de-sac* in terms of road system. It can also be explained by an important out-migration of youth whose chances of finding a job are very limited. In Piring, though their effects were detectable and positive, rural-urban commuting was not very frequent and was undertaken almost exclusively by members of the public service.

Contrasting with the above, the overall size of agricultural plots is much lower in Bandung which is located at a short distance from the town of Bantul and at a short commuting distance from Yogyakarta. In most instances, farming in Bandung is not an adequate source of income due to the small size of agricultural plots. Also, many inhabitants are landless due, in particular, to the mechanisms of inheritance.

Gardens and trees are much more sparse in Bandung than in Piring and population and building concentration is significantly higher in Bandung. Inhabitants have therefore very clearly responded to the latter in *diversifying* their activities away from agriculture. Thus, there is a very marked shift from agriculture to nonfarm activities which are not dependent on land or, to some extent, because they require limited space and because land is expensive and limited in supply in transit corridors (the supply of land where buildings can be legally erected is restricted by a regulatory system which forbids the conversion of irrigated agricultural land into dry land), can be undertaken in the main dwelling building (*toko* - *i.e.* retail shops sometimes specialized in a certain category of goods, which are larger than the grocery shops called *warung* which sometimes include a small restaurant - *warung*, small workshops, etc.).

A very large share of such nonfarm activities are associated either with urbanization (including such activities as construction; *mandor* - recruiters or foremen hiring construction labourers; land dealers; construction material dealers and producers), or with trades usually oriented towards the urban sector (including *makelar* - intermediate traders purchasing goods from small rural producers to resell them at regional markets or in town; settled traders in the markets of Niten or Yogyakarta; makers of *tempe* - a sort of fermented soybean cake, who sell their products in Yoyakarta; workers at markets; and cattle dealers who resell their fattened animals in Yogyakarta or Bantul, for example). Further nonfarming activities consist in the urban public service category, primarily in Yogyakarta but also in Bantul, or in cottage industry activities which are subcontracted from Yogyakarta including such activities as bag making and silverware craft. It is interesting to note that virtually no cases of wage workers from the urban private sector could be found, whereas many cases of urban civil servants were identified. In both studied communities, when they existed, linkages with Yogyakarta were found to clearly outdo linkages with any other secondary urban centres that proved

Figure 6.10   Surroundings of the Studied Lowland Villages

1.   Construction of apartment buildings near Maguwoharjo.

2.   Making bricks by using the clay from paddy fields.

Source: Photographs by the author.

very limited. The latter proved true for the nearby town of Bantul in particular, confirming the relatively weak regional growth role of this secondary town.

Micro-scale Differences among Communities as a Function of their Distance from Regional Roads

In the transit-corridor communities, shops and small-scale industries are rapidly developing. Types of buildings, built with more modern construction materials and techniques, are different from those within the hinterland a few kilometers away. Far fewer farmers (primary occupation) can be recorded in these communities, whereas in sharp contrast the share of farmers of the total population still remains very high at a short distance within the hinterland. The share of residents in the transit-corridor communities not undertaking farming at all, even as a secondary activity, is very high as noted earlier in this study. As a matter of fact, concentration of shopowners, civil servants and people involved in small-scale industries is very high within transit-corridor communities. Furthermore, life-styles and consumption behaviour appear substantially different from within the hinterland, in spite of a frequently short distance between the two environments. This cannot be related only to differentials in purchasing power between the two environments. In short, the general atmosphere and socioeconomic and physical characteristics of both the Celep and Karanggondang-Cepit transit-corridor communities are of an almost urban nature. Also, a contrast in urbanization levels, including in levels of development of nonfarm activities, that can be detected at the micro-level between areas located immediately next to the main road and those located a few kilometres further away from the main road, can also be detected to a different extent and at the macro-level between, on the one hand, communities located closer to Yogyakarta (*i.e.* Bandung and Karanggondang-Cepit) or along important arterial roads and, on the other hand communities located further away from Yogyakarta (*i.e.* Celep and Piring) including those communities which are deadlocked within the intra- and extraregional transportation network.

Nature of Rural-urban Linkages

Mobility of Labour and Urban Remittances - Direct, Indirect and Dynamic Effects: Rural-urban linkages appear to constitute one very important factor contributing to the process of labour expansion and development in the hinterland of the D.I.Y. The effects of increasing rural-urban linkages upon local employment generation can be characterized thus:

- Access to urban jobs by rural residents through daily commuting.
- A significant share of urban remittances is spent by commuters on the rural construction subsector since urban commuters have houses built. This, in turn, is conducive to the creation of locally-based rural jobs.
- Urban remittances, in particular generated by commuting, deeply impact on the rural economy. However, urban jobs which are accessible to commuters remain mainly confined to: (a) governmental and other public jobs in education, health, etc.; (b) trading jobs in urban markets; (c) jobs in the urban construction subsector for private housing while the rural construction subsector is very active also; (d) other jobs of the urban informal sector: rickshaw drivers, etc. – Figure 6.9.
- Even though the growth role of tourism is important in Yogyakarta and around a few regional landmarks, it is remarkable that the influence of tourism upon the economy of the two villages that were studied seems today particularly weak. In particular, according to the result of field interviews with small rural middlemen who are not involved in larger-scale urban construction works, most of the construction work which is generated by tourism in Yogyakarta (construction of hotels, etc.) would be often dominated by construction workers coming from the poorest areas of the D.I.Y., *i.e.* mainly from areas in Gunung Kidul District.
- The main reason for the latter seems to be that workers from the poorest parts of the D.I.Y. - upland communities and those which are remote from urban areas - would accept very low wages which would be almost always the rule in the case of large construction works where manpower is generally recruited through middlemen. In other instances, manpower reportedly comes from the place of origin of middlemen, and is recruited through a system of local clientelism.
- Urban remittances from sources other than commuting. A few households including international migrants to Singapore or the Middle-East were found in the hamlet which is the most distant from Yogyakarta. This hamlet shows many cases of permanent migrations to major cities located outside the D.I.Y., mainly Jakarta - Table 6.4.

The possibility of easy commuting - in particular, not requiring a motor vehicle - to Yogyakarta, reduces the need for finding extraregional employment on the part of rural dwellers.

Capital Mobility and Formation: There is a steady demand for retailing commodities and consumer goods in the countryside and, simultaneously, still low competition on the supply side due to the paucity of capital available to rural residents. Many rural residents cannot afford to acquire capital goods or the shops and merchandise which are necessary for initiating small-scale industries or initiating or expanding trading activities. Instead, a noticeable number of urban traders who are attracted by the low competition in the countryside and sometimes also pushed out from the city by increasing competition in the urban trading sector, are moving to the countryside, purchasing land and opening retail shops along the main roads. The strategy of the latter is clearly to capture the effective demand for consumer goods in the still largely untapped rural market, and to a probably much lesser extent for consumer durables.

The movement of urban traders to the countryside can be seen as a form of urban investment in rural economic activities, since in such a case the geographical origin of investors in rural trade is urban.

The effective demand for consumer goods in the countryside of the D.I.Y. stems from (a) an increasingly monetized rural economy; and (b) rising standards of living in the countryside which have brought about aggregate rural surpluses (such an assumption is made notwithstanding the issues of a probably uneven distribution of such surpluses among the rural population, and of out-migration of people possibly forced out of agriculture through the process of landlessness who may have swollen the ranks of workers in the urban informal sector).

Such surpluses may in turn be traced back to: (a) the increase of agricultural yields in the District of Bantul over the past decades (as a consequence of programmes of agricultural modernization); (b) the creation of many public jobs in urban but also rural areas of the D.I.Y. over the past decades, and also; (c) an increasing amount of urban remittance arising from increasing commuting to urban employment locations which, in turn, have fueled rural employment in certain sectors. Assumedly also, for various reasons that probably relate to sociological urbanization of hinterland areas of the D.I.Y., traditional products are produced more sparsely and rural people become both more dependent and more enthusiastic for manufactured consumer goods. Considering that most of the consumer and durable goods sold in the retail shops (*toko*), newly established in rural areas by urban settlers, are manufactured in urban areas, it must be pointed out therefore that an important share of rural surpluses is probably captured by the urban economy. On the other hand, through the opening of *toko* in urban corridors a few local jobs may be created such as shop employees and maids.

Also, in the wake of the deregulation of the banking system in Indonesia, banks are opening up new branches in the hinterland. This constitutes an attempt to extend credit availability to rural areas. But existing credit facilities through bank or traditional systems seem respectively rather ill-adapted or, in the case of traditional systems, quantitatively insufficient to accommodate the broader needs of those rural residents who would like either to invest in certain nonfarm activities, or diversify their existing agricultural activities to include for instance such activities as fish-breeding or cattle-fattening which seem promising. But some rural dwellers seem reluctant to borrow from formal banking institutions for fear of not being able to repay and probably also in many instances for fear of something that they are not used to, in cultural terms. Alongside the current paucity of capital in the countryside, lack of relevant vocational training and/or apprenticeship is likely to deter many farmers from initiating nonfarm activities. It is interesting that one of the very few large-scale inland fisheries currently under operation in the two villages, and by far the most sophisticated in terms of technology and also the most productive, was operated by a university graduate from a faculty of agriculture, who is also a commuter working primarily as a civil servant.

Forward and Backward Flows of Commodities, and Spread of Subcontracted Activities: Some farmers and middlemen-traders sell commodities produced in rural areas to local rural markets but also to urban markets where demand and prices are generally higher. In the meantime, some - though very few - agro-processing activities take place in the countryside where production costs remain lower (even after the deduction of transportation costs due in particular to low land prices), which are based on the processing of raw materials which are in most cases imported from outside the D.I.Y. and then re-exported, once processed. It must be emphasized that the D.I.Y. imports most fruits, vegetables and other agricultural cash crops which are sold at the markets. Rice is an exception which can be said to constitute a quasi-monoculture in the lowland areas. Also, nonfarm activities are subcontracted from

Yogyakarta to rural residents. In the case of the traditional *batik* industry, Piring has a tradition for well-organized subcontracted activities. Further activities, which today seem to have a brighter economic future are also subcontracted (*e.g.* making 'sport-type' bags).

Diffusion of Information: The role of urban areas (particularly urban markets) as regional nodes of communication must be emphasized. The diffusion throughout the hinterland of information pertaining to marketing potentials for certain crops and types of nonfarm activities often occurs together with and also partly as a result of the reinforcement of urban-rural linkages.

Regarding Employment Multiplicity

The results of the fieldwork conducted in the Plain of Bantul show that urbanization and the strengthening of rural-urban linkages in terms of employment generation clearly constitute an escape for residents of suburban rural areas where demographic pressures upon land are extreme. What is very important to stress is that, in many cases, the undertaking of such activities is not synonymous for local villagers with a sort of involutionary cycle and impoverishment, but, instead, enables a large share of them to make a decent living - see Table 6.2 and Figure 6.8. Nevertheless, existing nonfarm opportunities particularly for those which show relatively high levels of return are probably not accessible to the large majority of rural residents due to large disparities in terms of capital availability, education, and training, among households within communities, but also among communities by and large depending on their degree of proximity to Yogyakarta and to arterial roads.

Some of the studied communities are rapidly 'urbanizing' *in situ* as their economic base becomes increasingly diversified outside of agriculture, while, at the same time, their integration with existing urban centres is growing. Some main characteristics of such an 'urbanization' process can be summarized thus:

- The contribution of agricultural activities (renting land for agricultural purposes or nonagricultural purposes is not included) to household income becomes secondary in nature, while agricultural activities may be undertaken either part-time or by, or with the assistance of, household members: elderly, female workers, and teenagers;

- Individual-wise, employment multiplicity still exists but the number of activities undertaken by the same individual tends to be smaller. Tertiary activities undertaken by individuals that would be significant as for their share of contribution to the household income are probably becoming rare.
- Employment multiplicity may be stronger in poorer households, whereas in those households where for instance better-paid urban jobs which are accessible through commuting are available, there is less need and also less available time to undertake complementary activities;
- Household-wise, employment multiplicity exists. Women play an important role by taking some wage-employment such as clerical jobs in the public or private sector, but also continue playing a major role in trading activities. This latter role in trading is essential in the sense that trading activities are experiencing a rapid growth and probably also a change in character from petty trading to probably new and increasingly commercially and profit-oriented, as opposed to subsistence, forms of trading;
- As reviewed above, new employment opportunities are locally-based in trade and service sector activities, but also delocalized employment is accessible through commuting in Yogyakarta or in its urban fringes especially in the construction subsector;
- In turn, urban remittances, including in particular those generated by commuting, create a dynamics of growth triggered by the increase in the population's purchasing power. However, it is likely that a large share of local residents' expenditure goes on goods which are not locally-produced (*i.e.* consumer goods such as audiovisual equipment), thereby somewhat reducing the multiplier effects of urban remittances for local employment generation.

The ongoing process of change is multifaceted and complex, involving a very large number of factors. In that sense this process can also be termed a social movement. Thus, on the policy side, rather than a set of policies aiming at reinforcing rural-urban linkages as such, a set of integrated policies for rural and regional development in the D.I.Y. in the context of rising rural-urban linkages and of the urbanization of the countryside is needed. Some possible policy options are reviewed in Chapter 9.

Summary of Findings

The Importance of Communications/Disparities in Taking Advantage of Urban Opportunities

It is certain that important flows of rural residents commuting to Yogyakarta from the hinterland are nothing new, since they were already noticed by Seloesomardjan[10] nearly 30 years ago. An older source such as the *Kaart van de Residentie Djocjakarta* published around 1870[11] shows a concentration of settlements or hamlets along the road linking Yogyakarta to Bantul and stretching southwards suggesting the long history of flows of exchanges along this axis. Still, the frequency of public transport and ownership of motor vehicles, together with the provision of public amenities, have expanded over the past decades to the extent that an approach to rural and regional development and changes that would strictly focus upon land tenure, agricultural potentials, and demographic characteristics would prove clearly insufficient today for an understanding of changes occurring in this area. One must also bear in mind the tremendous impact of the opening up of historically still more backward areas of the D.I.Y. through transportation infrastructural development.[12]

The process of regional integration of the D.I.Y. occurs in the Plain of Bantul in a way in which not only capital, land and labour but also intraregional communications should be considered together as major intervening factors in the regional development process. A consequence of such developments is that uneven access to fast and affordable communications, and not only to land or capital or low skills of the labour force, should be regarded today as resulting in spatial and social disparities in development levels of local communities within the D.I.Y. not only among income groups within various communities, but also between suburban and other communities which are more remote from urban centres. Furthermore, as regional roads of the D.I.Y. can generally be considered convenient as a consequence of important physical infrastructural improvements realized during the former decades, disparities in access to urban employment opportunities relate to the following:

(1) commuting distance to urban centres;
(2) commuters' income levels (commuters must secure a profitability margin; what they can spend on transport fares depends on the level of return of the activity for which they commute), and;

(3) private vehicle ownership patterns, and availability, frequency, and speed of existing modes of public transport.

Examples drawn from the studied communities illustrate such disparities. In Piring for instance, the group of commuters working in town is predominantly recruited from higher-educated civil servant families whose income levels are above average. Moreover, Piring's outlying and remote location, means a somewhat lower frequency of service by public transport to Bantul town or Yogyakarta, and also a longer commuting time to be added to the time usually spent on necessary transfers. Hence, most civil servants choose to commute by means of a motorcycle that their regular wage activity enables them to afford and that they often acquire with some allowance from their office, or on credit from the motorcycle dealer upon certification of their employment status. In Bandung, relatively high aggregate income levels indicate that many residents are able to afford motorized transport, as confirmed by a relatively high ratio of per capita motorcycle ownership that also seems to show that a substantial share of commuters, even while living rather short distances away from their destinations, favour private motor vehicles over public transport. Furthermore, shorter commuting distances to Yogyakarta or - to a much lesser extent - to the town of Bantul enable residents of more suburban communities to undertake several consecutive daily activities more easily, such as an urban 'primary' activity - ranked as such in terms of share of income - together with a locally-based secondary activity such as trade or farming.

Increase and Diversification of Income

Agricultural Diversification: A 1991 study undertaken by the International Food Policy Research Institute[13] regarding the impact of high population pressures upon farmland in rural communities of Rwanda showed that in the studied area, agriculture tended to become a secondary subsistence activity when nonfarm employment alternatives were available. The fact that among the studied communities of the Plain of Bantul, many households derive some income, albeit in many instances only a small share of their total income, from agriculture, would seem to indicate a somewhat similar trend. Such a trend should be viewed positively. In suburban communities, indeed, higher human densities also mean smaller average sizes of agricultural plots. Individual plots of irrigated land are consequently becoming too small, as for *pekarangan* (dry land including the home compound and the adjoining garden usually planted with fruit trees) under pressure of construction, for agriculture to remain the primary household source of income. For most households, agriculture must therefore become a complementary and subsistence activity.

Simultaneously, it is probable that in such suburban communities agricultural diversification is hampered by lack of space and available time of suburban residents who usually would prefer spending their time on higher return nonfarm activities. For such residents renting out land or having it sharecropped may also constitute a possibility provided that the area of owned land is of adequate size. But, agricultural diversification is probably also hemmed in by the increasingly subsistence and complementary nature of agriculture which is likely to act as a disincentive to agricultural innovation when the only reason to cultivate a small piece of land is to secure rice as the household's main staple food.

Nonetheless, some diversified agricultural activities can be found more frequently in such suburban communities as Bandung or Maguwoharjo. For instance, cattle-raising seems more widely undertaken in such relatively suburban communities. Reasons for the latter probably relate to the fact that grazing land has disappeared from most areas of the Plain of Bantul having likely being converted into wet fields. Hence, the type of cattle-raising which is implemented in the Plain of Bantul can be described as 'zero-grazing'. Better communications and availability of transport enable suburban residents to obtain the fodder - rice stalks or some agro-processing by-products - which is needed. Also, suburban residents can afford to purchase cattle for commercial purposes, since higher incomes in the more suburban communities also mean a higher capacity to save and to borrow from banks. Last but not least, suburban residents' enhanced mobility allows them to obtain indispensable information concerning prices, supply, and marketing opportunities from other people, particularly at markets.

In a more 'peripheral' (*vis-à-vis* urban areas) and agrarian community such as Piring, agriculture remains largely undiversified in spite of lower man-land ratios and therefore a higher availability of agricultural land, apart from treecrops from which most households derive some income. As in other rural communities on the Plain of Bantul, three annual crops - two crops of rice and one of *palawija* (*i.e.* non-rice intermediary crops) - are the rule. Other agricultural income sources apart from treecrops, are small-scale fisheries or poultry-raising. Fish and poultry-raising as well as vegetable-growing and cattle-raising could probably be expanded considering the usually small-size and scarcity of currently existing schemes. This would require the establishment of specific programmes including the provision of credit aiming at strengthening such activities through bottom-up and community-based approaches so that resources can be pooled. Insufficient knowledge about marketing possibilities and technologies restrict the development of some high value crops such as vegetables, which are often considered as requiring too much time and care to be seriously undertaken. At the same time, low agricultural surpluses and the indebtedness of farmers, prevent risk-taking and, as such, act as disincentives to agricultural diversification, particularly for the smaller-scale farmers who, to an even larger extent, must live at subsistence levels.

Last but not least, certain existing official programmes whose aim is to promote nonrice crops, such as onions in the lowlands or cocoa in the uplands, should be reconsidered. The procedures to be followed by the farmers who join such programmes are often rigid and the interest of farmers in joining them are sometimes far from clear. The shortage of certain existing programmes and their lack of flexibility (to adapt the farmers' own interests) results in the misallocation of resources that could have been more efficiently and appropriately invested in agricultural diversification. Finally, the policy consisting in setting official prices which are below market prices, which existed for clove for instance (a crop which is grown in the uplands of Kulon Progo District) at the beginning of the 1990s, resulted in a considerably reduced income for upland farmers. This policy is also not conducive to agricultural diversification and probably even deters it.

Nonfarm Employment: As seen above, a large share of households in all communities derive an important share of their income from nonfarm activities.[14] Moreover, in the aggregate, such a sectoral employment shift has a positive impact upon household income levels in those suburban or transit-corridor communities, as it is shown by aggregate levels of both nonfarm employment and income which are higher than in a more outlying community such as Piring where nonfarm activities are much less developed.

In contrast, in a suburban community such as Bandung, an important share of households include members commuting to Yogyakarta or Bantul for primary activities. Such urban commuters work as government officials, *pasar* (market) traders, petty traders, construction workers, *becak* drivers, as well as in other urban services. This phenomenon contributes to raising aggregate income levels. In turn, higher aggregate income levels in such suburban communities translate into higher aggregate levels of household consumption which impact noticeably upon the construction subsector and retailing activity. Urban commuters, indeed, frequently spend a significant share of their income on new houses, as spacious traditional Javanese houses are increasingly viewed by young couples as too large and not suited to their changing needs. Also, such residents spend a significant share of their total expenditures on consumer goods, such as audio equipment and motorcycles.

A study of communities in upland Central Java by Tadjuddin Noer Effendi[15] shows a similar trend which, based on our observation, seems more accentuated in a suburban community such as Bandung than in the more rural community of Piring. As a broad consequence, allied services and trade grow steadily in the expanded hinterland of urban centres as an indirect and dynamic effect of the local spending of remittances stemming from commuting. Such services and trade mainly concern small restaurants and food hawkers, garage/repairs, plumbers, carpenters, masons, beauticians, tailors, or retail or wholesale (cooking oil, construction materials, etc.) traders. Accordingly, local levels of expansion of services relate, to some extent, to the distance to urban centres where employment is generated which determines aggregate commuting levels. In a nutshell, it is remarkable that many jobs are locally-generated as an indirect consequence of commuting. Nonetheless, the urban remittances which are spent on urban-produced consumer goods benefit the urban economy, but without creating local jobs except in retail trading whose capacity for labour creation is furthermore reduced by the fact that many retail traders are not native. They often originate from urban centres (Yogyakarta in particular) and labour in retailing is often comprised of members of the household.

There is a second distinct group of activities whose level of expansion remains conspicuously low, though to varying extents, in both relative and absolute terms in all studied communities. This is in the industrial sector. As seen earlier, apart from the case of rice-milling and a few other cases of traditional industries, those small-scale and cottage industries which are newly established tend to settle in the more suburban communities, preferably in urbanizing corridors. Industrial development in a more outlying community such as Piring remains stagnant. This is true even in a transit-corridor but a nonsuburban community such as Celep where, as seen earlier, industrial development has been largely overridden by the retailing activity and services (the situation is very different in the upland hamlet of Putat II in the District of Gunung Kidul, which is studied below). Moreover, it is questionable whether, within transit corridors which are more suburban, industrial growth results from endogenously-driven dynamics, whereby many native rural residents would shift from agriculture to industry, or is, instead, more of an industrial-growth-on-urban-peripheries' process. In the latter case, relatively few native residents but relatively many newcomers from urban areas would establish small-scale industries, and many new branches of expanding urban industries would be delocalized along transit corridors, where communications are the easiest and land cheap for a level of infrastructure development which compares with that of older urban areas.

In a community such as Celep, traditional *batik* painting is undertaken by a large number of housewives. Such an activity is usually subcontracted from Yogyakarta. Nevertheless, it constitutes a very low-paid activity whose future is bleak due to the decreasing demand of traditional garments not only in urban but also rural areas. In Bandung, the vicinity of Yogyakarta has a positive impact upon the development of some cottage industries. For instance, the making of bamboo baskets to be used in urban markets is subcontracted from Yogyakarta. So are some rare cases of more potent activities such as the sewing of sports bags. Regularly, inputs of both activities are delivered and outputs are collected by their respective urban subcontracting parties. A third group of activities concerns the trading of agricultural products. In Piring, many villagers can sell products of the gardens to Celep market which is held once every Javanese week which still follows a traditional calendar and consists of five days. Another type of activity seems, nonetheless, more promising in terms of anticipated returns. This is intermediary trading which often seems to be operated by women. Such intermediary traders' (*makelar*) business depends largely in size but by and large seems to be thriving. Their activities can range in size from a small *warung* (small grocery shop and/or restaurant) owner who carries one or two bags of rice a week, on his bicycle or in the bus, to be resold in the period preceding the harvest when the rural demand for rice is at its peak, or a seller who stands in the early morning along the main road purchasing fruits of the gardens such as bananas or coconuts from commuters en route to Yogyakarta, to larger-scale rice traders especially in the more outlying communities. By and large, when not a mere subsistence activity, the principal tenet of intermediary trading consists in formulating a strategy for purchasing and reselling at the most advantageous times and places based upon three main factors, *viz.* transportation costs, high seasonal sale prices on larger regional markets, and low seasonal purchasing prices of rice or other agricultural commodities from local producers which are also probably the lowest at harvesting time and in the most outlying communities. As far as the trading of rice is concerned, the development of such activities can probably be better understood in the context of growing commercialization of agriculture and probable concomitant diminution of the role of the village cooperatives (*K.U.D.* standing for *Koperasi Unit Desa*), whose role has been however instrumental for the modernization of rice-growing and which are liable to grant loans for small-scale - including nonfarm - enterprises. In more outlying communities (*vis-à-vis* urban areas), it is more likely that such activities are concentrated in the hands of a few big traders - not unusually the wife of large landowners - due to higher transportation costs and the much lower numbers of commuters who could undertake such activities on the basis of a secondary activity, and probably also to the general paucity of capital, particularly in such areas. Additionally, access to venture capital, the ownership of a private vehicle for essential mobility, the building up of a regional network of trading partners, a good knowledge of regional prices are all essential prerequisites which are not attainable for a large number of households. As a consequence, a higher volume of intermediary trading can probably be expected from less suburban communities which are also more agriculturally-oriented, but also probably a higher concentration of such activities. Furthermore, it should be noted that high levels of indebtedness and paucity of surpluses (if any) in more outlying communities such as Piring also mean that local farmers are obliged to sell a significant share of their rice after harvesting to repay part of their debts since they are permanently in a 'debt trap'. As a consequence, many farmers must purchase rice for home consumption after the second month following the first harvest but prior to the next one. This phenomenon is responsible for a rural demand for rice for home consumption from rice producers at relatively high prices from retail shops.

Conclusion

This study shows that the strengthening of communications and of various forms of rural-urban linkages is occurring steadily between Yogyakarta and its partly urbanizing hinterland. Such a process has a positive impact upon the extended periphery of Yogyakarta and along main transit corridors, in the sense that in such communities, employment is generated through commuting or, to a lesser extent, subcontracting. While this creates a dynamic with multiplier effects, the employment thereby created facilitates a decrease in out-migration rates in the more suburban communities. In more suburban communities, the sectoral shift occurring from agriculture to services seems to be accompanied by an increase in aggregate income levels which remain higher than those found in more outlying communities. In contrast, permanent out-migration is likely to continue occurring in response to the lack of local employment opportunities, in those communities which are more remote from urban centres and whose development is hampered by longer commuting distances. At the same time in such communities, remittances from permanent or circular out-migrants will probably continue to constitute an important supplement to household incomes. The main planning concerns should be to define strategies aimed at widening the access to urban employment and markets made possible by commuting to a broader segment of income groups. A closely related issue is the question of establishing a mass-transit system that would bring the most outlying communities of the Plain of Bantul closer to urban centres such as Wates, Bantul, and Yogyakarta. Nevertheless, as seen earlier, the attractiveness of Yogyakarta is predominant for hinterland commuters, while secondary urban centres such as Bantul or Wates, whose economic development remains low, do not generate enough employment opportunities to attract hinterland commuters. Also, an increasing number of local traders and producers may choose to sell their products in Yogyakarta where the largest markets are located and where broader marketing opportunities are available. If additional employment opportunities are not created in such secondary towns, would not the establishment of a regional public mass-transit system further aggravate the primacy of Yogyakarta? At the same time, the local retailing and wholesaling activity is relatively small and still rather remote areas may become affected by increasing opportunities generated for hinterland producers and to the increasing possibility for hinterland consumers to go shopping in Yogyakarta. Nevertheless, advantages generated for producers and consumers might balance disadvantages brought about on local retail and wholesale traders. Following the establishment of a regional mass-transit system, an increased number of urban residents belonging to higher income groups would probably settle into the enlarged periphery of Yogyakarta, possibly pushing away some of the native rural residents.

All in all, the possible implications of the establishment of a mass-transit system upon development are far from being clear.[16] In other terms, the issue that developing a mass-transit system in the D.I.Y., even if financially feasible, might lead to the reinforcement of urban primacy in the region and perhaps also to increased traffic congestion within and at the periphery of Yogyakarta, should not be overlooked. To compensate for these problems, it would be useful to develop a two-fold strategy aiming, through integrated policies, at a reduction in differential access to transportion among communities resulting from different locational characteristics, and within the same communities among different income groups, while at the same time generating locally-based activities that would contribute to a more endogenous form of development. The main purposes of the latter would be twofold:

(1) reducing high out-migration levels in outlying communities that increase urban congestion in other parts of Java, and;

(2) contributing to the increase in income levels of native rural residents so that they can garner a share of regional economic opportunities brought about by recent regional development.

This is to say that attempts should be made for linkages between Yogyakarta and its hinterland not to remain exclusively confined to the provision of labour supply in hinterland areas to urban services and trade, inflow of consumers goods being produced in urban areas and relayed to hinterland areas through Yogyakarta urban wholesalers, and the somewhat 'suburbanization' process of urban peripheral and transit-corridor communities. Instead, linkages should be further broadened to include increased flows of value-added products and raw materials originating from hinterland areas, by taking advantage of the dynamics created by reinforced communications between the hinterland and urban centres, with the target of strengthening locally-based or endogenous forms of development. Thus, active agricultural diversification policies should be undertaken in those areas which are relatively low-density and where nonfarm employment alternatives are rare, and where current levels of diversification are extremely low. Such policies cannot not succeed unless designed through and based upon a bottom-up and community-based approach. Also, strengthening the development of locally-based activities and expanding the existing ones to be undertaken by rural residents on the Plain of Bantul, would most necessarily require that integrated policies are established relating to the provision of credit, specialized training and education, and the diffusion of information regarding marketing possibilities and the provision of inputs. Furthermore, the issue of poverty alleviation should be carefully reviewed. In the studied lowland communities considered in the aggregate, income disparities remain very wide as shown by the Lorenz curve of income for all such communities combined. Further analysis of income disparities through a segmentation of the total sample into a more homogeneous grouping by community and further by sectors of activity (farm/nonfarm) would prove much more significant. This suggests that though aggregate levels of income are raised in hinterland communities through increasing commuting levels and urbanization, increase in income levels would be widely uneven among different communities, but probably also within the same community among different households. Specific steps should be taken to strengthen subsistence or very low return activities such as food preparation, hawking, and petty urban jobs.

Notes

[1] Maurer, 1986.

[2] Hardjono, 1987.

[3] The *mertelu* sharecropping system can be found in communities with dry land, where the supply of productive farmland is limited. In such communities, cultivators sharecropping dry land are forced to be less demanding. But even in the latter communities - based on the evidence from the communities studied in this book - the *mertelu* system is very rarely used (see the study on Putat II in Gunung Kidul District, in Chapter 7).

[4] 'Nonfarm' employment may be defined in several ways. One way is to consider it as synonymous with 'off-farm' employment. A definition of 'nonfarm' or 'off-farm' which is used in this book is summarized by Evers (1989) thus: 'Off-farm employment refers to "non-farm activities or occupations that are undertaken by any working member of a rural household" [...] As it refers to work of a non-farming nature, "it is thus synonymous with non-farm employment" (Shand, ed., 1986).

Non-farm type work in the (on-farm) home should be included (*e.g.* women's handicraft work).'

[5] The share of the agriculture in the total household income was constructed thus:

$$Yhh\text{-agr.} = \frac{\sum\limits_{i=1}^{n} (Z1i + Z.2i + Z3i) + Y6 + Y7 + Y8 + Y9}{Yhh} \times 100$$

where,

Yhh = total household income (constructed as above in the main text),

n = number of members in the household,

$Z1i$ = net annual return from primary farming activity of household member i (including cash equivalent of rice allowance to civil servants),

$Z2i$ = net annual return from secondary farming activity of household member i (including cash equivalent of rice allowance to civil servants),

$Z3i$ = net annual return from tertiary farming activity of household member i (including cash equivalent of rice allowance to civil servants),

$Y6$ = net annual return from treecrops,

$Y7$ = net annual return from livestock products (including fish, cattle, poultry); when primary, secondary or tertiary activity of one household member are related to livestock-raising, $Y7$ is adjusted in order to prevent double-counting,

$Y8$ = net annual return from renting land to sugar cane factory,

$Y9$ = annual cash equivalent of rice used for home consumption (food) which is grown by the household; $Y9$ is adjusted in order to prevent double-counting.

[6] This is the total household income calculated as shown in Part II.

[7] See footnote 2, Chapter 5.

[8] *Ibid.*

[9] In Wendt, ed., 1976.

[10] Selosoemardjan, 1962.

[11] Baron Melvill van Cambée and W.F. Versteeg, Atlas van Nederlandsch Indië, Uitgave van Gualtherus Kolff. The atlas was published in 1870; this map may have been drawn in 1857 (in Dutch).

[12] See for instance the case of Putat II, a hamlet of Gunung Kidul District, in Part II.

[13] Von Braun, de Haen, and Blanken, 1991.

[14] As seen in footnote 4, 'off-farm' and 'nonfarm' activities are considered here as synonymous, though some authors establish a difference between the two terms.

[15] Effendi, 1991.

[16] See for instance Overton (1990) with reference to the impact of road development upon a rural community.

7 Piedmont and Mountain Communities

- by Vincent Rotgé -

A Piedmont Community: Kembang Village

How Households Were Sampled in Kembang

In this village, human settlements concentrate around the market (*pasar*) and between the north-south road linking the village to Wates and the Progo River. The highest densities of human settlements are found near the *pasar*, while the area stretching from the *pasar* district up to the main road running north-south along the river is uninhabited, being fully covered by wet fields - Figures 7.2 and 7.3. A few shops, including small restaurants, the bus terminal and a branch of *Bank Rakyat Indonesia* (*BRI*) can be found along this road and near the bridge, suggesting the beginning of an urbanized corridor in this district. However, the high concentration of trading activities and retail shops near the *pasar* preclude any clear differentiation in terms of levels of human densities, nonfarm employment or concentration of service activities between clearly delineated transit-corridor and hinterland districts, as achieved in the case of the communities analysed in other sections of this study. It was therefore decided to analyse the data collected in Kembang in their aggregate. One hundred and thirty households were sampled.

Figure 7.1   Location of Kembang

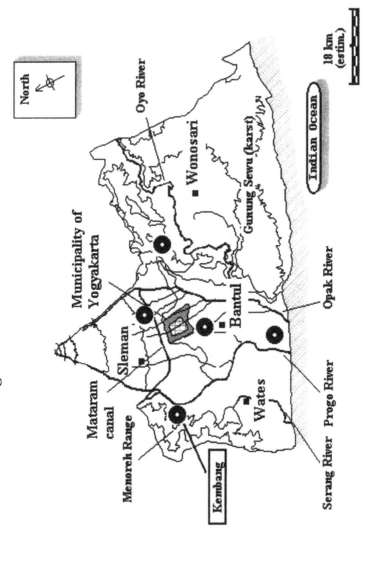

Source: Vincent Rotgé (December 1994).

Figure 7.2   Map of the Area Covered by the Study in the Village of Kembang (hamlets of Kenteng, Ngemplak, and Ngrojo)

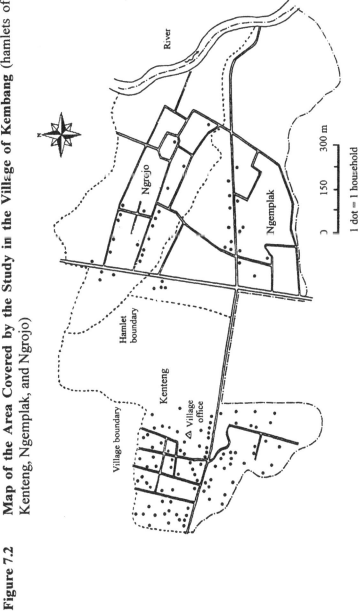

Source: Laboratory of Cartography, Faculty of Geography, Gadjah Mada University; acapted by Vincent Rotgé (1992).

Figure 7.3   Bird's Eye View of Kembang's Irrigation Network from the Menoreh Mountains towards the East

Legend: (S) : Wet fields   (T) : Dry fields (tegal)
                       (sawah)
                   (P) : Home gardens   [I2] : Secondary irrigation network
N ←⊕→ S   (pekarangan)   [I3] : Tertiary irrigation network
                   (M) : Market place   [I4] : Quaternary irrigation network
                       (pasar)

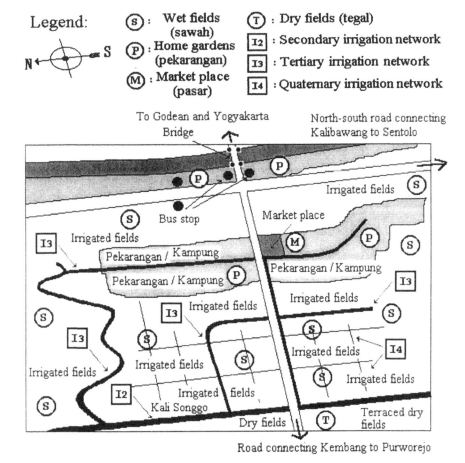

Notes:

- 'Irrigated field' refers here to a field irrigated through canals, not only rainfed. Given the specific agroecological characteristics of this lowland community, it is synonymous to 'wet field'.
- *Kampung* refers to built-up areas, *i.e.* the dwellings but also the home gardens which surround the dwellings.
- Villagers commonly use the word *pekarangan* to designate both the home garden and the area occupied by their dwelling, *i.e.* the home compound; but *pekarangan* is also often used by them to designate the home garden only.
- The word *kebun* is also used in lieu of *pekarangan*.

Source: Drawn by Vincent Rotgé (1994) based on a photograph taken by him from the Menoreh Mountains.

A Hamlet Situated in a Piedmont Plain on the Border between Two Sharply Contrasting Agroecological Environments

The village of Kembang is remarkable for its geographical setting, being located on the western bank of the Progo River on the piedmont plain next to the Menoreh range. Most of the area occupied by this community lies on flat irrigated land, albeit part of the agricultural land located alongside the westernmost fringes encroaches upon sloping terrain in the vicinity of the Menoreh range. Farmers cultivate wet rice on the flat irrigated land of Kembang in the same way as farmers do in most lowland communities. Still, the nature and levels of economic activities undertaken in this village relate to locational and agroecological characteristics, which essentially differ from those identified in the lowland communities analysed in the previous chapter of this study. As a matter of fact, Kembang can be pictured as a rural hamlet involved in trading across the border of two sharply contrasting agroecological environments:

(1) the wet rice communities located on flat irrigated land of the central Plain of Bantul and Kembang which share strong similarities in agroecological terms, and;

(2) further west, up the hill, the upland communities of the Menoreh range where permanent irrigation is scarce and where rural dwellers must rely for their survival to a very large extent on dry and rainfed cultivation, treecrops or the raising of goats and sheep which have little demand for fodder.

The *pasar* (marketplace) was built as a permanent structure before national Independence, when the market mostly specialized in the trading of cattle including cows and sheep. According to villagers, this specialization remained until an irrigation canal was built in the area allowing three crops a year to be grown by local farmers (two rice and one intermediary *palawija* crops), against only one crop prior to the development of permanent irrigation. But by the same token, it became impossible to utilize agricultural land for grazing and the production of fodder for even a part of the year. As a result, cows are no longer traded in the village of Kembang today and the local market has become a general market, which is held once a Javanese week (which is traditionally comprised of five days) and whose function is twofold:

(1) Selling retail commodities to the daily visitors living in the hills among which many are purchased from Yogyakarta, such as soap,

clothing, tobacco, agricultural tools, as well as both durable and fresh food, etc., and;

(2) Purchasing produce from upland farmers such as cloves, goats, sheep, poultry, and eggs to be resold by Kembang's brokers to larger Yogyakarta's wholesalers.

Impact of the Recent Construction of a Bridge

Around 1990, a bridge was built over the nearby Progo River. Prior to the construction of this bridge, travellers had to transit through the towns of Ngeplang and Sedayu located downstream to the south, from where they used to take a direct bus to Yogyakarta - this itinerary (but not the small town of Ngeplang) can be seen in Figure 3.2. Through the shortened itinerary, the distance from the village to the D.I.Y.'s capital by road was reduced by an approximate factor of three (down to about 17 km). This meant also a 50 per cent decrease in public transportation costs (from *Rupiah* 1,500 to *Rupiah* 800 for a round trip across the bridge, that is from US$0.75 to 0.40 at the early 1990s exchange rate, or from US$0.21 to 0.11 at the mid-December 1999 exchange rate). This recent development bears potential for future change. Kembang is now situated on a road linking two important Javanese urban centres, *viz.* Yogyakarta and the important city of Purworejo located in Central Java on the other side of the Menoreh range. Nevertheless, the geographical characteristics of the Menoreh range, including an undulating topography and a poor resource base, can probably be considered as adverse to the rapid building up of a corridor between the two urban centres. Shortly after the construction of the bridge, the government of Kulon Progo District (office of the *Bupati*) took the decision to establish a bus terminal in the close vicinity of Kembang, next to the bridge. Today, buses heading to Yogyakarta stop nearly forty times a day in the village of Kembang. About thirty buses a day connect Kembang to Wates, the capital of Kulon Progo District. Additionally many minibuses (known as *colt*) owned by small entrepreneurs serve the village. Such radical and sudden changes in communications are bringing about a series of changes in the economic activity of the hamlet, which can already be noticed.

Table 7.1   Kembang: Size of Land in m² Tenanted by Households, by Types of Land Tenure and Sharecropping Arrangements

	Number of occurences	Minimum size (in m²)	Maximum size (in m²)	Average (in m²)	Standard deviation
a. Dryland Farming (tegal)					
Sharecropping system:					
The household owns the land which is sharecropped: *maro**	1	500	500	500	
The household owns the land which is not sharecropped: The household operates the land:	6	500	5,000	2,667	1,763
b. Wetland Farming (sawah)					
Sharecropping system:					
The household owns the land which is sharecropped: *maro**	7	1,250	9,500	3,392	2,964
The household owns the land which is not sharecropped: The household operates the land: The household rents out the land:	50 6	100 600	100,599 199,398	4,907 36,566	14,072 80,133
The household leases the land: The household operates the land:	11	1,000	20,000	5,164	5,542
Other land tenure system:	3	1,000	18,000	9,667	8,505

*   *Maro*: A type of sharecropping arrangement, whereby half of the harvest goes to the cultivator and the remaining half to the landlord. Costs are also shared. It is by far the most common sharecropping system in use in all the communities which are studied in this book. See also Glossary.

Source: Primary data processed by Vincent Rotgé using SAS (fieldwork implemented in 1992).

Changes in Communications and Local Development

Some villagers, who prior to the construction of the bridge used to stay overnight or for some period of time in Yogyakarta as circular migrants in relation to their occupation (traders or students), can now commute. This also holds true for residents from the upland areas. However, though an important share of residents of neighbouring communities would now undertake commuting to Yogyakarta in relation to their activity, few among the residents of the village of Kembang actually do so. This is mainly because the local *pasar* (marketplace) provides them with locally-based employment. This is the case for *pasar* traders or the '*adang-adang*' intermediate traders who collect agricultural produce along the road early in the morning and then bring it to the *pasar* - see also glossary at the end of this study - while local shopowners benefit from the influx of visitors to the village. Hence, villagers in Kembang do not need, by and large, to find delocalized employment opportunities to the same extent as villagers in communities which are more dependent on farming do. Therefore, economic changes experienced in the village of Kembang as a consequence of changes in communications relate more to changing levels in trading relations - including changing levels of commuting associated with trade - rather than to an increase in delocalized employment accessible through commuting in the non-trade sectors. As a consequence, some residents of the village of Kembang, including local consumers and shopowners, now prefer conducting trading transactions in Yogyakarta instead of in the town of Godean, though the latter is located at a short distance from the village on the other side of the bridge. An essential reason for them to do so is that purchasing and selling prices in a smaller market centre, such as Godean, are less advantageous than in a much larger trading centre, such as Yogyakarta, where levels of both the demand for rural-produced goods and the offer for urban-produced commodities are higher. All in all, this - together with transportation improvement - contributes to an emerging positive trade-off between time and cost of transportation and comparatively lower purchasing costs and higher selling prices in Yogyakarta, which is itself conducive to making the regional capital city more attractive for trading.[1] Although it is true that the abovementioned process probably benefits some of Kembang's traders and local consumers, the emerging possibility of realizing trading transactions in Yogyakarta is at the same time available to the members of neighbouring communities, which prior to the construction of the bridge used to go to Kembang for trading purposes and probably also to some local consumers for certain types of goods. Some villagers from neighbouring upland communities eventually charter cars to Yogyakarta for trading purposes. A pessimistic view is that such a scenario may lead to the gradual erosion of the quasi-monopoly in trade previously held by the village of Kembang's traders in this district west of the Progo River. However, the construction of the bridge has also directly benefited Kembang's trading activity in enabling the village to capture the demand for commodities of neighbouring areas located on the other side of the bridge, thereby somewhat mitigating the possible consequences of the former scenario. Still, it is likely that benefits and disadvantages resulting from the bridge for Kembang's trading activity would to some extent balance each other. Supporting this latter view is the fact that market officials (civil servants in charge of collecting taxes from the traders) report that the volume of transactions in Kembang's market decreased in the aftermath of the bridge construction, but soon thereafter recovered to the level of the period preceding the construction. It is furthermore possible that changes brought about by the construction of the bridge by contributing to raising income levels in the upland areas, might ultimately bring longer-term benefits to Kembang's trading sector through creating a dynamic of growth in neighbouring communities, provided that the latter communities retain a sufficient level of trading relations with the village. Nevertheless, the long-term implications of improvement in communications upon the volume and nature of the trading activity in Kembang are complex and uncertain. In particular, it may be hypothesized that accessibility to potentials, as well as the capacity for facing competition, brought about by changes in communications might be unevenly distributed among the population of the village depending upon levels of mobility of households which relate to capital availability, vehicle ownership, and further possible factors such as landownership since credit availability is bound to the provision of collateral which often consists of a land registration act. But, in many instances and as in most rural areas in this region, land is occupied or used *de facto* without landownership being certified by the relevant land administration office.

Other Changes Brought about by Improved Communications

Improvement of communications has brought some positive impact upon certain types of local agricultural activities. For instance, poultry raisers can obtain fodder at lower costs from Yogyakarta and sell their products at higher prices in the town of Godean located on the opposite bank of the Progo River. A further significant side-effect of the construction of the bridge is that value of land has subsequently risen in areas of Kembang, as reflected by higher transaction costs being reported in the past two years. However, the volume of land transactions seems small in size, as only very few cases were reported. This process should benefit landowners by enabling them to access credit sources through using their land as collateral. At the same time, development pressures are probably still too low for smaller landowners to exchange their land for larger plots in communities where land is cheaper.

Types of Land-use and Tenure, and of Sharecropping Arrangements

Though this village encroaches upon sloping terrain which comprises of dry land, most of the agricultural land is irrigated and very few households cultivate dry land (*tegal*). Approximately 65 per cent of all households in the village of Kembang have access to a wet field (*sawah*). This is through various kinds of land tenure and sharecropping arrangements which are contained in Table 7.1. Still, most of the irrigated land is owner-cultivated (fifty plots of *sawah*), a small share of the land operated in the village being leased while a very small percentage is sharecropped through the *maro* system of sharecropping arrangements, whereby the cultivator and the landlord receive half of the crop and pay half of the costs each. The share of owner-cultivated plots of *sawah* falls in between the values found in Piring and Bandung hamlets where man-land ratios are lower and higher, respectively, than in the village of Kembang - Tables 6.1, b and d, and 7.1. At the same time, average size of owner-cultivated *sawah* in Kembang is close to 0.5 ha and is the largest among all studied communities. A likely explanation to the relatively low man-land ratio found in the village of Kembang could be that rainfed land that would have prevailed before was unable to support high carrying capacities of population, while permanent irrigation has penetrated the village relatively recently. Nevertheless, very large standard deviations and the wide range of sizes of *sawah* (from 0.01 ha to more than 10 ha) underscore the presence of very large disparities in the distribution of irrigated land, suggesting that there might be potentials for adjustments in land tenure in this village geared towards more equitable access to land - Table 7.1. Differently perhaps from the case of other communities where man-land ratios are considerably higher - especially of suburban lowland communities where the role of agriculture seems to evolve as a secondary activity of lesser importance - land tenure adjustments might be considered in Kembang as a possible way to achieve a more equitable access to resources, while not causing the fragmentation of land into land plots that would be too small to be operated with profit.

Demographic Structure

As compared to transit-corridor communities of the Plain of Bantul, such as Celep or Karanggondang-Cepit, Kembang shows a deficit in the segment of the population between 15-34 years old - Table 7.2. But such a deficit is much less accentuated in Kembang than in the peripheral hamlet of Piring, and actually compares with the deficit of population noticed for the same age group in Bandung. This suggests that, although permanent out-migration of the young people does occur in Kembang, some employment opportunities generated in the trade sector enable some of the youth who are entering working age to settle down in the village.

Table 7.2   Age Pyramid of Kembang

	MALES			Age		FEMALES		
(1)	(2)	(3)	(4)		(1)	(2)	(3)	(4)
1	1	0.40	0.40	90-94	1	1	0.37	0.37
5	6	2.00	2.40	80-84	4	5	1.47	1.84
3	9	1.20	3.60	75-79	2	7	0.74	2.57
12	21	4.80	8.40	70-74	12	19	4.41	6.99
18	39	7.20	15.60	65-69	11	30	4.04	11.03
11	50	4.40	20.00	60-64	16	46	5.88	16.91
12	62	4.80	24.80	55-59	12	58	4.41	21.32
15	77	6.00	30.80	50-54	21	79	7.72	29.04
6	83	2.40	33.20	45-49	6	85	2.21	31.25
8	91	3.20	36.40	40-44	16	101	5.88	37.13
16	107	6.40	42.80	35-39	18	119	6.62	43.75
18	125	7.20	50.00	30-34	17	136	6.25	50.00
24	149	9.60	59.60	25-29	33	169	12.13	62.13
30	179	12.00	71.60	20-24	19	188	6.99	69.12
23	202	9.20	80.80	15-19	25	213	9.19	78.31
19	221	7.60	88.40	10-14	28	241	10.29	88.60
19	240	7.60	96.00	05-09	12	253	4.41	93.01
10	250	4.00	100.00	00-04	19	272	6.99	100.00

```
                18   14   11   7    4           4   7   11   14   18
                     Percentage                      Percentage
```

Note: Column (1): Number of cases; Column (2): Cumulative number of cases; Column (3): Per cent of the total population; Column (4): Cumulative per cent of the total population.

Source: Primary data processed by Vincent Rotgé using SAS (fieldwork implemented in 1992).

Table 7.3   Kembang: Per Cent of Workers Engaged in a Primary Activity, for Workers above 15 Years of Age (percentages)

	Agriculture	Cottage / small-scale industry*	Transport	Civil service	Trade at market	Peddling trade	Settled trade	Other non-trade services	Other	All
Males	45.6	2.5	7.7	19.8	2.5	3.4	2.5	11.2	4.3	# 100
	(53)**	(3)	(9)	(23)	(3)	(4)	(3)	(13)	(5)	(116)
Females	32.2	5.5	0	8.8	11.1	14.4	15.5	10	2.2	# 100
	(29)	(5)	(0)	(8)	(10)	(13)	(14)	(9)	(2)	(90)
All	39.8	3.8	4.3	15	6.3	8.2	8.2	10.6	3.3	# 100
	(82)	(8)	(9)	(31)	(13)	(17)	(17)	(22)	(7)	(206)

*:   Employing up to 19 workers.
**:   Figures in parentheses represent number of cases.

Source: Primary data processed by Vincent Rotgé using SAS (fieldwork implemented in 1992).

**Table 7.4   Employment Structure in 1992: Kembang -
For Male and Female Workers** (primary activity)

(i) Government

HEALTH ------	NURSE	1	
PUBLIC ------ +--	TEACHER OF ELEMENTARY SCHOOL	4	1
EDUCATION ------ +--	MAINTENANCE WORKER	1	
+--	CASHIER / BOOK-KEEPER	1	2
DEFENSE ------	MILITARY (ON THE ACTIVE LIST)	2	1
PUBLIC WORKS ------	RESEARCHER	2	
CIVILIAN CLERICAL ------ +--	HIGHER CLERICAL ------- MANAGERIAL STAFF	1	1
+--	INTERMEDIATE AND LOWER CLERICAL	4	3
+--	TRAINEE (LOWER CLERICAL)	1	
+--	LOCAL RURAL DEVELOPMENT CADRE	5	

Table 7.4 (continued)

(ii) Non-government

```
FARM ----+                                            +-- LANDOWNER OR TENANT (DOES NOT SHARECROP) .. 47   23
         |                                   +-- LABOURER ------+
         +-- SELF/HOUSEHOLD ---------+       |                  +-- SHARECROPS (TENANT, NOT LANDLORD) .........  1    1
         |   EMPLOYED                +-- FISH/POULTRY RAISER  ......................................  2
         |
         +-- HIRED LABOURER ---------+       +-- SEASONAL LABOURER  .....................................  2    2
                                     |
                                     +-- CASUAL LABOURER  .....................................  1    3

                                     +-- BUS DRIVER .........................................  1
                    +-- TRANSPORTS ------+-- TRADITIONAL TRANSPORT (OTHER THAN RICKSHAW)  ........  1
                    |                    +-- OTHER .............................................  1

                                             +-- COOKED FOOD ..........................................  1
                                             +-- TRADITIONAL MEDICINES ...........................  1

NON- --+--SELF/ ----+                +-- PASAR TRADER --+-- CRAFTS NOT-PRODUCED BY TRADER'S HOUSEHOLD .  1    1
FARM   |   HOUSEHOLD |                                  +-- OTHER FOOD PREPARED BY TRADER'S HOUSEHOLD .       2
       |   EMPLOYED  |                                  +-- NON-PERISHABLE FOODSTUFFS .................       1
       |             |                                          +--- TOBACCO / CIGARETTES                 2
       |             |                                          +--- GOLD AND JEWELLERY ...............    1
       |             |                                          +--- PALM SUGAR ........                   1
       |             |                                          +--- CONFECTION / FOOTWARE ............  1  2
       |             |                                          +--- TRADITIONAL MEDICINES ............  1
       |             |                                          +--- HOUSEHOLD UTENSILS ...............      1
```

Table 7.4 (continued)

```
NON-
FARM --+--SELF/ --+--TRADE ----------+--AMBULANT TRADER ----+--CRAFTS NOT-PRODUCED
       |  EMPLOYED |                  |                      |    BY TRADER'S HOUSEHOLD .......  1      4
       |  HOUSEHOLD|                  |                      +--CONFECTION / FOOTWARE .......  1      1
       |           |                  |                      +--FRUITS .......
       |           |                  |                      +--FOOD PREPARED BY TRADER'S
       |           |                  |                      |    HOUSEHOLD .......                   2
       |           |                  |                      +--FOOD NOT-PREPARED BY TRADER'S
       |           |                  |                      |    HOUSEHOLD .......                   2
       |           |                  |                      +--AGRICULTURAL PRODUCTS NOT-PRODUCED
       |           |                  |                      |    BY TRADER'S HOUSEHOLD .......       2
       |           |                  |                      +--OTHER .......  1                      1
       |           |                  |
       |           |                  +--WARUNG -------------+--COOKED FOOD .......  2               2
       |           |                  |                      +--BEVERAGE .......                      1
       |           |                  |                      +--BUILDING MATERIALS .......            1
       |           |                  |                      +--OTHER GOODS NOT-PRODUCED BY
       |           |                  |                      |    HOUSEHOLD OWNING WARUNG .......     1
       |           |                  |                      +--GROCERY .......  1                    2
       |           |                  |
       |           |                  +--TOKO ---------------+--HARDWARE SELLER .......               1
       |           |                  |                      +--GENERAL STORE .......                 5
       |           |                  |
       |           |                  +--OTHER TRADE --------+--POULTRY SELLER .......                1
```

Table 7.4 (continued)

```
NON- --+--SELF/ ----+
FARM   | HOUSEHOLD |
       | EMPLOYED  |
       |           +-- NON-TRADE SERVICES ---+--- GARAGE / REPAIR ............ 4      1
       |                                     +--- NURSE ...................... 1
       |                                     +--- PHYSICIAN .................. 1
       |                                     +--- BARBER / BEAUTICIAN ........ 1
       |                                     +--- TAILOR ....................
       |                                     +--- CARPENTER .................. 2
       |                                     +--- SHOEMAKER .................. 1
       |                                     +--- PHOTOGRAPHER ............... 1
       |                                     +--- OTHER ...................... 4      4
       |
       +-- CLERICAL (NON-PUBLIC) -----------+--- TRAINEE (LOWER CLERICAL) .... 2      2
       |
       +-- COTTAGE INDUSTRY (LESS THAN 5 WORKERS) -+--- TRADITIONALLY MANUFACTURED
       |                                            |         PLANT PRODUCTS ....
       |                                            +--- OTHER ................ 1      1
       |
       +-- DOMESTIC SERVANT ----------------------- ..................... 1
       +-- TRANSPORT ------------------------------ TRUCK DRIVER ......... 1      1
       +-- INTERMEDIATE LARGE INDUSTRY (50 TO 100 WK) - SKILLED WORKER
                                                        IN MECHANIZED WEAVING       1

EMPLOYEE -+-- COTTAGE INDUSTRY (LESS THAN 5 WORKERS) --+--- BAMBOO PRODUCTS ...... 1
          |                                            +--- WEAVING (HAND LOOMS) --      2
          |                                            +--- OTHER ................ 1
          |
          +-- OTHER NON-TRADE SERVICES --+--- DAILY WORKER (PRIVATE BUSINESS) .. 1      1
                                         +--- OTHER ........................... 2

RETIRED PENSIONEE -------------------------------------------------------------       2
```

Source: Primary data processed by Vincent Rotgé using SAS (fieldwork implemented in 1992).

Structure of Primary Employment

Farm versus Nonfarm Activity: The share of agriculture as primary activity in the village of Kembang falls in between the values found in the lowland communities of Piring and Bandung respectively, suggesting that Kembang occupies an intermediate position in terms of dependency upon the agricultural sector for primary employment, between the two lowland communities. Thus, though a large percentage of the households have access to land and though the man-land ratio is relatively low in the studied area, about 40 per cent of workers are involved in farming as a primary activity - Table 7.3. This may be explained by the fact that many farmers are tenants of plots of land which are small, and also by the presence of opportunities in the nonfarm sectors, including in trade, which reduces local dependency upon agriculture. Thus, 60 per cent of the labour for primary activity is absorbed by trade and non-trade services (37.6 per cent), followed by the public sector (15 per cent, including clericals, extension workers, teachers and other employees of the educational sector), and other nonfarm activities. As in most other studied communities apart from Putat in Gunung Kidul Regency, especially in relatively peripheral and deadlocked communities, it is remarkable that nonfarm primary activities in Kembang remain restricted to trade and other services, while the role of local industry - including small-scale industry - is rather small as far as primary activity is concerned – Table 7.3. A rapid historical overview of the development of small-scale industry in Kembang casts light on today's low level of development. Numerous looms were operated in Kembang, prior to the 1970s producing a type of traditionally-woven belt for traditional Javanese female garments. Some villagers are still operating such handlooms today. One large entrepreneur, for instance, has ten looms operating in his house by elderly female employees. This entrepreneur owns fifteen further looms which are operated in the house of employees who work part-time as farmers and part-time on the looms. The belts are sold either in Godean or to traders in Yogyakarta. Nevertheless, the demand for such products has been decreasing for decades as the taste for traditional garments is diminishing. The long-term decline and today's stagnation of this industry cannot be related, therefore, to such a factor as the penetration of urban values in the village since the market for such products is not domestic but regional and even extra-regional, but rather to a change in life-style probably also associated with a change of generation among customers who, for many of them, live outside the community. On the other hand, a traditional Kembang industry such as mat-making using a type of locally-grown grass, is affected by the competition with mats which are manufactured by urban industries out of synthetic materials, probably in the same manner as construction materials such as woven bamboo panels made in lowland areas are disappearing due to the severe competition with new and cheaper construction materials.

Important Women's Role in Primary Employment in Kembang: An analysis of the structure of primary employment by gender in Kembang shows a clear female specialization in trade, *i.e.* retail and peddling trade, and trade at *pasar*. Such a specialization is often described in the literature for rural Java.[2] Women in Kembang are more mobile than males as far as primary employment is concerned, and hence play an essential role in the regional integration process of Kembang. This is not to say, however, that women do not assist in agriculture at all. They do so as a secondary, part-time, and also seasonal activity, especially during harvesting. At that time, agricultural tasks are very much labour intensive and spread over a relatively short period of time, requiring a high work participation within the household and the community.

Location of Primary Employment: Few village residents work outside the village or the Subdistrict (*Kecamatan*) on a permanent basis - Figure 7.4. Among the few who do so, half work in Subdistricts located on the other side of the Progo River, who may not have held such jobs prior to the construction of the bridge. At the same time, half of them are involved in clerical positions. Thus, primary employment in Kembang remains very largely locally-based. Also, the fact that only two years after the construction of the bridge, half of the few delocalized jobs are located in Districts east of the Progo River may suggest that - increasingly over time - new forms of employment may be secured by Kembang's residents in or in the vicinity of Yogyakarta. Furthermore, it is remarkable that none of Kembang's residents work undertake a primary activity in the capital of the Regency, Wates, though the village was closer by road to the village than to Yogyakarta prior to the construction of the bridge. It can be assumed, therefore, that further development that may be triggered by improved communications between Kembang and the eastern side of the Progo River may fully cut off Kembang from all interaction with Wates, even though one may wonder whether any significant level of interaction exists or has ever existed. As in the case of Bantul, the capital of the Regency of Bantul, this may also mean that improved communications between Yogyakarta and its extended periphery may have left unaltered and may have even worsened the slow development of secondary towns (the capitals of Regencies). In the context of improved regional communications, it is quite possible that the role of Yogyakarta and its extended periphery in offering delocalized forms of employment accessible from the hinterland through commuting will be further reinforced, while the growth and employment generation potential of secondary towns will remain weak if not insignificant.

A further important observation is that long-distance commuters tend to be those who hold a stable wage position especially as public or private clerical workers. In that sense, higher mobility in terms of distance of commuting in relation to employment, is very often associated with higher income status, as noticed by N.T. Effendi in the case of rural communities of West Java.[3] This is particularly true in communities which are more remote from urban areas where relatively better-paid jobs are created, such as Kembang or the hamlet of Piring in the village of Murtigading-Srigading which is studied above and which is located near the southern coast in a rather deadlocked part of the Plain of Bantul. This trend must not only be related to higher transportation costs which might be afforded by a significant share of villagers in a mechanistic manner, but also to a more uneven access to education in such communities and other possible factors. There are other forms of interaction between Kembang and other regional localities. Villagers commute to communities outside the village (mostly in relation to a primary activity) which are not fixed and may even vary over time. Nevertheless, such commuting remains mostly concentrated within neighbouring Districts, though it includes some trips to locations outside the Regency such as Yogyakarta in relation to trading which also includes such activities as securing goods which are then resold in Kembang. In a nutshell, the level of commuting between Kembang and Yogyakarta for both fixed or varying destinations over time remains considerably lower than the level of commuting between Yogyakarta and, for instance, the rather suburban hamlet of Bandung, in Pendowoharjo village in the Plain of Bantul which is studied above. But, at the same time, Kembang is a local trading centre in which the important level of interaction in trade with neighbouring communities generates locally-based employment.

Level and Share of Income Derived from Agriculture

In Kembang village, as in the rather deadlocked hamlet of Piring (in Murtigading-Srigading village) in the Plain of Bantul, about 60 per cent of households derive between 0 and 25 per cent of their income (calculated per capita) from agriculture - Table 7.5.[4] Nevertheless, as compared to Piring, more households in Kembang are widely dependent upon agriculture for their income: 27 per cent of all households in Kembang derive from 50 per cent up to 100 per cent of their income from agriculture - Tables 6.2 and 7.5. At the same time, it appears that in Kembang as in other studied communities, the more diversified the household income outside of agriculture the higher its level. Nevertheless, income levels in Kembang are by and large significantly lower than in other villages of the Plain of Bantul (Pendowoharjo and Murtigading-Srigading). Though the possibility that villagers may have under-reported their actual income cannot be fully discounted, such low levels of average income may be explained by:

(1) The low level of delocalized urban employment in Kembang (this, however would not be enough to explain large differentials in income levels with Piring which is similar to Kembang in that respect);

(2) Lower agricultural yields than in other lowland communities, and;

(3) The nature of trading activities in Kembang which generate employment but have low levels of return, as Ever noticed in another piedmont community of Central Java.[5]

It must be further noted that a larger household size in Kembang compared to the hamlet of Piring in the Plain of Bantul, may have somewhat increased income differentials between the two communities.

Figure 7.4   Kembang: Location of Settled Primary Employment in the D.I.Y. and outside Nanggulan Subdistrict

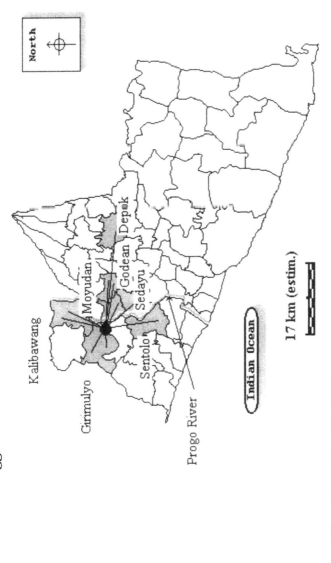

Source: Vincent Rotgé (December 1994).

Table 7.5   Kembang: Income Groups by Per Cent of Total Household Income Derived from Agriculture

0 per cent from agriculture			0⁺ to 25⁻ per cent from agriculture			25⁺ to 50⁻ per cent from agriculture		
No. of Cases	Row per cent	Annual average income (*Rupiah*)	No. of cases	Row per cent	Annual average income (*Rupiah*)	No. of cases	Row per cent	Annual average income (*Rupiah*)
25	20.16	778,230	50	40.32	716,518	15	12.10	510,876

50⁺ to 75⁻ per cent from agriculture			75⁺ to 100⁻ per cent from agriculture			All households		
No. of cases	Row per cent	Annual average income (*Rupiah*)	No. of cases	Row per cent	Annual average income (*Rupiah*)	No. of cases	Row per cent	Annual average income (*Rupiah*)
10	8.06	505,880	24	19.35	241,253	124	100	595,110

*   Total household income weighted by the number of members within household, as defined in Chapter 6.

Source: Primary data processed by Vincent Rotgé using SAS (fieldwork implemented in 1992).

Policy Implications and Conclusion

An important conclusion is that diversification of employment outside of agriculture in Kembang, as in the other studied lowland communities, impacts positively upon the income level of households. But also, as opposed to the communities of the Plain of Bantul, types of nonfarm activities which are undertaken in Kembang generate much lower levels of return and show a low level of interaction with Yogyakarta, while economic activities remain generally locally-based and/or oriented towards trading activities with the surrounding communities. A general explanation of the relatively low level of incomes in Kembang, as opposed to other communities of the Plain of Bantul which have been analysed in other sections of this study, is suggested below which relates to the interplay of geographical, historical, and economic factors.

In flatland areas, roads and irrigation canals frequently developed in tandem. Villages which had better accessibility to urban areas were therefore situated in flat and fertile lowland areas, which, due to the fact that they had been irrigated for longer periods, had, at the same time, generated a certain level of capital accumulation. In such communities, segments of the population would benefit from such accumulation. Furthermore, the varying degree of proximity of Yogyakarta for communities of the lowland areas has fostered - to a varying extent - the expansion of diversified forms of employment which may have furthermore benefited from financial transfers from the agricultural sectors in the wake of programmes of intensification of the rice subsector of the past decades (such as in the case of agroprocessing industries or other nonfarm activities undertaken by large-scale farmers). At the same time, the proximity of Yogyakarta particularly for suburban communities of the lowland areas has made it possible for many households to undertake two simultaneous activities, in many cases agriculture has gradually been overtaken by nonfarm activities as a primary activity. This scenario has generated a growth dynamic in many communities.

On the other hand, less accessible communities such as Kembang have not experienced the latter scenario. The development of a set of factors which is conducive to socioeconomic achievement (capital availability, etc.) has thereby been hampered. All in all, this has led to lower average income levels in such communities. Moreover, though diversification of employment outside of agriculture is important in Kembang, including employment mostly in the trade sector, any further expansion is limited by a set of factors including remoteness from Yogyakarta - where there are better paid jobs - which plays a very significant role, while most existing nonfarm locally-based activities do not yield such wages. In Kembang, such a basic scenario has been further compounded by the gradual disappearance of nonfarm activities which have traditionally been specific to the community, such as weaving or cattle trading for reasons which have been reviewed above. Simultaneously, retail trading continues to play an important role in Kembang for employment generation, and actually captures the demand from both local consumers and consumers originating from neighbouring communities. But its prospect is limited by the weak purchasing power of most of the households living in this area. Simultaneously, the future of local trade is made uncertain by the competition for consumers living in the surrounding areas west of the Progo River which, somewhat paradoxically, the construction of a bridge in 1990 may have facilitated between Kembang's traders and Godean's and Yogyakarta's traders. But, it is also true that the construction of the bridge has also introduced changes which have impacted positively upon certain types of activities. On the policy side, agricultural diversification in Kembang may prove promising due to the relative availability of land in the community, in contrast to communities of the Plain of Bantul where land is very much fragmented and man-land ratios are very high. Nevertheless, it is essential to stress that external and public intervention in this matter should be very cautious as any attempt to impose fixed prices (as it is currently the case for certain agricultural produce in some parts of the D.I.Y.) or too much public regulation upon farmers' initiatives will undoubtedly lead to passivity and mistrust, as well as to inhibiting spontaneous trends towards agricultural commercialization of products directly from the producers' cooperatives to the urban markets. In contrast, NGOs' assistance may prove useful in collaborating with local community-based organizations in, for instance, expanding credit facilities and providing further assistance in such areas as management and the marketing of crops. Furthermore, it may be desirable to try combining relevant public policies aimed at introducing adjustments in land tenure with NGOs' activities in Kembang. For instance, land-use regulations to prevent the use of sloping terrain for overintensive cultivation which may lead to environmental degradation should be considered. Other forms of public intervention could consist of studying forms of land tenure adjustments. Another possible form of public intervention would be to help the establishment of local industries with the main aim of compensating for the probable continued stagnation of retail trading in Kembang due to emerging competition between local and urban traders. In particular, specific programmes designed to enhance the role of women in the socioeconomic life of the community may find a very favourable environment in this community with a traditional background for important women's participation in local socioeconomic activities. It is also very likely that the community will increasingly integrate in the regional economy, as a consequence of recent developments in communications. Specific programmes aimed at raising education levels in the community that would target a broad segment of the population regarding, in particular, vocational education in activities which are likely to grow alongside urbanization (such as construction) could be considered.

Local development policies should be followed in Kembang which, in parts, may be similar to policies advisable for lowland communities, but which should also include policies adapted to the very specific characteristics of this piedmont community. This includes steps aimed at supporting the growth of endogenous activities, through, for example, promoting diversification of agriculture and possibly at introducing some small-scale industries to be identified in the context of increasing regional integration and rural-urban linkages. In particular, ways of diversifying the nature of linkages between Kembang and the neighbouring communities should be actively searched for, for at least two important reasons. First, due to new alternatives offered to villagers of upland communities in trading their goods to urban centres on the opposite (eastern) bank of the Progo River, trading relations with Kembang and these communities may be reduced in a manner that would probably benefit upland communities but would also affect Kembang's resource base. It would therefore be advisable to try to establish new types of economic relations between Kembang and the neighbouring communities, including upland communities to avoid the decline of Kembang as a local centre of economic activity. It is also advisable that efforts should be actively pursued towards integrating the development of Kembang with that of the surrounding communities, as neighbouring upland communities are even poorer than Kembang. Also, the need for external assistance and subsidies is certainly stronger in such a community as Kembang than in the relatively suburban communities of the Plain of Bantul where the proximity of Yogyakarta fosters a momentum for growth. In the former community (Kembang), public intervention or NGOs' assistance should be actively geared towards creating employment and economic growth and towards the provision of education and credit and other essential facilities and infrastructure. In the latter communities of the Plain of Bantul, priority for public action and for NGOs' assistance relates more to monitoring growth such as with regard to urban land-use and avoiding the widening of socioeconomic disparities as a result of uneven access to newly emerging opportunities. Considering that there is a momentum for economic growth in the latter communities which accompanies the urbanization process, available resources should be allocated, above all, to poverty alleviation schemes aimed at reducing disparities among social groups within urbanizing areas and, second, at reducing intraregional disparities between lowland and the more peripheral (*vis-à-vis* urban areas) upland and piedmont communities.

Figure 7.5   Views of Kembang

1.   View towards Kembang piedmont plain. The secondary irrigation canal (Kali Songgo) in the middle of the photograph illustrates the sharp boundary between wet and dry land. The dry land in the front cannot be irrigated because it is situated higher than the canal (no pumping device is currently available). The hand-shaped monument near the entrance gate of a neighbouring village stands here to remind villagers of the official family planning slogan: '*dua cukup*', *i.e.* 'two [children] are enough'.

2.   Weighing cloves sold by the inhabitants of the Menoreh mountains.

Source: Photographs by the author.

An Upland Community: the Hamlet of Putat II

Environmental Impediments to Development

The studied area coincides with the hamlet of 'Putat II' which is an administrative division of the village of Putat in Patuk Subdistrict. Putat lies in the Regency of Gunung Kidul, on the road linking Yogyakarta to Wonosari, the Regency capital, at an equal distance (15 km) from each of the two urban centres - Figure 7.6. The Regency of Gunung Kidul has been known in the geographical and development literature for lagging behind in terms of socioeconomic development and including some extreme cases of rural poverty. Fundamental reasons for such socioeconomic 'backwardness' relate to the District's very dissected topography and the scarcity of flatland apart from in the central area of the basin, which render communications difficult and are responsible for patterns of human settlements of a very sparse and scattered nature. In turn, human settlement patterns hamper the growth of certain types of economic activities. Moreover, in a very large part of the Regency, water is scarce. Permanently irrigated cultivation being impossible in many parts of Gunung Kidul including many upland areas of the hamlet of Putat II, dry rice is cultivated in such areas throughout the year.

Also, environmental degradation over many decades due to deforestation in this previously densely forested District (for the purposes of opening new agricultural land or charcoal-making) has led to the general impoverishment of upland areas. Such a process is not recent, as it probably stems from the last century, originally triggered by historical causes, as has been argued by scholars.[6] Nonetheless, afforestation policies are aimed today at upgrading the environment through the introduction of trees that can be harvested for their crops. Thus, forest resources can be tapped in a way which is environmentally sound, while the income of local farmers can be raised. Reasons for the low level of local socioeconomic development may be further cited which probably relate to local mismatches between labour and raw material inputs. They are developed in reference to the hamlet of Putat II later in this study where it is argued that both lack of storage and immediate need for cash, which force farmers to sell their crops after harvesting (also noticed in the case of lowland communities)[7] prevent the processing of agricultural products locally

Figure 7.6   Location of Putat

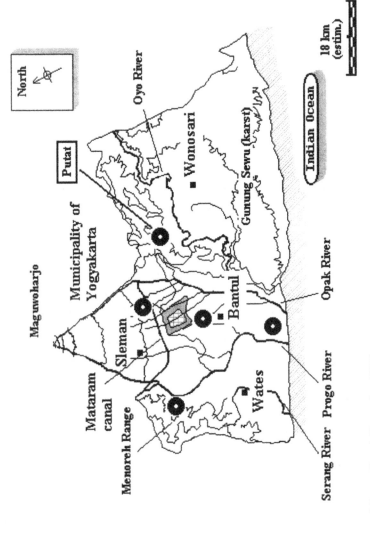

Source: Vincent Rotgé (December 1994).

Figure 7.7   Map of the Area Covered by the Study: Hamlet of 'Putat II' in Putat Village

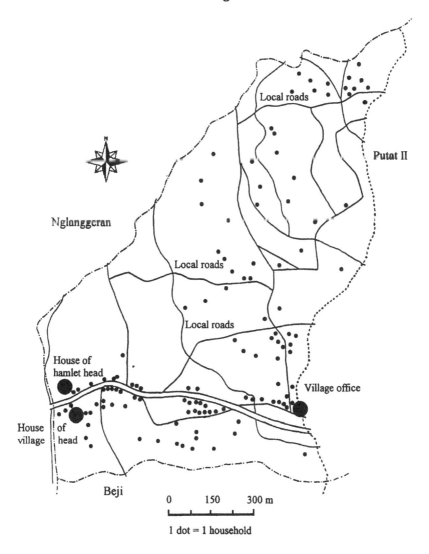

Source: Laboratory of Cartography, Faculty of Geography, Gadjah Mada University; adapted by Vincent Rotgé (1992).

Figure 7.8   Densities* in 1990 (inhabitants per km²) by *Desa* (administrative villages), Putat's Surroundings

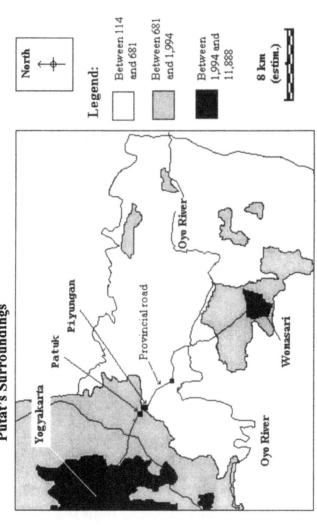

Legend:

☐ Between 114 and 681

▨ Between 681 and 1,994

■ Between 1,994 and 11,888

8 km (estim.)

*   These data are based on calculations from official registration acts. Assumedly, these demographic data are less reliable than those of the decennial census. In this study, they are only used to give a general view of densities by *desa*.

Source: Numerical data are from: *Penduduk, Kabupaten Bantul, Kabupaten Kulon Progo, Kabupaten Sleman, Kabupaten Gunung Kidul, Tahun 1992*, published separately by the statistical office of each Regency (*Kabupaten*). Data mapped by Vincent Rotgé (1994).

Figure 7.9   **Annual Population Growth Rate by Desa** (administrative villages), **Putat's Surroundings: 1980-1990, in percentages**

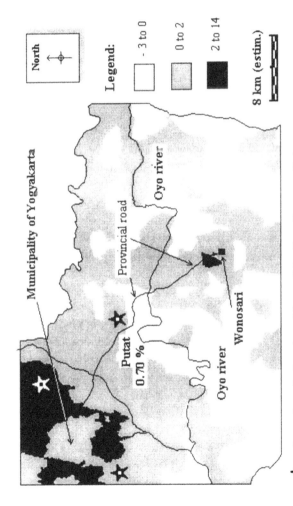

Source: For the numerical data: *Penduduk, Kabupaten Bantul, Hasil Sensus Penduduk 1990* (Yogyakarta: Provincial Statistical Office, February 1991) (and the same for, respectively, Kabupaten Sleman, Gunung Kidul, Kulon Progo and Koytamadya Yogyakarta); data mapped by the author; Vincent Rotgé (1994).

during the dry season. The crux is that such a process occurs when local labour (especially from those households living on sloping terrain not having access to wet land) would have been available for undertaking nonfarm activities during the period when rainfall is not available. A further impediment to local economic growth has been stressed, *viz.* the fact that the very specific nature of human settlements in hills of this Regency hampers the growth of industries producing or trading non-durables due to the lack of local marketing opportunities and difficulties for storing or carrying such types of goods over long distances without proper transportation facilities. This latter aspect is, indeed, essential since storage facilities - even for those consisting of a simple shed for storing harvested crops - are not available to a large number of households.[8]

Mitigating Factors

Still, all things being considered, Putat II can be regarded today as a relatively better-off hamlet in Gunung Kidul, whose population's socioeconomic characteristics compare very favourably with those of many more isolated and dryer hinterland areas of the Regency. In spite of its generally sloping and dissected terrain and rather unfavourable soil characteristics, Putat II has indeed benefited from a set of mitigating factors including the relative proximity of both Yogyakarta and Wonosari, together with the considerable improvements in public transportation transiting through or serving the village, which have taken place over the two last decades. Moreover, permanent irrigation is possible in Putat II in areas located in the valley where the groundwater does not lie very deep, though it is not possible in some elevated areas. Furthermore, the hamlet is conveniently located, for it does not lie at the dead end of a road heading to Yogyakarta. The town of Wonosari, lying east of Putat II, constitutes an active trading centre - more active than Wates, the capital of Kulon Progo Regency, for instance, and probably more than Bantul, the capital of the lowland District bearing the same name. Active trading in Wonosari can be explained in turn by the fact that this town lies at the centre of a basin while being relatively distant from Yogyakarta. Hence, as the capital of the D.I.Y. is located too far for some wholesale traders and retailers of Wonosari's hinterland to find any trade-off advantage in commuting to Yogyakarta, Wonosari's markets are probably spared a fierce competition with Yogyakarta's, while wholesalers from Yogyakarta come to purchase local commodities and cattle in Wonosari. A further asset of Putat II is that the hamlet lies along the road heading to the tourist site of Baron Beach.

Impact of Improved Communications

The magnitude of changes brought about in the hamlet of Putat II by improved communications can be better understood if one bears in mind that less than three decades ago local roads were in such bad condition and public transportation so limited that villagers planning to travel by bus needed to be wait-listed and to obtain an official letter of permission. Local villagers, not uncommonly, resorted to traveling by foot to nearby towns. Today, the regional road crossing the village has grown into an extremely busy thoroughfare with many local, regional but also extraregional bus lines (one line links Semarang to Jakarta for instance). Such a radical improvement of communications makes possible or facilitates trading activities, but also creates opportunities in the transport and other relevant service sectors (garages and retail trading to some extent). Simultaneously, better intra- and interregional communications and decreasing transportation fares on long and short distances facilitate all types of migrations including those related to economic purposes such as to secure employment outside the village. Links with permanent or circular outmigrants who are the relatives of local villagers are made easier especially at the time of *Lebaran* (a major holiday), making possible the diffusion of information regarding employment and other economic opportunities outside the village and the region to permanent residents of the village. The sending of remittances from circular and permanent migrants to relatives back home is also facilitated. Also, one can note at least one case of a permanent migrant living in Jakarta who has a secondary residence built in his native village, thereby creating some employment for construction and housekeeping. It is doubtful whether they would have done so, if the improvements in communications had not taken place between the hamlet of Putat II and Jakarta. Furthermore, circular migrations are facilitated during the dry season, thereby reducing the need for permanent out-migrations.

Types of Land-use and Tenure, and of Sharecropping Arrangements

A higher share of households than could be expected in this community located in a largely non-irrigated area, has access to a wet field (*sawah*) in the hamlet of Putat II which coincides with the studied area. In this regard, the village may be relatively exceptional within the Regency of Gunung Kidul, in the sense that the groundwater is shallow in the valley, enabling local farmers to irrigate their fields throughout the year by drawing water from wells adjacent to the *sawah* or by tapping water from nearby rivulets. About 53 per cent of studied households in the hamlet of Putat II have access to a *sawah* - Table 7.6. This level is approximately the same as in the suburban lowland hamlet of Bandung in Pendowoharjo village which is facing high population pressures analysed earlier. The low accessibility to *sawah* in the hamlet of Putat II results from the limited acreage of agricultural land that can be irrigated. Still, the ratio of the total area of *sawah* per capita is likely to be higher in Putat II than in Bandung. Average size of *sawah* in Putat II (0.3287 ha in Putat II's hinterland for owner-operated land) falls below 0.5 ha which is often considered as the minimum size for a *sawah* to support the annual household needs - Table 7.7a.[9]

Table 7.6   **Putat II: Access to *Sawah*, Including All Types of Land Tenure and Sharecropping Arrangements***
(percentages)

	No access to *Sawah*	Access to *Sawah*	All households
Transit Corridor	53.33 (16)**	46.66 (14)	# 100 (30)
Hinterland	44.44 (40)	55.55 (50)	# 100 (90)
All	46.66 (56)	53.33 (64)	# 100 (120)

*   Refer to following table.

**   Figures in parentheses represent the number of cases.

Source: Primary data processed by Vincent Rotgé using SAS (fieldwork implemented in 1992).

Furthermore, the high share of landowners not cultivating their land by themselves in communities of the Plain of Bantul indicates a positive trade-off between agricultural and nonfarm activities to the advantage of nonfarm activities, as far as the types of activities which are undertaken by the better-off socioeconomic group of landowners are concerned - Table 6.1. Conversely, the high share of owner-cultivated *sawah* which is found in the hamlet of Putat II and especially in the community's hinterland, seems to support the view that there would be no advantage for landowners in renting out their land or having it sharecropped. This suggests that nonfarm activities that are better-paid than agricultural activities are far fewer in Putat II than, for instance, in a relatively suburban hamlet such as Bandung where an important share of local landowners hold relatively well-paid positions in activities associated with the urbanization process, while raising an additional income from sharecropping or renting out their land. Such a high share of owner-cultivated *sawah* in Putat II tends to indicate that most nonfarm activities which are undertaken in this village are probably not only characterized by low levels of return, but probably also, if one refers to the whole year, by very low levels of labour-intensity. Therefore such nonfarm activities leave available time to farmers, for those at least who are not involved in activities requiring time-consuming daily commuting. This time can be spent on farming, either on an annual part-time or seasonal basis. Moreover, the high share of owner-cultivated *sawah* found in Putat II seems to indicate that there might not be any advantage for farmers who own a *sawah* in undertaking nonfarm activities due to the difficulty in accessing nonfarm activities which show a higher level of return than farming in the irrigated parts of Putat II - Table 7.7a. In a nutshell, it can be said that neither farming nor nonfarm activities would alone raise enough income to support the needs of households in this community. Also, households in Putat II live at a level of subsistence which is probably even more accentuated than in any other of the communities which have been studied in this work - Tables 6.2, 7.5 and 7.12.[10] Furthermore, as in other studied communities, but probably to a larger extent in Putat II, very wide disparities in size of *sawah* which are owned by households are suggested by important standard deviations. Such wide disparities can be identified in particular in the transit corridor - Table 7.7a. Apart from *sawah* many households operate dry fields (*tegal*) in Putat II. The fact that average size of *tegal* in Putat II is considerably higher than the corresponding figure for *sawah* should not be surprising. Nevertheless, high levels in average size of dry fields ought not to obscure the fact that such fields are also very often characterized by low yield levels, and in sloping terrain a very fragmented topography that makes these fields difficult to cultivate or access. In such fields, indeed, crops are grown such as peanuts, 'yard long beans' (*kacang panjang*), maize, a variety of rice grown in dry land, cassava, etc., which are usually mixed with other crops such as trees or bushes which are tapped for charcoal-making. Other treecrops have recently included cacao.

Demographic Structure

Demographic and household structure in Putat II are characteristic of a poor community with a low capacity for locally-based employment expansion. Thus, population deficit in the 20-35 year age group is very important, due to the paucity of employment opportunities for youth entering the work force. Such a deficit is also more accentuated for males than for females as rural males are usually more mobile than females - Tables 7.8 and 7.9. Simultaneously, the average household size in Putat II as a whole (including transit-corridor and hinterland communities) is the smallest among all studied communities, ranking last after the nonsuburban village of Murtigading-Srigading in the Plain of Bantul (including the hamlets of Piring and Celep). Also, a severe population deficit in the 20-29 year age group in the transit corridor - Table 7.8 - suggests that the fast and recent developments in communications experienced in Putat II may have fueled emigration from the transit corridor where average levels of income are higher for those households which derive more than half of their income from nonfarm activities - Table 7.11. This supports the view whereby in poor and remote communities, individuals originating from upper socioeconomic groups will be more mobile.[11] Such a level of youth emigration from the transit corridor of Putat II may be opposed to the pattern found in the more suburban hamlet of Karanggondang-Cepit in the village of Pendowoharjo, Plain of Bantul, where, on the contrary, youth within the 20-29 year age group tends to stay in the community to a larger extent than in the community's hinterland. Likely, the improvement of communications in a hamlet such as Putat II, where employment opportunities offering a sufficient level of earning are rare, leads to increased youth migration, in contrast to rather suburban areas where some locally-based and delocalized employment opportunities accessible through commuting are available.

Structure of Primary Employment

Farm versus Nonfarm Activity: An analysis of the structure of employment by sectors of primary activity in Putat II reveals that the share of agriculture for primary employment falls below 50 per cent in both the transit corridor and hinterland of Putat II (respectively 36.4 per cent and 48.3 per cent; Table 7.10). At the same time, a very clear female specialization in agriculture can be identified. As a matter of fact, 45.8 per cent and 69.5 per cent of all females in, respectively, the transit corridor and hinterland of Putat II are engaged in primary activity in the agricultural sector. This pattern is particularly remarkable for it contrasts sharply with patterns of female employment in all other studied communities. In all such communities apart from Putat II, indeed, agriculture constitutes a very clear male specialization, while females do participate in agricultural activities, but to a lesser extent, and frequently as a secondary activity. Such a peculiarity of Putat II's structure of employment can be explained by the low labour-intensive nature off-season of agricultural activity in this community, where many households own dry rather than wet fields. At the same time, the difficult topographic conditions, the nature of soils and impractical and non-permanent irrigation or unavailability of irrigation on undulating terrain, and second, the small size of wet fields in the valley are all together responsible for the low productivity of farming in Putat II. While agricultural activity in upland areas of Putat II is probably time-consuming, the income which it generates is insufficient, creating a stringent need for complementary nonfarm activity(-ies) within the household. Therefore, household members must look for employment outside of agriculture. But nonfarm employment in this nonsuburban and poor community, where the socioeconomic development level and the level of training of labour are low, are somewhat restricted to a range of low-skill activities frequently involving physical hardship or requiring circular migrations, which are mostly undertaken by males, *viz.* repair work, carpentry, garage work, masonry, quarrying, bus or truck driving, road construction work, etc. Male specialization appears also but to a lesser extent in the cottage industry sub-sector and in the public.

A number of important conclusions can be drawn:
(1) In both the transit corridor and hinterland of Putat II, primary employment is very widely diversified;
(2) Even in Putat II's hinterland, the level of employment diversification for both males and females is still higher than in the hinterland of any

other of the studied communities, including suburban wetland communities;

(3) Level of employment diversification in Putat II is higher in the transit corridor than in the hinterland;

(4) If only males are considered, the levels of employment diversification in both transit-corridor and hinterland areas are among the highest, if not the highest, among all studied communities, including the suburban lowland and wetland community of the hamlet of Bandung. As a matter of fact, a very large share (more than 65 per cent) of all males in Putat II's hinterland are engaged in a primary activity belonging to the following sectors: non-trade services (20.4 per cent), trade (settled, peddling and at market: 13.5 per cent), industry (12.4 per cent), public sector (civil servants: 10.2 per cent), and transport (9.1 per cent);

(5) In sharp contrast to all the other studied communities, *female, not male specialization in agriculture* can be identified in Putat II. Thus, about twice as many females as males, in relative terms, are engaged in a primary activity in agriculture.

The main conclusion to this section is that it is paradoxical only at first glance that the highest level of primary employment diversification can be found in Putat II, which is characterized by the lowest level of socioeconomic achievement among the studied communities and is not a suburb either of Yogyakarta or of a regional secondary town. In reality, the low agricultural potential of land in Putat II renders such a pattern inevitable. However, as confirmed below, such a high level of nonfarm employment diversification means that a significant share of villagers are engaged in low-skill activities characterized by low levels of return. In this respect, nonfarm employment in Putat II contrasts sharply with the type of nonfarm employment found in suburban communities which are located in the lowland and wetland area of the Plain of Bantul. Thus, it can be assumed that in the peripheral hamlet of Piring located in the Plain of Bantul and characterized by very fertile agricultural land and very high man-land ratios, the growth of nonfarm employment has been inhibited by negative locational factors (the distance of the community to Yogyakarta), but also by positive factors relating to the quality of agricultural land and infrastructures which reduces the need for alternatives. In Putat II, on the other hand, low agricultural potential has clearly provided an incentive to nonfarm diversification. But, nonfarm employment in most cases has not

Table 7.7 **Putat II: Size of Land in m² Tenanted by Households, by Types of Land Tenure and Sharecropping Arrangements**

a. **Wetland Farming** (*wet fields or sawah*)

	Number of occurences	Minimum size (in m²)	Maximum size (in m²)	Average (in m²)	Standard deviation
a.1 Putat II's Transit-Corridor					
Sharecropping system:					
The household owns the land which is sharecropped: *maro**	4	110	2,500	1,327	1,111
The household owns the land which is not sharecropped: The household operates the land:	8	600	100,999	15,037	34,965
a.2 Putat II's Hinterland					
Sharecropping system:					
The household owns the land which is sharecropped: *maro**	1	500	500	500	.
The household owns the land which is not sharecropped: The household operates the land:	46	100	22,000	3,287	3,560
The household rents out the land:	1	1000	1000	1000	.

* See Glossary.

Source: Primary data processed by Vincent Rotgé using SAS (fieldwork implemented in 1992).

Table 7.7 (continued)

b. Dryland Farming (dry fields or *tegal*)

	Number of occurences	Minimum size (in m²)	Maximum size (in m²)	Average (in m²)	Standard deviation
b.1 Putat II's Transit-Corridor					
The household owns the land which is sharecropped:					
Sharecropping system:					
*maro**	2	3,000	10,000	6,500	4,949
*mertelu**	5	3,500	10,000	7,100	2,924
The household owns the land which is not sharecropped:					
The household operates the land:	19	100	20,000	5,842	5,742
The household rents out the land:	1	5,000	5,000	5,000	
b.2 Putat II's Hinterland					
The household owns the land which is sharecropped:					
Sharecropping system:					
*maro**	2	500	2,000	1,250	1,060
*mertelu**	2	5,000	5,000	5,000	
The household owns the land which is not sharecropped:					
The household operates the land:	58	500	102,499	8,592	13,781
The household rents out the land:	1	6,200	6,200	6,200	

*   See Glossary.

Source: Primary data processed by Vincent Rotgé using SAS (fieldwork implemented in 1992).

Table 7.8   Age Pyramid of Putat II's Transit Corridor

MALES (1)	(2)	(3)	(4)	Age	FEMALES (1)	(2)	(3)	(4)
0	0	0.00	0.00	90-94	1	1	1.56	1.56
1	1	1.45	1.45	85-89	0	1	0.00	1.56
1	2	1.45	2.90	80-84	0	1	0.00	1.56
0	2	0.00	2.90	75-79	2	3	3.12	4.69
1	3	1.45	4.35	70-74	1	4	1.56	6.25
2	5	2.90	7.25	65-69	0	4	0.00	6.25
3	8	4.35	11.59	60-64	3	7	4.69	10.94
1	9	1.45	13.04	55-59	4	11	6.25	17.19
1	10	1.45	14.49	50-54	4	15	6.25	23.44
4	14	5.80	20.29	45-49	2	17	3.12	26.56
4	18	5.80	26.09	40-44	3	20	4.69	31.25
6	24	8.70	34.78	35-39	7	27	10.94	42.19
5	29	7.25	42.03	30-34	6	33	9.38	51.56
1	30	1.45	43.48	25-29	6	39	9.38	60.94
4	34	5.80	49.28	20-24	0	39	0.00	60.94
14	48	20.29	69.57	15-19	6	45	9.38	70.31
13	61	18.84	88.41	10-14	10	55	15.63	85.94
3	64	4.35	92.75	05-09	6	61	9.38	95.31
5	69	7.25	100.00	00-04	3	64	4.69	100.00

Percentage (Males): 18   14   11   7   4

Percentage (Females): 4   7   11   14

Note: Column (1): Number of cases; Column (2): Cumulative number of cases; Column (3): Per cent of the total population; Column (4): Cumulative per cent of the total population.

Source: Primary data processed by Vincent Rotgé using SAS (fieldwork implemented in 1992).

Table 7.9   Age Pyramid of Putat II's Hinterland

	MALES			Age		FEMALES		
(1)	(2)	(3)	(4)		(1)	(2)	(3)	(4)
1	1	0.51	0.51	95–	1	1	0.52	0.52
0	1	0.00	0.51	90–94	1	2	0.52	1.04
1	2	0.51	1.02	85–89	0	2	0.00	1.04
3	5	1.53	2.55	80–84	2	4	1.04	2.07
2	7	1.02	3.57	75–79	0	4	0.00	2.07
3	10	1.53	5.10	70–74	0	4	0.00	2.07
2	12	1.02	6.12	65–69	2	6	1.04	3.11
8	20	4.08	10.20	60–64	6	12	3.11	6.22
6	26	3.06	13.27	55–59	4	16	2.07	8.29
5	31	2.55	15.82	50–54	10	26	5.18	13.47
7	38	3.57	19.39	45–49	6	32	3.11	16.58
9	47	4.59	23.98	40–44	12	44	6.22	22.80
22	69	11.22	35.20	35–39	12	56	6.22	29.02
12	81	6.12	41.33	30–34	21	77	10.88	39.90
10	91	5.10	46.43	25–29	15	92	7.77	47.67
16	107	8.16	54.59	20–24	15	107	7.77	55.44
16	123	8.16	62.76	15–19	18	125	9.33	64.77
29	152	14.80	77.55	10–14	23	148	11.92	76.68
26	178	13.27	90.82	05–09	24	172	12.44	89.12
18	196	9.18	100.00	00–04	21	193	10.88	100.00

Note: Column (1): Number of cases; Column (2): Cumulative number of cases; Column (3): Per cent of the total population; Column (4): Cumulative per cent of the total population.

Source: Primary data processed by Vincent Rotgé using SAS (fieldwork implemented in 1992).

Table 7.10 Per Cent of Workers Engaged in a Primary Activity, for Workers above 15 Years of Age (percentages)

a. **Putat II's Transit Corridor**

	Agriculture	Intermediate large industry*	Cottage / small-scale industry**	Transport	Civil service	Trade at market	Peddling trade	Settled trade	Other ***	All
Males	29 (9)****	3.2 (1)	3.2 (1)	9.7 (3)	16.1 (5)	6.4 (2)	3.2 (1)	3.2 (1)	25.8 (8)	# 100 (31)
Females	45.8 (11)	8.3 (2)	8.3 (2)	0 (0)	4.2 (1)	8.3 (2)	4.2 (1)	8.3 (2)	20.8 (5)	# 100 (24)
All	36.4 (20)	5.4 (3)	5.4 (3)	5.4 (3)	10.9 (6)	7.3 (4)	3.6 (2)	5.4 (3)	23.6 (13)	# 100 (55)

*: Employing between 50 and 100 workers.

**: Employing up to 19 workers.

***: Includes tailoring, repairwork, carpentry, masonry, garage work, and others.

****: Figures in parentheses represent number of cases.

Source: Primary data processed by Vincent Rotgé using SAS (fieldwork implemented in 1992).

Table 7.10 (continued)

b. Putat II's Hinterland

	Agriculture	Intermediate large industry*	Cottage / small-scale industry**	Transport	Civil service	Trade at market	Peddling trade	Settled trade	Other ***	All
Males	34.1 (30) ****	1.1 (1)	11.4 (10)	9.1 (8)	10.2 (9)	4.5 (4)	7.9 (7)	1.1 (1)	20.4 (18)	# 100 (88)
Females	69.5 (41)	1.7 (1)	0 (0)	3.4 (2)	1.7 (1)	5.1 (3)	10.1 (6)	3.4 (2)	5.1 (3)	# 100 (59)
All	48.3 (71)	1.4 (2)	6.8 (10)	6.8 (10)	6.8 (10)	4.8 (7)	8.8 (13)	2 (3)	14.3 (21)	# 100 (147)

*:   Employing between 50 and 100 workers.
**:   Employing up to 19 workers.
***:   Includes, quarrying and carpentry and others.
****:   Figures in parentheses represent number of cases.

Source: Primary data processed by Vincent Rotgé using SAS (fieldwork implemented in 1992).

Table 7.11a   Employment Structure in 1992: Putat II's Transit Corridor - For Male and Female Workers (primary activity)

(i) Government

```
DEFENSE ----------- MILITARY (NOT RETIRED) ........................ 1

                +- INTERMEDIATE AND LOWER CLERICAL  ............... 1
CIVILIAN CLERICAL --------+
                +- LOCAL RURAL DEVELOPMENT CADRE: IRRIGATION/WATER-PUMP SUPERVISOR . 1

PUBLIC EDUCATION ------------ TEACHER OF ELEMENTARY SCHOOL ........ 2
```

(ii) Non-government

```
       |-- SELF/HOUSEHOLD-EMPLOYED ---- LABOURER ----- LANDOWNER OR TENANT (DOES NOT SHARECROP). 8   1
FARM ---+
       |-- HIRED LABOURER -------------- DAILY LABOURER ........... 1   11
```

Table 7.11a (continued)

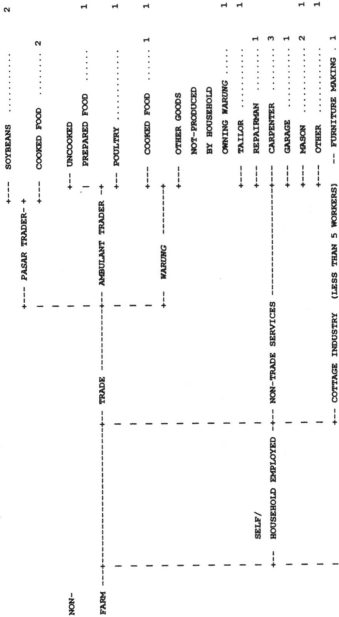

	PASAR TRADER	SOYBEANS	2
		COOKED FOOD	2
		UNCOOKED	1
TRADE	AMBULANT TRADER	PREPARED FOOD	
		POULTRY	1
	WARUNG	COOKED FOOD	1
		OTHER GOODS NOT-PRODUCED BY HOUSEHOLD OWNING WARUNG	1
		TAILOR	1
NON-TRADE SERVICES		REPAIRMAN	1
		CARPENTER	3
		GARAGE	1
		MASON	2
		OTHER	1
COTTAGE INDUSTRY (LESS THAN 5 WORKERS)		FURNITURE MAKING	1

NON-FARM — SELF/HOUSEHOLD EMPLOYED

Table 7.11a (continued)

```
NON-
FARM ---+
        |           +-- DOMESTIC SERVANT  -----------------------------------  1
        |           |
        |           +-- TRANSPORT  --------+-- BUS DRIVER   ............  2
        |           |                      +--- TRUCK DRIVER ............  1
        +----- EMPLOYEE ---------+--                                
        |           INTERMEDIATE LARGE                              
        |           INDUSTRY (50 TO 100 WK) -----+-- EXTRACTIVE INDUSTRY  ....  1
        |           |                            +-- PLASTIC PRODUCTS   ......  2
        |           |
        |           +-- OTHER NON-TRADE SERVICES -----+-- DAILY WORKER  ...........  1
                                                      |   (ROAD OR CONSTRUCTION)
                                                      +-- OTHER DAILY WORKER  .....  1

RETIRED PENSIONEE   --------------------------------------------------------  1
```

Source: Primary data processed by Vincent Rotgé using SAS (fieldwork implemented in 1992).

**Table 7.11b   Employment Structure in 1992: Putat II's Hinterland -
For Male and Female Workers (primary activity)**

(i) Government

DEFENSE ----------------- MILITARY (ON THE ACTIVE LIST)	1
+- INTERMEDIATE AND LOWER CLERICAL	6 1
CIVILIAN CLERICAL ----+	
+- LOCAL RURAL DEVELOPMENT CADRE: IRRIGATION/WATER-PUMP SUPERVISOR	1
PUBLIC EDUCATION ------ TEACHER OF ELEMENTARY SCHOOL	1

Table 7.11b (continued)   (ii) Non-government

```
FARM --+
       +-- SELF/
       |   HOUSEHOLD-EMPLOYED -- LABOURER - +
       |                                    +-------- LANDOWNER OR TENANT (DOES NOT SHARECROP) .....  29   37
       |                                    |
       |                                    +-------- SHARECROPS (TENANT, NOT LANDLORD) ..........        1
       |
       +-- HIRED LABOURER ----- DAILY LABOURER -+
                                                +--------- SEASONAL  ..............................  1    1
                                                |
                                                +--------- CASUAL  ................................       2

SELF/HOUSEHOLD
 +- EMPLOYED --------+
                     +-- PASAR TRADER -+--- SOYBEANS  ............................................  2    2
                     |                 +--- CASSAVA  .............................................  2    2
                     |                 +--- OTHER AGRICULTURAL PRODUCTS  .........................  1
                     |
                     +--- SOYBEANS  ..................................................................  1    1
                     +--- UNCOOKED PREPARED FOOD  ....................................................  1    1
                     +--- BAMBOO PRODUCTS  ...........................................................  1
                     +--- OTHER TRADITIONALLY MANUFACTURED PLANT
                     |                                                PRODUCTS  ....................
                     +--- POULTRY  ...................................................................  1    2
                     +--- TRADITIONAL MEDICINES  ...................................................        2
 +- TRADE + AMBULANT TRADER +--- OTHER FOOD PREPARED BY HOUSEHOLD  ..................................  1
                            +--- VEGETABLES  ........................................................  1    1
                            +--- OTHER  .............................................................  1    1
```

Table 7.11b (continued)

```
                    +- TRADE +
                    |        +--- GROCERY ........................ 1
                    |        |
                    |        +-- WARUNG ---+
                    |        |             +-- OWNING WARUNG ........ 1
                    |        |             +-- OTHER CRAFTS PRODUCED BY HOUSEHOLD
                    |        |
                    |        +--- OTHER SETTLED TRADE ------- CONSTRUCTION MATERIALS ...... 1
 SELF/HOUSEHOLD     |
  +- EMPLOYED ------+                                    +-- QUARRYMAN ........... 5
  |                 |                                    +-- CARPENTER ......... 2
  |                 +-- NON-TRADE SERVICES --------------+-- OTHER ............ 2
  |                                                      +-- TRADITIONAL GARMENTS . 1
  |
NON- |
FARM -+                                                        +-- SILVERCRAFT ...... 1
  |  +-- COTTAGE INDUSTRY (LESS THAN 5 WORKERS) ---+-----+-- OTHER ............ 8
  |  |                                                   +-- BUS DRIVER ......... 1
  |  |
  |  +-- TRANSPORT ----------------------------------+-- TRUCK DRIVER ........ 2
  |  |                                               +-- OTHER ............ 5
  +- EMPLOYEE ---------+-- INTERMEDIATE LARGE INDUSTRY (50 TO 100 WK) ------ PLASTIC PRODUCTS ...... 1
     |                 |
     |                 +-- MEDIUM-SIZED INDUSTRY (20 TO 49 WK) ------------+-- CHEMICALS ............. 1
     |                 |
     |                 +-- OTHER NON-TRADE SERVICES -------------------- DAILY WORKER
     |                                                                  |  (ROAD OR CONSTRUCTION) . 7
     +                                                                  +-- OTHER DAILY WORKER .... 2
```

Source: Primary data processed by Vincent Rotgé using SAS (fieldwork implemented in 1992).

Figure 7.10 Putat II's Transit Corridor: Location of Settled Primary Employment in the D.I.Y. and outside Patuk Subdistrict

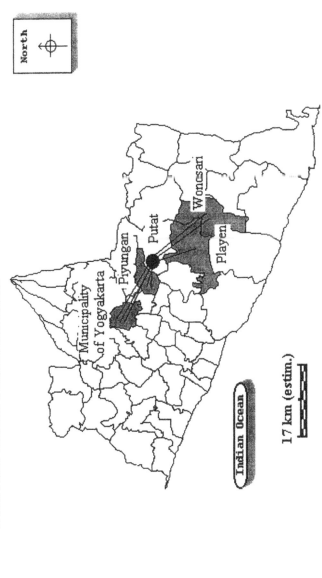

Note: The boundaries of the Subdistricts of destination which are located within the Municipality of Yogyakarta are not shown on the map. These Subdistricts are: Danurejan, Umbulharjo, Jetis.

Source: Vincent Rotgé (December 1994).

Figure 7.11   Putat II's Hinterland: Location of Settled Primary Employment in the D.I.Y. and outside Patuk Subdistrict

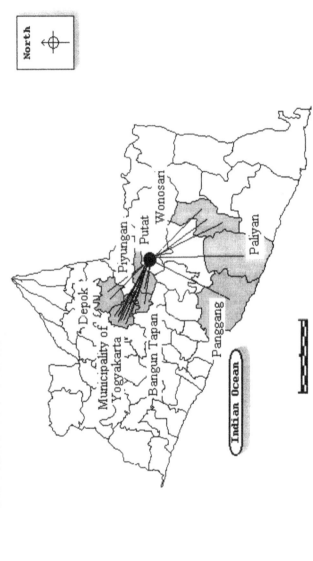

Note: The boundaries of the Subdistricts of destination which are located within the Municipality of Yogyakarta are not shown on the map. These Subdistricts are: Mantrijeron, Umbulharjo, Pakualaman, Gondomanan.

Source: Vincent Rotgé (December 1994).

Figure 7.12   Views of Putat II

1.   The traditional house of a poor family.

2.   The 'urbanized' house of an urban migrant.

Source: Photographs by the author.

been chosen in Putat II as a positive trade-off with agriculture, but simply out of absolute necessity. Putat II's villagers, who are presumably less educated and trained for holding clerical jobs than in better-off agrarian communities of the Plain of Bantul, are also more inclined to take up low-return jobs in the urban sector. At the same time, the process of capital accumulation has been somewhat possible in lowland and wetland communities which are endowed with fertile agricultural land (though probably restricted to a relatively small group of residents). This has also rendered possible in such communities a shift to nonfarm activities through the investment of some agricultural profits into the education of the youth or/and in fixed capital for nonfarm activities, including agricultural processing activities. The crux is that such a process could not be realized in areas with low agricultural potential where even more farmers live at a critical level of subsistence.

In some instances, low levels of economic return from activities in Putat II relate to the difficulties faced by villagers in entering competition in, or simply gaining access to, the regional and urban markets. For instance, some existing - though very few - local activities, such as mask-making, address the urban tourism sector. Nonetheless, the products are not sold directly by the craftsmen to the tourists, but through an urban wholesale trader who operates the finishing (painting) and reaps the largest share of the final profit. This example illustrates the inability of some workers from Putat II to take advantage of existing possibilities in the urban market in a fully competitive way, in spite of real local advantages such as low wages and, in some cases, real expertise in wood-carving or processing. Such an inability can be traced back, in turn, to the small size of locally-based enterprises (small enterprises concentrating on production at subsistence level without having the financial or manpower resources for dealing with marketing), insufficient private transportation or inadequate training and information regarding management and marketing. In other instances, Putat II's workers display a real ability in gaining access to employment opportunities outside the village, but their success in doing so partly stems from a competitive edge arising from their acceptance of low wage levels. Thus, road and construction workers from Putat II work on a non-permanent basis outside the village, in urban or urbanizing areas of the D.I.Y. where employment is created in this subsector, or outside the region altogether. Some of these workers working on large construction sites may be hired in preference to local workers who are usually paid less than locally-based workers. The existing system of labour recruitment, which involves middlemen (*mandor*) who, in turn, frequently subcontract their work but keep the differences between the contracted and actual wage, fuels such a process. The crux is that, apart from excesses such as in working conditions and possible embezzlement, such a system draws wages down to the bottom line. And, if it may be considered as somewhat benefiting poor communities in generating employment for its members, it also rests on the readiness of the poorest communities to supply low-skilled labour accepting low wages below contracted wages and in difficult working conditions.

Location of Employment: Nearly 13 per cent of all workers in Putat II are engaged in primary activity, which is a regular and settled activity based outside Patuk Subdistrict where Putat II is located. It is remarkable that all such jobs are located either:
(1)   Within the Municipality of Yogyakarta (38.5 per cent);
(2)   Within close proximity of the Municipality of Yogyakarta (19.2 per cent);
(3)   In Wonosari (19.2 per cent), or;
(4)   In other Subdistricts of the D.I.Y. which include a small urban centre located at crossroads (19.2 per cent).

This is to say that more than one worker out of ten engaged in a primary economic activity in Putat II is involved in a regular and settled activity - mostly in services - which is located in an urban or urbanizing area of the D.I.Y. Very few among these workers work for a non-service activity (only 7.7 per cent do so for the small-scale and cottage industry). Worth noting finally is that clerical employment as a form of urban employment accessible through commuting is clearly under-represented in Putat II, as urban low-paid activities largely dominate. Only regular and settled activities have been considered so far in this section. However, some villagers from Putat II work on an irregular and seasonal basis in urban areas located within the D.I.Y. or in other Javanese urban centres which have direct bus connections with the village. This holds true in particular for Jakarta in the case of construction workers. In short, a significant share of Putat II's villagers hold a regular position or undertake irregular activities in urban or urbanizing areas of the D.I.Y., while a few work occasionally outside the D.I.Y., mostly in Jakarta. Among the former, most work or undertake irregular activities in the Municipality of Yogyakarta or in its outskirts, but also in Wonosari or in smaller urban centres such as for instance the nearby piedmont trading centre of

Piyungan - Figures 7.10 and 7.11. Hence, it would be misleading to regard Putat II as an isolated community that could be characterized by a low level of interaction with the regional economy and probably also to some much lesser extent with the national economy. On the contrary, among the studied communities, Putat II is one of the most extrovert in terms of labour flows (but not in terms of inward and outward flows of commodities).[12] The crux is that delocalized clerical employment in urban areas that was rather common in suburban hamlets of the Plain of Bantul, is exceptional in Putat II where the employment base remains restricted to relatively low-paid cottage industries or unskilled activities.

Level and Share of Income Derived from Agriculture: An analysis of the share of income which is derived from agriculture in Putat II indicates that - Table 7.12:

(1) Less than a third of all households derive between 75 per cent and 100 per cent of their income from agriculture;

(2) About another third derive between 25 per cent and 75 per cent of income from agriculture;

(3) The last third derive some income but less than 25 per cent of income from agriculture, and;

(4) A very small share of all households does not depend at all upon agriculture.

Also, data show that the average level of income is very low in Putat II, as compared to other studied communities, being about 20 per cent lower than in the piedmont community of Kembang and more than 63 per cent lower than in all studied communities of the Plain of Bantul when considered in their aggregate. Furthermore, it must be stressed that in Putat II, the level of income does not seem to be correlated with the share of this income which is derived from agriculture. This fact is particularly remarkable in so far as it contrasts sharply with existing trends noted in all other studied communities, whereby level of income and the share of this income which is derived from agriculture are inversely related. This confirms that in Putat II, nonfarm diversification of employment is necessary for a very large share of households, but also that at the same time, nonfarm employment generates by and large very low levels of return.

Table 7.12   Putat II: Income Groups by Per Cent of Total Household Income Derived from Agriculture

	0 per cent from agriculture			0⁺ to 25⁻ per cent from agriculture			25⁺ to 50⁻ per cent from agriculture		
	No. of cases	Row per cent	Annual average income (*Rupiah*)	No. of cases	Row per cent	Annual average income (*Rupiah*)	No. of cases	Row per cent	Annual average income (*Rupiah*)
Putat II Transit corridor	-	-	-	12	38.71	429,833	10	32.26	541,205
Putat II Hinterland	6	6..9	540,650	27	31.03	417,055	16	18.39	452,348
All	6	5.08	540,650	39	33.05	420,986	26	22.03	486,524

	50⁺ to 75⁻ per cent from agriculture			75⁺ to 100⁻ per cent from agriculture			All households		
	No. of cases	Row per cent	Annual average income (*Rupiah*)	No. of cases	Row per cent	Annual average income (*Rupiah*)	No. of cases	Row per cent	Annual average income (*Rupiah*)
Putat II Transit corridor	3	9.68	426,138	6	19.35	223,153	31	# 100	425,399
Putat II Hinterland	9	10.34	673,343	29	33.33	501,093	87	# 100	486,595
All	12	10.17	611,542	35	29.66	453,446	118	# 100	470,518

*   Total household income weighted by the number of members within household, as defined in Chapter 6.

Source: Primary data processed by Vincent Rotgé using SAS (fieldwork implemented in 1992).

This also confirms that:

(1) Nonfarm employment is undertaken at subsistence level in Putat II;
(2) Agricultural and nonfarm income complement each other in such a way that in a great many cases neither agriculture nor nonfarm employment can be considered as marginal within the same household.

On the contrary, employment multiplicity within the household is high in Putat II given the general paucity of productive activities which make villagers look for all possible means to increase their low incomes. Nonetheless, in contrast with the hamlet of Bandung, it is likely that the former type of employment multiplicity is hampered by the time-consuming nature of commuting from Putat II to Yogyakarta and to Wonosari. This observation is likely to apply particularly to male labour in Putat II who commutes to urban areas. A further important observation is that in Putat II, level of income for all households is surprisingly lower (by 12 per cent) in the transit-corridor, than in the hinterland area. This is probably related to the fact that irrigation in the land bordering the main road which is located at some elevation seems to be less developed than in the valley further away down the road for reasons explained earlier in this study. Second, types of retail trading (*warung*) undertaken along the transit corridor are also characterized by very low levels of return, which are limited by the weak purchasing power of the very large majority of households.

Policy Implications and Conclusion

This study of the community of Putat II suggests that given the paucity of locally-based productive activities, a possible local development policy may consist in raising the chances of Putat II's villagers to gain access to regional employment opportunities, including those which are located at a commuting distance. This type of approach might indeed be more realistic and feasible than one that would consist in attempting to solve the whole dimension of the problem of employment expansion in Putat II at the local level. This is particularly true as local purchasing power is very low, reducing the scope for any rapid and significant growth of the locally-based activities in trade and other services which target local consumers, if the level of external remittances is not increased. Educational and vocational training programmes should be set up, commensurate with the educational level of local youth, of the standard required for qualifying for urban sector positions, or for job opportunities such as those provided through the existing work-abroad programmes, and also the public regional work programme. Such programmes would be efficient, if they are combined with transportation policies aimed at providing relevant assistance to individuals and small-scale enterprises, such as in the form of allowances or subsidized credit for acquiring private motorized transportation suitable for local topographic conditions (few local villagers own bicycles for this reason). The feasibility of providing local villagers with public transport allowances for economic purposes could be studied as a possible alternative. Simultaneously, both public and NGOs' efforts should be directed towards strengthening local activities, such as wood-processing (furniture-making, mask-carving), or cattle-raising and treecrops.

Notes

1   This recalls the low attractiveness of the town of Bantul mentioned in a previous section of this Research Report for residents of the hamlet of Bandung, who - albeit living closer to this town - prefer to sell and purchase goods in Yogyakarta.

2   See for instance Evers, 1989.

3   Effendi, 1987.

4   The basic formula used for calculating household income in the communities of the Plain of Bantul (Murtigading-Srigading and Pendowoharjo villages) was also applied to the communities of Kembang, Maguwoharjo and Putat II. However, in those latter communities, the system of data collection was improved to take into account annual cash equivalent of *palawija* crop - *i.e.* an intermediary crop between two rice crops - which is grown and used for home consumption (food) by the household. While, indeed, the omission of this variable was probably not too much fraught with consequences for the calculation of total household income in the case of lowland communities where *palawija* crops play a lesser role, taking into account cash equivalent of *palawija* crops for home consumption (food) was more significant in the case of communities where dry land can be found and where non-rice crops are much more frequent than in the wetland areas of the central alluvional plain of D.I.Y.

5   See for instance Evers, *op.cit.*

6   Khan, 1963 and 1964; Nibbering, 1991.

7   See for instance Rotgé, 1992.

8   *A fortiori* more sophisticated storage facilities such as by refrigeration are not affordable to cottage enterprises involved in trading perishable food. In rural communities, the few existing refrigerators are used for the commercial production of

ice not for the storage of food. The use of refrigeration for commercial purposes other than ice-making is unthinkable in today's local socioecomic context and level of development.

9   See for instance Hardjono, 1987.

10   This matter is further analysed below with regard to the questions of employment and of contribution of nonfarm and agricultural activities to the household income.

11   Effendi, *op.cit.*

This is not to say that only more mobile individuals belong to upper socioeconomic groups. This, indeed, often constitutes the direct consequence of holding a position such as within the urban sector, though all positions involving mobility are not necessarily characterized by very high levels of income. This also means that individuals born within upper socioeconomic groups are more likely to hold those better-paid positions involving mobility.

12   Apart from economic linkages with extraregional urban areas through occasional or seasonal employment, such economic linkages are likely to be enhanced through the sending of remittances from permanent migrants.

8 Focus on Nonpermanent Migrations

- by Ida Bagoes Mantra -

Definitions Recalled by the Editor

'Commuting' refers to an absence from home for more than six hours but less than twenty-four hours (commuters do not sleep at their destination). 'Circular migration' or 'circulation' refers to an absence of at least twenty-four hours from home for an indefinite duration but with the intention of returning in the future. 'Permanent migration' refers to an absence with the intention of never coming back except for short-term visits such as on the occasion of holidays (*Lebaran*, for instance). Other possible definitions are not used in this study.

Introduction

Standing on the side of the road leading into Yogyakarta, in the early morning, it is always possible to see a stream of labourers, traders, officials, and school students heading for the city. These people usually ride bicycles, motorcycles, or use public transport. In the afternoon we could observe the opposite stream going home from their work in the city. They are the commuters who work in the city during the day and go back home to the village to be with their families. The magnitude of the flow of population mobility from the rural to the urban areas during the day and back again in the late afternoon has caused the number of people in the urban areas to be larger during the daytime than during the night. Besides the rural dwellers who commute, there are also people such as construction workers, hawkers, and domestic servants, who board in the city and are fewer than the commuters.[1] The improvement of transportation facilities which connect the urban with the rural areas, and the increasing number of (mini)buses which connect rural communities with other rural or urban localities has modified the patterns of population movement. There has been a dramatic increase in the number of commuters who often commute over great distances. Today, most village dwellers prefer to commute rather than to undertake circular migrations. If a potential destination is beyond commuting distance, while there are compelling reasons that force people from these areas to stay away from their usual place of residence, then they will only stay as briefly as possible. As a result, the frequency of circular migration decreases as the duration of absence from the village lengthens. Circular migrations can be subdivided into several groups, such as periodic, seasonal, and long-term. Noting this, three main questions must be addressed. First, what factors have compelled these people to adopt population mobility from rural to urban areas? Second, why did not these people choose to become permanent migrants instead, that is, to leave their village of origin on a permanent basis? Third, what is the impact of population mobility on the socioeconomic conditions of the households as well as of the community in the places of origin?

Decisions to Move or to Stay

The type of model often used to analyse the population migration of a certain region is the 'push and pull' model. The socioeconomic conditions in the place of origin do not enable one to meet the basic needs, and thus forces some individuals to leave their village in order to find an occupation and to earn an income. It has been noted above that a person will become mobile if he/she is not able to meet his basic daily needs. It is to understand that every individual has his own different needs, hence he has his own evaluation towards his place of origin. Thus, the process of decision making of each individual is also different.

Todaro[2] and Titus[3] are of the opinion that the primary motivation for an individual to move is economic. Todaro[4] considers it as a rational economic consideration, where moving to the city has two expectations: the hope of finding an occupation and of earning an income higher than what can be earned in the village. Hence, rural-urban mobility reflects some imbalance between rural and urban areas. The population then tends to move to the cities, which have relatively larger economic power and which are expected to be able to meet the economic needs of the individuals. The course of population movement is determined by several other increasingly interrelated factors, such as distance, costs, and information. Yet, in spite of improved transport and reduced transportation costs, distance has remained an important factor in determining the course or at least the type of mobility preferred by the inhabitants. Residents from villages which are the most remote (*vis-à-vis* an urban area where employment is available) tend to become permanent migrants; those with moderate distances tend to perform circular mobility, whereas people who live within short distances of urban areas prefer commuting. Also, distance does not affect all rural dwellers in the same way, depending on the socioeconomic conditions of the potential migrants in the village and on the information brought home by returning migrants who, not infrequently, have stayed in urban areas for a considerable period. It was observed that the contribution of the earlier migrants has substantially helped many new migrants from the village or from the same regions, particularly during their first stages of adaptation in the city. When they first arrived in the city, the new migrants were not only housed initially with their fellow migrants from the same village, but the latter also provided them with food and help for them to seek occupations according to their respective skills or abilities.[5] This phenomenon frequently caused certain occupations in certain cities to be dominated by migrants coming from certain villages, since the process of finding an occupation is generally due to the related migrants from the same village of origin. Relations between migrants and their home villages in developing countries are on the whole very close. These relations are generally realized in the form of remittances and goods sent directly or indirectly to families in the village, or even in the form of ideas to the development of the village of origin. The intensity of relations is determined among others by the distance of migration, transport facilities, duration of migration, marital status, and kinship. Mantra[6] noted that there is an opposite correlation between distance and intensity of relation: the shorter the distance from the village, the higher the frequency of visits they made to the home villages. This intensity of relation will certainly affect the intensity of the impacts of mobility in the village or in the village of origin.

Starting from the models mentioned above, the process of rural-urban population mobility in the D.I.Y. will be discussed by taking case studies from two hamlets[7] of Piring (in the village of Murtigading-Srigading) and Bandung (in the village of Pendowoharjo) both in Bantul District - Figures 6.1 to 6.3. Neither the hamlet of Celep located in the village of Murtigading-Srigading, nor the hamlet of Karanggondang-Cepit included in the village of Pendowoharjo, studied in earlier sections, are analysed below. On the other hand, the hamlets included in the villages of

Maguwoharjo (in Sleman District - Figures 6.1 and 6.4), Putat (in Gunung Kidul District - Figures 7.6 and 7.7), and Kembang (in Kulon Progo District - Figures 7.1 to 7.3) which were analysed in the previous chapters, are studied below with a focus on migration. Data used here for the villages of Maguwoharjo, Putat, and Kembang come from the same fieldwork conducted by V. Rotgé and I. B. Mantra in 1992. However, data used below for the hamlets of Piring and Bandung come from fieldwork conducted by Haruo Kuroyanagi from September 1989 to February 1990. Such data were used with the permission of Kuroyanagi, for the writing of a paper presented by Mantra at the second Country Seminar on Regional Development and Planning of Daerah Istimewa Yogyakarta, in Yogyakarta in August 1991. This paper is presented here in a revised form.

Piring and Bandung

Introduction

The hamlet of Piring is located in the village of Murtigading-Srigading in the Subdistrict of Sanden, Bantul District. It has an area of 0.184 km². In 1988, the region had only 350 inhabitants, or 1902 people per km². The region itself consists of fertile ricefields situated on a plain fertilized by volcanic materials which is located near the southern coast of the D.I.Y. Piring is located about 27 km to the south of the urban core of the city of Yogyakarta and is flanked by two main roads. The main road in the west connects Yogyakarta with the village of Sorobayan, whereas the main road in the east connects the city with the tourism area of Samas Beach. Almost every ten minutes there is convenient public transport available passing along these main roads, so they enable rural dwellers to reach the city within less than 45 minutes.

Bandung, which is situated about 10 km from the southern outskirts of Yogyakarta, but approximately 15 km away from the city centre, stands on a plain also fertilized by volcanic materials, about 200 m away from the road which connects the city with Samas Beach. Bandung could be called a peripheral area of Yogyakarta. Administratively, the hamlet of Bandung is located in the village of Pendowoharjo, Sewon Subdistrict. In 1988, its population numbered 709 persons, while the area was about 0.30 km². With 2,355 inhabitants per km², its population density was therefore higher than that of Piring.

Table 8.1 **Wet (irrigated) Field Ownership in Piring and Bandung** (1989)*

Size of land (Ha)	Piring		Bandung	
	Number of cases	Per cent	Number of cases	Per cent
< 0.050	8	9.41	7	5.93
0.050 – 0.100	11	12.94	9	7.63
0.101 – 0.150	7	8.24	5	4.24
> 0.150	11	12.94	7	5.93
Does not own land	48	56.47	90	76.27
Total	85	100	118	100

* These 1989-90 research areas included the hinterland communities, but not the transit corridors, that V. Rotgé studied in 1991 (see Chapter 6).

Source: Primary data from H. Kuroyanagi's fieldwork (1989); quoted by courtesy of H. Kuroyanagi in Ida Bagoes Mantra, 'Nonpermanent Population Mobility in the Rural Areas: A Strategy to Increase the Household Income - A Case Study of Two Dukuhs in Bantul Regency' [Paper presented at the second Country Seminar on Regional Development Planning of Yogyakarta, Yogyakarta, 3-6 September 1991].

To study the population mobility behaviour of these two regions, some data results of a 1989-90 study of these two hamlets by Kuroyanagi were used.[8] Accordingly, as much as 56.5 per cent of the respondents of Piring owned no wet fields (*sawah*), whereas for Bandung the percentage was higher, *i.e.* 76.3 per cent. Every household head of Piring and Bandung owned wet fields of about 0.19 ha and 0.12 ha respectively; it is impossible for a household to depend for their livelihood wholly on agriculture. In the 1970s, Singarimbun and Penny[9] who conducted fieldwork in Sriharjo, Bantul District, stated that the average agricultural landownership per household head during the period of study was 0.22 ha. A household was considered self-sufficient or *cukupan*[10] if it owned 0.7 ha of wet land and 0.3 ha of dry land. If this norm of *cukupan* is applied to the inhabitants of these two study areas, it is obvious that the Sriharjo inhabitants lived below the *cukupan* line. Eighteen years later in 1989, this *cukupan* margin experienced some changes due to the increase of rural dwellers' basic household needs. Considering the average wet field ownership in Piring and Bandung which is even smaller than 0.2 ha, the figure is thus far below the *cukupan* margin.

To be able to overcome the hardships of the household economy, much of the labour force of these two hamlets found employment outside the agricultural sector. Besides, almost all respondents had supplementary occupations to increase their household income. In Piring, only 49.4 per cent of the people worked in agriculture either as farmers or as farm labourers, while in Bandung the percentage was even lower (37.3 per cent) - Table 8.2. As much as 28.8 per cent of the respondents in Bandung worked as construction workers. Other occupations available in this hamlet are clerical jobs, both government or private, 14.4 per cent or as traders, 6.8 per cent. Occupations in the nonagricultural sector often take place in Yogyakarta. Those who undertake such occupations generally commute - leaving in the morning for their places of work and returning home in the late afternoon.

The percentage of construction workers in Piring is lower than that in Bandung - 7.1 per cent compared to 28.8 per cent. As much as 10.6 per cent of respondents work in the handicrafts industries in the city, whereas those who are employed as nongovernment clerical staff or civil servants - often as primary school teachers - represent also about 10.6 per cent - Table 8.2. The share of those who work in their community of origin is larger in Piring (61.2 per cent) than in Bandung (43.2 per cent). On the other hand, more respondents in Bandung work outside the hamlet, generally in Yogyakarta – Table 8.3. The larger number of respondents in Bandung who work in Yogyakarta, and who mostly work outside agriculture, is mainly caused by the relatively small distance between the hamlet and their places of work; whereas for the respondents of Piring, very few commute to Yogyakarta because the city is around 27 km away, and is considered beyond commuting distance. To increase the household income, many of the household members, particularly the respondents' children, search for employment outside the D.I.Y. The results of Kuroyanagi's study show that as many as 149 of the respondents' children in Piring have an occupation, while 142 of those in Bandung do the same.[11] From this number, as many as 78 (52.4 per cent) of the total working respondents' children of Piring find employment outside the D.I.Y, while the corresponding percentage for Bandung is smaller (30.9 per cent) - Table 8.4.

Tables 8.2   Main Occupation of Respondents (household heads), **Piring and Bandung** (1989)*

	Piring		Bandung	
	Number of cases	Per cent	Number of cases	Per cent
Farmer	38	44.71	35	29.66
Farm labourer	4	4.7	9	7.63
Trader	4	4.7	8	6.78
Government official	9	10.59	11	9.32
Non-gov. clerk	0	0	6	5.08
Construction worker	6	7.06	34	28.81
Handicraft labourer	9	10.59	1	0.85
Domestic servant	0	0	2	1.7
Self-employed	0	0	2	1.7
Retired	4	4.70	4	3.39
Unemployed	2	2.35	0	0
Others	9	10.59	6	5.08
Total	85	100	118	100

*   Same as Table 8.1.

Source: Same as Table 8.1.

Table 8.3   Place of Work of Respondents (household heads), **Piring and Bandung** (1989)*

	Piring		Bandung	
	Number of cases	Per cent	Number of cases	Per cent
The same hamlet	52	61.18	51	43.22
The same village	6	7.06	7	5.93
Other village, same Subdistrict	2	2.35	3	2.54
Other Subdistrict, same District	9	10.59	90	7.63
Other District within the D.I.Y. **	4	4.71	41	34.75
Central Java	1	1.18	1	0.85
East Java	0	0	0	0.85
Does not work	11	12.94	5	4.24
Total	85	100	118	100

*   Same as Table 8.1.
**   The Municipal District of Yogyakarta (*Kotamadya Yogyakarta*) or one of the three Districts (*Kabupaten*) that the D.I.Y. comprises.

Source: Same as Table 8.1.

Table 8.4   **Place of Residence of Working Respondents' Children, Piring and Bandung** (1989)*

	Piring		Bandung	
	Number of cases	Per cent	Number of cases	Per cent
The same hamlet	19	12.75	63	44.37
Other hamlet, same village	6	4.03	11	7.75
Other village, same Subdistrict	11	7.38	7	4.93
Uther Subdistrict, same District	12	8.05	8	5.63
Other District within the D.I.Y.**	23	15.44	9	6.34
Central Java	8	5.37	8	5.63
East Java	6	4.03	4	2.82
Jakarta	31	20.80	12	8.45
West Java	7	4.7	2	1.41
Sumatra	21	14.09	14	9.86
Other	5	3.36	4	2.82
Total	149	100	142	100

*   Same as Table 8.1.
**   The Municipal District of Yogyakarta (*Kotamadya Yogyakarta*) or one of the three other Districts (*Kabupaten*) that the D.I.Y. comprises.

Source: Same as Table 8.1.

In conclusion, in both Piring and Bandung, most rural dwellers could not succeed in making a living by depending for their livelihood on the agricultural produce of their land, unless they found other occupations or employment outside agriculture often in Yogyakarta or even in other Provinces. Most of them are nonpermanent migrants, *i.e.* they either commute or circulate. The inhabitants of Bandung who find work in Yogyakarta mostly commute. These people do construction labour, perform trading, find employment as government or nongovernment officials, or are self-employed. As outlined earlier, not many inhabitants from Piring commute to Yogyakarta since it is beyond commuting distance. These people prefer to go much farther from their village to places such as Jakarta, West Java, or Sumatra. In these places they retain their status as nonpermanent migrants who board in the places where they work.

Reasons for Nonpermanent Migration

The level of education of the respondents in the two hamlets is low. In 1989, less than 25 per cent had only studied beyond primary school - Table 8.5. The point is that only casual labour is usually available for poorly educated individuals, such as construction labour, retail trading, or domestic work.

Table 8.5   Educational Level of Respondents (household heads), Piring and Bandung (1989)*

	Piring		Bandung	
	Number of cases	Per cent	Number of cases	Per cent
No schooling	19	22.4	30	25.4
Did not complete primary school	13	15.3	24	20.3
Completed primary school	32	37.6	36	30.5
Completed junior high school	8	9.4	8	6.9
Completed senior high school	10	11.8	17	14.4
University / Academy	3	3.5	3	2.5
Total	85	100	118	100

*   Same as Table 8.1.

Source: Same as Table 8.1.

Most of these people have very low incomes: a construction worker generally received around *Rupiah* 3,000 per day in the late 1980s (US$1.50 at the early 1990s exchange rate, or US$0.42 at the mid-December 1999 exchange rate), which made it impossible for him to move with his family to the city or other places. To enable these rural dwellers to maintain a livelihood they have to engage both in agriculture in the village and in nonagricultural work in the city. Coming back to the village in the afternoon they continue to work, tending their land in order to supplement the income gained in Yogyakarta. This life-style entails one foot in the city and one in the village, and requires commuting or permanent or circular migrations. In general, there are various forces, which induce people to move from, or to stay within hamlets such as Piring or Bandung. Mitchell[12] has grouped such forces into the centrifugal and the centripetal. The first set induces individuals or small groups of people to leave the village whereas the second set leads people to resist such action. Whether mobility is present or absent in a certain place - in this case Piring and Bandung - depends upon the balance between these two conflicting sets of forces.

Centrifugal forces identified in the two study areas reflect the agricultural economy, formal education, and social obligations, of which dissatisfaction with the local wet rice economy is the most significant factor. The tiny size of each family's ricefield means that not even through the use of agricultural innovations will the farmers be able to produce sufficient food to meet the basic needs of their households. In addition, the chances to find local occupations outside agriculture are very few and characterized by very low levels of income.

There are five sets of centripetal forces that encourage people to remain in Piring and Bandung, among which two will be discussed. First, the close kinship ties among village inhabitants. Ties are also maintained with wider kindred, or groups of relatives, among whom reciprocal obligations exist.

Second, local communities are founded upon, and practice, the principle of *gotong royong*, or mutual self-help. Living together in this type of society means a life of a corporate family type, where individuals must help one another, and where everyone must collectively participate in community life and its various activities. Ways of sharing and redistributing wealth among households in such hamlets have evolved, but there is still a strong relationship between patron and client involving a bond of mutual responsibility between the rich and the poor. As members of such a community, individuals need not worry about starvation as long as they remain with their kin. Consequently it would be a high risk to leave the community for long periods, because of the uncertainty of whether paid employment could support them at their destination. The majority, whose socioeconomic status is low, prefer to remain in the hamlet and work as farm labourers rather than to move elsewhere. Even though local incomes are low, the inhabitants of Piring and Bandung feel far more secure by remaining in their hamlet than migrating. If these two sets of centrifugal and centripetal circumstances are viewed from the standpoint of a hamlet community, it can be observed that the situation is highly contradictory. Village people face a grave dilemma of whether to remain in their community and endure both the hard economic life and the lack of educational facilities, or to move away to leave their land and birthrights, and to be separated from family, kin, and relatives. This dilemma is resolved in Piring and Bandung by adopting an alternative strategy by commuting or circulation, which is essentially a compromise between total immobility and permanent relocation.

The Utility of Remittances

Nonpermanent migrants are still officially registered as legal residents in their places of origin. Usually, children, spouse, and parents remain in the village. This brings closer and stronger relationships between migrants and their places of origin. The primary aim of migrants in going to the city is to find employment or an occupation to earn something to bring home as remittances. Nonpermanent migrants and their families form one extended kinship economic unit, and the remittances form part of the household income in the two study areas. A migrant always tries to spend his income earned in the city as economically as possible with the aim of sending as much money as possible to the village. The volume of remittances sent to the home village depends on the type of migrant. Commuters are migrants with the largest amount of remittances sent home, followed by migrants who board in their places of work, whereas the smallest remittances are usually sent by permanent migrants. To most permanent migrants, remittances are usually more socioeconomic in value. That is to say that they maintain social ties rather than promote economic well-being. The volume of remittances sent home by Bandung's migrants is usually larger. This can be easily detected by the number of houses of the Bandung inhabitants which have been renovated, and by the neatly kept yards and fences built of red bricks, and by the clean surroundings and the better village households. The situation in Piring is quite different. Most of the houses, which were built many years ago and which should by now have experienced reparations or renovations, have remained the same. No new settlements have been made in this area, and only a few houses have external brick fences surrounding the home compounds. All this indicates that the average distribution of income of the people of Bandung, including remittances, is better than that of Piring. Nonpermanent movement is considered a strategy not only to improve the household economy and the distribution of income in rural areas but also to speed up the development of the village of origin of both commuters and circular migrants. In his study, H. Kuroyanagi did not analyse in detail the size of remittances sent by nonpermanent migrants to their home village.[13] The results of Sunarto's study conducted in the villages of Mulusan and Sodo, Gunung Kidul District, will be mentioned here for comparison.[14] This study reveals that remittances affect, among other things:

(1) The volume of money circulating in the village of origin;
(2) A more even distribution of income within the community;
(3) A decrease of population pressure on agricultural land, and;
(4) An improvement in households' welfare.

Volume of Remittances

One of the impacts that arise due to population mobility is the increase of households income in the village of origin. In 1986, there was an average of at least one migrant in every five households in Gunung Kidul District. If, in 1986, there were 130,306 households, it means that there were 26,061 people who were circular migrants. Remittances have made a considerable contribution to the village, which has been known as a critical region. According to the abovementioned study by Sunarto, the per capita income increased by as much as 15.6 per cent because of the remittances.

Community Income Distribution: The imbalance of distribution of community income is usually calculated by using Gini coefficients (or indexes: G.I.) whose value ranges between 0 and 1. The lower the value of the G.I., the more even the distribution of income of the community of a certain region. G.I. figures in Sunarto's study[15] are as follows:

Nonmigrant   = 0.39

Circular migrant after remittance calculation   = 0.21

It can thus be concluded that remittances of circular migrants may improve the imbalance of income distribution of the community in the village of origin.

Population Pressure on Agricultural Land: The intensity of population pressure on agricultural land (T.P.) could be used to identify the size of economic costs to support the livelihood of the population. According to Soemarwoto,[16] T.P. could be distinguished according to the following:

> *T.P. <1* : means that the region can still receive additional population
>
> *T.P. >1* : means that demographic pressure upon land has reached its critical point

The higher the T.P. value, the more critical the region becomes.

The result of the study shows that the T.P. prior to the remittances is calculated as much as 6.31, whereas after the remittances the T.P. becomes 2.43. This means that remittances sent by circular migrants have considerably reduced the value of T.P.

Improvement of Household Welfare: Sunarto's abovementioned study also reveals that seventy-five out of eighty-one circular migrants' wives stated that the economic situation of their households has, on the whole, improved. None reported that their economic situation has worsened after their spouses performed nonpermanent mobility to work outside the village. The role of remittances in increasing the household standard of living is confirmed by other researchers. Some of them believe that remittances not only have positive influences on household welfare, but also bring significant progress to the neighbourhood. Hugo who studied fourteen villages of West Java reached the conclusion that remittances bring prosperity to circular migrants' households.[17]

Maguwoharjo, Putat II and Kembang

Setting of the Three Further Research Communities

The three further research communities, *i.e.* the hamlet of Putat II (Figures 7.6 and 7.7) and parts of the villages of Maguwoharjo (the hamlets of Ringinsari, Nanggulan, Kradenan and Gondangan - Figures 6.1 and 6.4) and Kembang (the hamlets of Kenteng, Ngemplak and Ngrojo - Figures 7.1 to 7.3) are situated outside the Plain of Bantul where the two hamlets which have been studied previously - Bandung and Piring - are located. These three further research communities are located in different geographical settings.

Maguwoharjo is situated in Sleman District, on a lower footplain of the Merapi Volcano, whereas Putat II and Kembang are geologically occupying part of the Sentolo formation and the Sewu Mountain range respectively. Maguwoharjo, which is also partly an urbanized village, represents a very fertile area with a well-developed irrigation network initiated by the Dutch government prior to the Second World War. The location of Maguwoharjo near Yogyakarta explains the steady conversion of some fertile agricultural land to accommodate nonfarming activities. Private agricultural universities, companies, factories, hotels, and trading activities compete for the limited land belonging to the native inhabitants due to the improvements of village accessibility. A ring road connecting the northern and the eastern parts of Yogyakarta city has recently been finished. This also provides economic opportunities for both villagers and people from outside Yogyakarta, apart from the possible negative impacts on the environment and the socioeconomic life and norms.

As seen in previous sections, the hamlet of Putat II faces a water shortage problem during the dry season. This village is situated in the hills on the road connecting Yogyakarta and Wonosari, the capital of Gunung Kidul District. Irrigation can only be carried out on the lower parts of the area, especially on some narrow flatland, utilizing spring water. A large-scale irrigation network will not be possible due to the rough topography of the area and its low water-retaining capacity.

Kembang, which belongs to Kulon Progo District, is situated on an elevated plain about 17 km from Yogyakarta to the west via the small town of Godean east of the Progo River. The irrigation network of this village uses water brought through a canal connected in the north to the Progo River, which makes at least two crops of rice a year possible. In the last five years, a bridge connecting the village to Yogyakarta has been constructed, providing better regional accessibility and enabling people to commute to the city. Prior to this, people commuted to Yogyakarta for various purposes via the towns of Ngeplang and Sedayu in the southwest. This itinerary was considerably longer and was more expensive in terms of transport costs than today's straight route to Yogyakarta across the newly built bridge (see Chapter 7). The mobility patterns to Yogyakarta have experienced a shift from circulation to commuting. These three case study villages indicate differences in their potentials and constraints relating to their natural resources and use. The way in which people make their living clearly shows considerable varieties as discussed below.

Socioeconomic Background

The populations in the villages vary greatly in size and structure. The village of Maguwoharjo had a population of 21,491 in 1990, followed by the village of Kembang which had 4,119 and by the village of Putat which had 3,131 making population densities of 1,431, 806, and 436 inhabitants per km² respectively (these figures are for the whole villages in which the studied communities are located - see Table 5.1). The difference in population density partly reflects the intensity of population pressure on the agricultural land of the villages, in which there is a growing trend towards greater dependency on nonagricultural activities, as agricultural income is not sufficient to meet household needs. The insufficient availability of agricultural land seems to be the main factor which forces people to diversify their activities. In this regard, nonagricultural activities have contributed to a more significant role in improving the household income. This phenomenon is shown by the occupational structure of the three studied communities as discussed in the following section.

The suburban village of Maguwoharjo: This village, especially, has experienced a great shift in its occupational structure. Out of 3,000 farmers living in the whole village of Maguwoharjo, some 2,600 are working in various nonagricultural activities (these figures are for the whole village and come from official village statistics; the size of the population that was sampled and that is studied below is smaller in size). These activities are mostly related to services or processing industries: employment as government employees, traders, bricklayers, carpenters, employees of small or medium-sized industries, but also self-employed activities. The types of small and medium-sized industries found in this village are - among others - the leather industry producing export goods which employs about one hundred workers. Several furniture-making workshops also produce household utensils supplying the urban markets of Yogyakarta.

The upland and partly dryland hamlet of Putat II: Putat II does not show distinct occupational diversification since most of the people are engaged in farming as their main activity. Only about 200 out of 2,500 of the working population can be assumed to be working in nonagricultural activities which are mostly related to the utilization of local natural resources such as woodcarving, wood trading, charcoal making, carpentry, and agricultural product trading (these figures cover the whole village and come from official village statistics). However, seasonal shortage of raw materials in this partly dryland community forces people to commute or to circulate, especially during the dry season. Generally, those who leave the village prefer to find jobs in the town.

The piedmont village of Kembang: This village has shown socioeconomic progress over the past two decades. Only recently the village has been conveniently linked to Yogyakarta with a bridge and bus services which provide better economic opportunities to the village. Although agricultural activities make an ample contribution to the local job opportunities, the growth of other services and certain crafts (confection) are also worth mentioning. Better connection with Yogyakarta has been anticipated by investing greater capital in the existing activities or in establishing completely new nonagricultural activities. The steady growth of nonagricultural activities along the road leading to Yogyakarta shows that the provision of infrastructure has attracted and generated new activities. Nevertheless, a major impact of the above is the fact that many inhabitants of Kembang now prefer to make purchases in Yogyakarta.

From the above it can be observed that natural resource endowment, the utilization and potentials, and constraints, have all had an impact on the way the people make their living. The inadequacy of the people's income from agriculture is followed by the occupational multiplicity in the nonagricultural sector. This type of social mobility is also combined with geographical mobility involving a temporal or permanent change of residence in the forms of migration, circulation, and commuting.

Demographic Structure

Strong linkages with urban areas are reflected in the population structure of the research villages (in this section, villages are considered in their totality and the figures which are referred to come from official village statistics, not from fieldwork). The dependency ratio is:

> [...] the ratio of the number of people who cannot be gainfully employed in a population (the dependants) to the number who are actively or potentially active (the employed or employable).[18]

The villages of Maguwoharjo and Kembang are characterized by a low dependency ratio of 50.3 and 56.1 per cent respectively. This ratio is expressed here as a percentage by considering the number of dependants for every one hundred active individuals. The same figure of dependency ratio for the village of Putat is 68.3 per cent. Population structure by gender in the research villages is also worth noting. Maguwoharjo, the most urbanized village, shows a male/female ratio of 101.2 per cent - considerably higher than those of Putat and Kembang - indicating that there are more males than females (this ratio is the number of males divided by the number of females, shown here as a percentage, by calculating it for every one hundred females in the villages' population). The presence of more male than female population in many cases reflects the high portion of migrant population. In other words, the level of migrations is especially high in Maguwoharjo. This is further confirmed by the greater proportion of population below the productive age groups in Maguwoharjo.

Welfare

Besides income levels, a common method of measuring the welfare of a particular population group is to examine the housing conditions. The available information about housing such as the size and type of house, family size, status of housing ownership, condition of water availability for drinking and for other household use, lighting system, and types of roofing do not show any significant difference among the three case study villages in terms of welfare. In most cases, the locally available materials determine the type of housing materials used.

Table 8.6   Types of Flooring in the Three Research Areas (1992)*

Types of floor	Maguwoharjo		Putat II		Kembang	
	Number	Per Cent	Number	Per cent	Number	Per cent
Tiles	36	24.5	11	9.2	22	16.9
Cemented floor	95	64.6	43	35.8	78	60
Uncemented bricks	2	1.4	4	3.3	3	2.3
Earthen floor	10	6.8	60	50	27	20.8
Rock	4	2.7	2	1.7	0	0
Total	147	100	120	100	130	100

* They are the same population samples as studied by Rotgé in previous sections. However, while V. Rotgé divided the data for Putat II and Maguwoharjo in two sets corresponding to a hinterland and transit-corridor community, data here are taken in their aggregate.

Source: Primary data processed by the Computing Department of the Faculty of Geography of Gadjah Mada University (fieldwork implemented in 1992).

The most representative variable to measure the welfare of population in the case study villages is the type of floor of the house. The above table shows that the most prosperous community among the three further studied communities is in Maguwoharjo (hamlets of Ringinsari, Nanggulan, Kradenan and Gondangan), followed by Kembang (hamlets of Kenteng, Ngemplak and Ngrojo) and the hamlet of Putat II, if one assumes that the type of flooring in each house reflects the inhabitants' capability to invest a part of their income - Table 8.6. Nearly a quarter of the households in the research area in Maguwoharjo (24.5 per cent) occupy houses with roofs of tiles, while about 64.6 per cent occupy houses with cement or tiled floor. The proportion with earthen floor or uncemented brick floors is negligible. The percentages of households with cemented floors in the research areas in Kembang and in the hamlet of Putat II are 60 and 35.8, respectively, whereas the houses with earthen floors still predominate (20.8 per cent and 50 per cent, respectively).

Population Mobility

It has been mentioned above that there are two patterns of nonpermanent population mobility in these three studied communities, *i.e.* commuting and other categories of migration. These patterns of movement do not occur only in the three studied communities, but also in almost every village throughout the region. In terms of frequency, commuters are greater in numbers than other types of migrants (circular and permanent).

Commuting: Putat II and Kembang are rather distant from Yogyakarta (more than 15 km away), while Maguwoharjo is located in the urbanizing periphery of Yogyakarta. Thus, more people from Maguwoharjo commute to Yogyakarta to work or trade than from the other two study villages. Although most workers in Maguwoharjo work in the agricultural sector, many work in Yogyakarta as construction workers. As the income that they obtain from the nonagricultural sector in the city is higher, most of their time is taken up by working in the city. Formerly, they used to commute to the city by bicycle, many use motorcycles or take public transport. They go to the city in the morning and return to the village in the afternoon on the same day. Arriving home, after resting, they continue to work tending their ricefield(s). The situation of Kembang is rather different. Before the bridge existed, rural dwellers sold agricultural goods only at the local market. The traders sold their commodities in Wates, Muntilan, or Godean. Most of the people commuted. The frequency of commuters to Godean or Yogyakarta increased when the bridge linking Kembang and Yogyakarta began to function. Almost every fifteen minutes there is a bus, which departs to Yogyakarta. Now many inhabitants prefer to make purchases such as agricultural tools, ready-made clothes, and other daily necessities in Godean or Yogyakarta. Wider ranges of choice and quality of goods are available in these markets. Few respondents from Putat II commute to Wonosari (the capital of Gunung Kidul District) and Yogyakarta - Table 8.7. The location of these cities is beyond commuting distance either by bicycle or on foot. Only civil servants, traders, police, and army people who work in these two cities commute every day. Usually they ride motorcycles or use public transport.

There are several reasons why rural dwellers prefer to commute rather than to undertake circular migrations, though all relate to their home community as the focus of their lives and the basis of their social security. One is that rural dwellers prefer, of course, living with their family. When rural dwellers must travel away from their home villages, they always tend to return home on the same day. If they have to stay away overnight, either because of the great distance or because they have to help relatives in the fields, they tend to try to remain for the shortest possible time.

Given the low level of most rural incomes, by and large, there is rarely any surplus money available to allow family members to remain in town or other areas for any length of time. By staying in the village where the cost of living is far lower, rural dwellers who have permanent and temporary jobs can still cultivate their ricefield(s) after working hours and can thus maximize their income. Since 1972, in addition, this ability has been greatly assisted by the improvement throughout the D.I.Y. of the road network that connects the city with its hinterland. Thus, the considerable reluctance of rural dwellers to stay overnight in another place has been reinforced by the improvement of transport facilities which used to permit them to return by nightfall.[19]

Reasons for Commuting

In the study of population mobility it has often been found that a journey has more than one objective. For example, an individual who goes to the market to sell agricultural products will also visit or meet relatives living near to the marketplace. It is sometimes difficult to understand how much mobility results from multiple objectives. In the three case study areas the primary objective of commuting is economic. Respondents who commute mentioned that their primary objective was to look for an occupation. Those who commute to work in the city try to obtain permanent employment. As their level of education is low, and job opportunities in the cities are very limited, not all of them could succeed in finding a job in the formal sector, such as government positions. The second objective in moving is noneconomic: visiting relatives, attending cultural events (births, circumcisions, marriages, funerals) or other events marking familial or individual events. By nature, such movements are not regular. The third objective in moving is attending school. In Maguwoharjo, for instance, almost all students who attend high school or university commute to Yogyakarta. The distance from Putat II and Kembang to Yogyakarta is beyond commuting distance. High school as well as university students have to board in the city. Only civil servants or traders who work in Yogyakarta can commute; most use motorcycles.

Frequency of Commuting: Commuting or daily circulation can be divided into regular (or periodical), nonregular (nonperiodical), and seasonal circulation. In the study, a regular commuter travels regularly although not necessarily daily, to a place, outside the village to work, to trade, or to go to school. A nonregular commuter is a person who travels occasionally to a place outside the village to purchase items such as clothes, agricultural tools, or to visit relatives or friends. A seasonal commuter is someone who goes daily to other places at particular times of the year, for example, to work in the ricefields outside the village boundaries during harvest seasons. In the three studied communities, the frequency of commuting is shown in Table 8.7.

Table 8.7   Weekly Frequency of Commuting in the Three Research Areas (1992)*

Frequently of weekly commuting	Maguwoharjo		Putat II		Kembang	
	Number	Per Cent	Number	Per cent	Number	Per cent
2	0	0	0	0	2	2.3
3-4	8	4.3	1	3.1	2	2.3
5-6	159	85	17	53.1	59	68.6
7	18	9.6	7	21.9	15	17.4
Non-regular	2	1.1	7	21.9	8	0
Total	187	100	32	100	86	100

*   Same as Table 8.6.

Source: Primary data processed by the Computing Department of the Faculty of Geography of Gadjah Mada University (fieldwork implemented in 1992).

In addition, more than 50 per cent of the commuters are of the regular group. In Maguwoharjo the number of regular commuters is higher than in Putat II and Kembang. This reflects the fact that a large majority (85 per cent) of respondents work or go to school in Yogyakarta. There are more commuters in Kembang than in the community of Putat II, which is located in a hilly environment. The main destinations of Kembang's commuters are the towns of Godean, Wates, or Yogyakarta. In Putat II, commuters, who mostly consist of civil servants, students, and small-scale traders, commute to their destinations particularly to Yogyakarta and Wonosari by motorcycle. Due to the topographic conditions, it is impossible for commuters to commute by bicycle to Wonosari or Yogyakarta. Hence, the number of regular commuters from Putat II was very small compared to Kembang. Nonregular commuters usually go to Yogyakarta or Wonosari either by motocycle or public transport. The greater significance in Maguwoharjo of commuting to earn a living is a simple function of distance and topography from the places of work. Since Maguwoharjo is close to Yogyakarta, many people prefer daily commuting in contrast to Kembang and Putat II. Only civil servants and traders from Putat II who work in Wonosari or Yogyakarta regularly commute from their villages. Other people commute incidently to Wonosari or Yogyakarta for certain purposes. The mobility behaviour of the people of Kembang is the same as that of Putat II. Most of them undertake nonregular commuting.

Circular Migration: Beside practicing commuting as one of the mobility patterns, some of these urban dwellers stay in the places where they work. They sometimes stay for months with no intention of living permanently at the place of destination. This only occurs if their working places are generally beyond commuting distance. The mobility behaviour of the circular migrants of the three studied communities will be discussed below.

Characteristics of Circular Migrants: Maguwoharjo lies within commuting distance from Yogyakarta, whereas Putat II and Kembang are beyond commuting distance if rural dwellers are meant to use bicycles. Accordingly, there is a larger number of commuters from Maguwoharjo going to Yogyakarta rather than from Putat II and Kembang. The potential migrants from Putat II and Kembang are mostly either circular or permanent migrants. The number of respondents who are circular migrants are thirty-one from Maguwoharjo, and forty-four and fifty from Putat II and Kembang, respectively. Rather interesting is the case of Kembang where members in about thirteen households, each of which consists of more than one household member, are circular migrants. Some work as shoemakers in Tangerang near Jakarta in West Java Province.

Table 8.8   Number of Circular Migrants per Household in the Three Research Areas (1992)*

Number of circular migrants per household	Maguwoharjo			Putat II			Kembang		
	HH	Migrants		HH	Migrants		HH	Migrants	
	(a)	(b)	(c)	(a)	(b)	(c)	(a)	(b)	(c)
1	23	23	74.2	37	37	84.1	21	21	42
2	4	8	25.8	2	4	9.1	10	20	40
3	0	0	0	1	3	6.8	3	9	18
Total	27	31	100	40	44	100	33	50	100

*   Same as Table 8.6.
**   HH: Household; (a): number of households in the sample including one circular migrant or more; (b): number of circular migrants; (c): per cent of households including circular migrants in the research area.

Source: Primary data processed by the Computing Department of the Faculty of Geography of Gadjah Mada University (fieldwork in 1992).

A majority of Kembang's inhabitants are Catholics. Some youth receive guidance from a Catholic organization and are then sent to the shoemaking industries in Tangerang near Jakarta. Earlier migrants usually help newly arrived relatives from the village, so that they do not have to find housing when they first arrive. This kinship and friendship network is effective in taking care of the basic needs of migrants immediately after their arrival, which leads to the process of chain migration. In the hamlet of Putat II there are three households (consisting of more than one household member) who also practice circular migration. Most of them work as drivers, either as truck drivers operating between Jakarta and Bandung, or as drivers of public transport operating between Wonosari and Yogyakarta. In Maguwoharjo there are fewer circular migrants. Here, the proximity of Yogyakarta, which brings local or urban opportunities at a short commuting distance, may explain why inhabitants do not need to resort to circular migrations to the same extent as in more peripheral communities.

Objectives of Circular Migrations: The main objectives of circular migrations in Maguwoharjo and Putat II are socioeconomic, while in

Kembang the main reason is educational. The frequency of visiting relatives occupies second position (20.6 and 9.7 per cent respectively) in Putat II and Maguwoharjo, and third in Kembang (6.0 per cent) - Table 8.9.

Table 8.9   Number of Circular Migrants and Reasons for Migrating in the Three Research Areas (1992)*

	Maguwoharjo		Putat II		Kembang	
Reasons	**Number**	**Per Cent**	**Number**	**Per cent**	**Number**	**Per cent**
Wage work	26	83.9	33	74.9	14	28
Education	1	3.2	0	0	31	62
Visiting relatives and trade	3	9.7	9	20.6	3	6
No record	1	3.2	2	4.5	2	4
Total	31	100	44	100	50	100

*   Same as Table 8.6.

Source: Primary data, processed by the Computing Department of the Faculty of Geography of Gadjah Mada University (fieldwork in 1992).

Places of Destination: Circular migrants who work in other regions and stay there for some time mostly work outside the D.I.Y. For example, about twenty circular migrants from Maguwoharjo work in Jakarta, and three even work in the female labour force in the Middle East. In Putat II, 38.3 per cent of respondents work in Jakarta, and 27.3 per cent in Yogyakarta. Fourteen people (28 per cent) from Kembang work as casual labourers in the shoemaking industry in Tangerang near Jakarta - Table 8.10.

Table 8.10   **Places of Destination of Circular Migrants from the Three Research Areas (1992)***

Places of destination	Maguwoharjo		Putat II		Kembang	
	Number	Per Cent	Number	Per cent	Number	Per cent
Within same Subdistrict	0	0	2	4.6	0	0
Yogyakarta Municipality	1	3.2	12	27.3	31	62
Other within D.I.Y.	0	0	6	13.6	1	2
Jakarta	26	83.9	17	38.6	0	0
Tangerang	0	0	0	0	14	28
Abroad	3	9.7	1	2.3	0	0
Other	0	0	4	9.1	2	4
No record	1	3.2	2	4.6	2	4
Total	31	100	44	100	50	100

*   Same as Table 8.6.

Source: Primary data, processed by the Computing Department of the Faculty of Geography of Gadjah Mada University (fieldwork in 1992).

Many people who were born in, or originally came from, the three case study communities now live in neighbouring or distant places, yet still maintain contact with their relatives. As has been mentioned, almost all migrants in Indonesia are from 'bi-local' population. During the *Lebaran* (first day after the Moslem fasting month) the people have a strong moral obligation to be home with their relatives and to pay homage to the graves of their ancestors. Ancestors' graves could thus be regarded as a means of uniting all the village people descended from their respective ancestors, and the *Lebaran* itself as a specific time of reunion to everyone who feels they belong to a particular rural community.[20]

Conclusion

This study suggests that nonpermanent movement is not a new phenomenon in Indonesia and that it has intensified considerably since the country's Independence. This is mainly caused by the improvements of the transportation network among villages and urban areas, the scarcity of work opportunities in the villages, and above all, the desire of the villagers to supplement their household income and to raise their standard of living by finding employment in urban areas located in and/or outside the D.I.Y. Nonpermanent movement is a form of linkage between rural and urban areas and is important in achieving a closer interaction between rural and urban residents. Through commuting and circulation, the villagers become more familiar with different work and residential environments, and with the different social environments that make up the urban areas. Thus, nonpermanent forms of movement, far more than permanent migration, have the potential of spreading new ideas, attitudes and knowledge to rural areas and contributing greatly to the processes of social change. By itself, nonpermanent movement creates its own momentum as more and more village people experience the benefits of a wider range of contacts and work experience with the minimum costs for permanent residence in towns and cities. Returning home, commuters can still continue to work on their land in the village in the afternoon in order to gain supplementary income. Nonpermanent population mobility is considered a strategy not only to improve the household economy of the villagers but also of speeding up the development of the villages of origin of both commuters and circular migrants.

Notes

[1] Mantra, 1981.

[2] See for instance Todaro, 1971.

[3] Titus, 1982.

[4] See Todaro, *op. cit.*

[5] Soeratman, 1978.

[6] Mantra, 1979.

[7] Administratively, villages (*desa*) are subdivided into hamlets (*dukuh* also called *dusun*).

[8] The study was conducted in 1988 by interviewing eighty-five household heads in Piring and one hundred and fifteen household heads in Bandung.

9   Singarimbun and Penny, 1976.

10   *Cupuk* means 'enough' in Bahasa Indonesia. *Cukupan*, literally having 'enough', was given the explicit meaning of 'real income of 1,200 kg of (husked) rice (or its equivalent) per year.' It was assumed that each household comprised of 4-5 members (Singarimbun and Penny, *op. cit.*). See also glossary.

11   Kuroyanagi, 1990 and 1991.

12   Mitchell, 1961.

13   See Kuroyanagi, 1990 and 1991.

14   Sunarto, 1991.

15   *Ibid.*

16   Soemarwoto, 1988.

17   Hugo, 1975.

18   Clark, 1985; p. 162.

19   Mantra, 1981.

20   *Ibid.*

9 Regional Development Policies in the Context of Emerging Rural-Urban Linkages in the D.I.Y.

- by Vincent Rotgé -

Foreword

In this part, some general regional approaches to dealing with employment shortages and demographic pressure in rural areas are summarized in the context of rising rural-urban linkages in the D.I.Y., and an agenda for policy recommendations is outlined.

General Approaches: Scope and Limits

Limits to Cultivated Land Expansion

The option to expand areas under cultivation is either very limited, or would show adverse ecological side-effects that might ultimately lead to a general decline in agricultural productivity. The point, indeed, is that, apart from wooded uplands, there is almost no additional land available that can be reclaimed for agricultural purposes in the D.I.Y. or even Java as a whole. Thus, expanding cultivated areas would mean encroaching upon wooded catchment areas of rivers, risking ecological degradation, and hence an ultimate decrease of agricultural productivity in the lowlands, subsequent to a degradation of the irrigation system, that would result from the degradation of the regional watershed in the upland areas. More relevant than an unattainable expansion of areas under cultivation is the issue of how to deal with the reduction of the total cultivated area following a general trend towards the conversion of farmland to residential and urban land-use categories.

Providing Irrigation to Dryland

Such an alternative is limited for at least the following two reasons:
(1) Providing dryland with irrigation is difficult in certain areas of the D.I.Y. due to specific geological conditions, as for instance in a large part of the District of Gunung Kidul.
(2) Second, irrigating new land facilitates an increase in output. This benefits those who have access to land and is obviously desirable especially in areas of the District of Gunung Kidul, if technically possible. But this would not necessarily be directly conducive to significant employment expansion. However, it would probably have indirect and dynamic effects on employment, especially in local services, in raising the level of income of rural dwellers.

However, there is probably still some room left for local irrigation schemes, especially in upland areas where rainfed fields are numerous. Thus, in the hamlet of Putat II in the District of Gunung Kidul, villagers who own land along a small river pooled their resources to build a dike containing a small river. The purpose of this scheme is to raise the level of the waters in order to irrigate elevated fields by means of bamboo pipes. But this scheme is constrained by the paucity of financial and technological resources available to the farmers.

Increasing Yields

The modernization of the rice subsector has been steadily implemented over the past two decades. This has been done through the provision of inputs (fertilizers, pesticides, high-yield seeds, etc.), through mechanization such as tractors, and by providing the credit facilities in particular through cooperative-based organizations, in order to enable peasants to acquire such inputs, tools, and machines. The point would now be to expand the benefits of modernization to further crops, the returns from which are higher than that of rice. There is however, largely untapped potential in lowland areas for growing vegetables and for treecrops and cattle-raising in upland areas. These two areas could possibly feed a growing demand from restaurants and other urban consumers.

Undertaking Land Reform

Could land reform resolve the question of declining access to land and of related widening disparities in rural Java? Certain scholars contend that in Java, an overall land reform would not make much sense when there is not enough land to be shared, and would result in very tiny holdings. The French geographer Pierre Gourou suggests instead local adjustments, and points out that land reform alone would be an insufficient answer to population pressures upon the land.[1] Evidence from the communities analysed in this study suggests that land reform does not make much sense in suburban communities where man-land ratios are very high and where land is very fragmented, though there are still some large-scale landowners in such communities. Instead, local policies for the regrouping of land would be much more relevant. As a matter of fact, regrouping of land does occur through private initiatives on the part of small farmers (*i.e.* those whose household owns less than 0.5 ha) who are willing to exchange their valuable land in transit corridors for larger plots in hinterland locations. It may be desirable to coordinate such spontaneous trends at community-level. In less suburban communities where man-land pressures are not too excessive (*i.e.* where average size of wet fields is not falling too far below 0.5 ha), land tenure adjustments may be considered. This would be particularly relevant where large-scale landowners - those owning a few hectares of wetland - are not working their own land by themselves, but are undertaking nonfarm activities.

Reducing the Rate of Population Growth

Through Family Planning: In the first half of the 1990s, the rate of increase in the population of the D.I.Y. has been the slowest in the country - see Chapter 3. This is due to strong out-migration, but also to efficient family planning policies. Today, most rural families have a maximum of two children, which is the target of family planning policies (reflected by the widespread slogan '*dua cukup*', meaning: 'two [children] are enough' - see photograph 1 in Figure 7.5) which are enforced by all levels of government. One can note the role of village and hamlet heads and of local women's associations which are especially active in this field.

Through Transmigration: The transmigration programme has been changing its focus since the 1980s. Efforts are now being focused on consolidating already initiated schemes, while 'spontaneous migrations' to outer islands continue.[2]

Decentralization of Public Finance

It can be argued that increasing local public revenues can help developing peripheral Provinces and Districts. Towards that end, it has been suggested in various studies to carry out a decentralization of public finance in Indonesia. The national government subsidizes local governments through grants. For all regions of Indonesia, including the D.I.Y., the central government's contribution to first stage region receipts - that is at provincial level – has been high - Table 9.1. Some scholars contend that '[such a situation of central fiscalism in Indonesia] makes all regions truly dependent on the central government though there is the possibility of the region increasing its income from its own local sources'.[3] Therefore, certain scholars argue that it would be desirable in Indonesia to reduce the level of local taxes that go to the national government and to redirect them to local governments.[4] Furthermore, studies of intragovernmental public finance relationships stress that nationwide, 'increasing gross domestic product does not enhance the provincial and local government's tax revenues proportionately'.[5]

Table 9.1   Per Cent of Central Government Contribution to First Stage Regional Receipts, D.I.Y., 1981-1982 to 1985-1986
(as a percentage of total)

	1981-82	1982-83	1983-84	1984-85	1985-86
Current receipts (percentages)	78	74	89	75	78
Development receipts (percentages)	77	77	71	62	71

Source: Vincent Rotgé, calculated from Regional Statistics of the D.I.Y., and; State and Local Governmental Financial Statistics, First Stage Region (Province), (1981/1982 to 1985/1986) (Jakarta: Indonesian Central Bureau of Statistics, 1988).

However, one might question the short-term necessity for, as well as the possibility of, redirecting local taxes to Provinces nationwide. If not very carefully managed, attempts in this direction may help increase provincial receipts from oil- or timber-producing regions, and reduce total receipts in other regions, thereby leading to income disparities in public revenues among regions. Furthermore, notwithstanding the oil and timber industries, would redirecting provincial fiscal revenues to local governments bring about any significant increase in local governments' revenues at all in those regions - including the D.I.Y. - whose tax base, even if broadened, would probably continue to be weak and which would therefore need continued grants from the central government if current levels of public expenditures are to be maintained? A second important observation relates to second stage (*i.e.* District or Regency level) public receipts in the D.I.Y. It must be stressed, indeed, that for many years central and provincial governments have been reapportioning an important share of total public receipts into public development expenditures in the poorest areas of the D.I.Y., such as in the District of Gunung Kidul. Such a long-term approach is now yielding good results. In fact, the rural-urban social disparities gap is narrowing in the D.I.Y. and life quality indices (reflecting life-expectancy, child mortality, etc.) were among the very best in the country in the first half of the 1990s. In spite of a rather slow rate of gross regional domestic product (GRDP) increase, such a very positive trend can probably be related to the abovementioned policy approach of continued public expenditure in rural 'backward' areas such as for the provision of health infrastructure, electricity, and schools. At the same time, it is clear that the latter areas have lacked a sufficient tax base, and that local public development expenditures cannot be offset by local receipts, whereas the local tax base in urban areas is significantly higher due to higher receipts from certain categories of activities which remain very largely concentrated in urban areas. The latter include activities which are taxable under the entertainments and hotel and restaurant taxes which have been traditionally the highest in the Municipal District of Yogyakarta and the neighbouring and largely urbanized District of Sleman.

Therefore, one might fear that decentralizing public revenues *imprudently* in Indonesia might harm the growth of a large number of regions, such as the D.I.Y., whose tax base is clearly insufficient. If second stage public receipts are also concerned, this would also be true for the development of Districts that are lagging behind in socioeconomic terms, because of their soil or their remote locations from important infrastructures, especially within Provinces such as the D.I.Y. whose Districts are socioeconomically and geographically very diversified. Longstanding efforts which have been undertaken by various levels of government to provide the latter Districts with infrastructure, schools, and other public amenities should be continued. Failing to do so on the part of higher levels of governments, would ultimately lead to an increased burden of public expenditures in regional and extraregional urban areas, which would have to absorb increased in-migration from rural 'backward' areas.

Also, the urban-rural social disparities gap is narrowing in the D.I.Y., in contrast with the rest of Java.[6] Such a positive and exceptional trend must be partly related to continued public expenditures in rural areas. If it can be proven to be desirable for the sake of any better efficiency or increased devolution to local governments, altering current patterns of public finance should be realized, but with great care. In particular current patterns of public expenditures allocation ought not to adversely affect 'backward' regions on their way to a more sustainable form of development.

Furthermore, public revenues could be increased in the D.I.Y., like elsewhere in Indonesia, through improving the efficiency of the system of tax collection. In particular, land prices should be assessed regularly so as to take into account any current increase in land prices. Such assessment should be undertaken within short periods of time in areas where land prices are rapidly rising.[7] Efforts should be made for such assessments to accurately reflect real land prices based on market prices. The latter is required so that public revenues can increase proportionately with land prices, and in turn so that governments are able to finance the public expenditures needed in urbanizing areas to answer mounting congestion:[8] *e.g.* new infrastructure such as sewerage, water mains, electricity supply, and realizing planning policies which need public land acquisition and whose cost, therefore, is dependent on current land market prices. It is also cautiously suggested that the introduction of some kind of mechanism be studied - such as a special system of value added tax to be applied in specific sectors - so as to enable public authorities to reap a share of the added value of land especially when the construction of public infrastructure in the vicinity of the land - such as the 'ring road' in the D.I.Y. - has significantly boosted land prices - Table 9.4.

A final important remark relates to the possibility of a decline in revenues generated by oil and other natural resources in the future. If this happens, Indonesia would lose an important part of its financial resources for allocation to rural development unless other revenues such as those generated by taxes levied on industries or others can bridge the gap in the meantime. It is therefore increasingly essential to better integrate rural and urban areas, as far as fiscalism and revenue-sharing are concerned, so as to prepare for a possible post-petroleum economy in Indonesia. This remark holds true for the D.I.Y., where fiscal revenues are still very limited especially in the hinterland.

Industrial Development

Industrial development of the D.I.Y. will remain limited, if it does not succeed in attracting industrial investment from outside the region, and in exporting manufactured goods to other regions. National or international investors could be attracted by low wages, a relatively well-educated labour force and good regional infrastructure including a domestic airport whose role could significantly evolve in the future, especially if it is allowed to accept direct international connections. Thus, it is a common, but suitable, recommendation that incentives should be made at the national level to decentralize industrial investment outside a few existing growth centres in Java into more peripheral regions including the D.I.Y.[9] Possibilities may be explored of subcontracting industrial activities for export industries that are located in other parts of Indonesia, such as the Balinese textile industry which already imports *batik* from Central Java. Possible ways to establish linkages with transnational corporations (TNCs) via subcontracting should also be explored in parallel. Diversification of agriculture could lead to the establishment of new agroprocessing industries and existing agroprocessing industries could be expanded. Linkages should be established between tourism and industries that should be encouraged to grow together.

Still, in the course of regional industrialization, small-scale and cottage industries should definitely not be neglected within the context of any general framework for industrial expansion in the D.I.Y. It seems indeed that the large number of small-scale and cottage industries that can be found in the D.I.Y. is characteristic of the Special Region. Any rapid and uncontrolled alteration of such a pattern would probably entail severe social problems in particular - and not only - in the rural areas. Hence, particular care should be given to reviewing possibilities of expanding small-scale and cottage industries. The building materials sector in particular, which could benefit directly from rapid urbanization, could be expanded on a cooperative basis and building materials' enterprises could be introduced to new building made essential by urbanization (*e.g.* multistoried construction which is not traditional in rural areas) with the asssistance of governments and NGOs. The introduction of industries in transit-corridor communities, where private investments are still mostly directed to enterprises of trade, may be advisable. This may be partly achieved by providing tax incentives to urban industrial enterprises that are moving to transit corridors, while hiring local labour. However, for environmental reasons, it may be desirable to direct such policies to upland areas, not to lowland transit-corridor communities where the best agricultural land is located. Supporting the latter is the fact that upland communities are more in need of local employment base expansion than lowland communities which benefit from better access to urban employment through commuting.

Outline of an Agenda for Integrated Rural-Urban Development

Policy recommendations are reviewed below in the context of increasing rural-urban linkages in the D.I.Y. and of the related need for integrated rural-urban development.

Improving Education in Rural Areas

General Education: As mentioned earlier, the rural-urban social disparities gap seems to be narrowing in the D.I.Y., whereas this gap is actually widening in other areas of Java (and of Indonesia).[10] On the other hand, the level of education of rural populations is still significantly lower than that of urban populations. This is not really surprising considering the very high concentration of higher education institutions and universities and therefore of residents who are students especially in Yogyakarta and in the District of Sleman (where the campus of Gadjah Mada University and other educational institutions are located). More significant, however, is the fact that educational levels in rural areas and, in particular, rates of literacy seem to be significantly lower than in urban areas. Public efforts to improve education including higher education in the rural areas of the D.I.Y. should be continued so as to further reduce the still important rural-urban gap in this regard.

Rural dwellers are aware of potentials emerging from a better education for their children. This is clearly reflected in Figure 9.1 which shows the share of the six most important economic alternatives to owning land in the opinion of villagers, based on interviews conducted in Putat II and Kembang, *i.e.* the upland and piedmont communities (using the same questionnaire as designed by Brookfield, *et al.*,[11] for their study of urbanizing communities around Kuala Lumpur). According to observations realized by Kuroyanagi during fieldwork conducted between September 1989 and February 1990 in the hamlets of Piring and Bandung, local villagers follow specific familial strategies concerning education, which are determined by the geographical and socioeconomic characteristics of their hamlets of residence,[12] Thus, although based on a limited sample, it would seem that educational levels in the hamlet located furthest away from Yogyakarta (Piring), would in reality be *higher* than in the hamlet (Bandung) located in the vicinity of, and at short commuting distance, to Yogyakarta, where the range of employment opportunities showing a higher level of return - either local or accessible through daily commuting - than agricultural activities is much broader than in Piring.

Such a situation, if it can be confirmed, could be explained by, firstly good educational infrastructure in Piring or, secondly, an agricultural income which is relatively high in Piring (probably due to a larger overall size of agricultural plots and strong out-migration) which might partly offset the lack of nonfarm alternatives, while enabling households to afford a relatively good education for their children, but also; thirdly, by a probably *deliberate strategy* on the part of households to provide their children with an adequate level of education to enable them to find a job, such as for instance in the civil service, often outside the hamlet.[13] The above observations would tend to indicate that the rule whereby, 'the more rural the location, the lower the level of education' would not always apply under certain geographical and socioeconomic circumstances. It would also be consistent with another observation made in rural communities in a number of countries concerning a correlation between levels of education and of out-migration.[14] Such a positive correlation may find itself somewhat reduced in today's context of increasing rural-urban linkages, which make possible job alternatives for rural residents either locally through rural-urban linkages, or through rural-urban commuting. The evidence of such a strategy is indicated by the fact that villagers borrow money in Piring to a large extent to cover the costs of education for their children.

If confirmed, such a trend should be definitely reinforced through policies for employment expansion aiming at providing rural residents not only with a job near or at commuting distance from their residence, but also subsidized credit, and other incentives such as of a fiscal nature, etc., but also with the kind of relevant education which is required in the first place to qualify for the job or to start a small-scale enterprise. However, the main factor of disparities in accessing education for rural dwellers remains financial as the costs of higher education are beyond the capacity of most households. In fact, a major reason for rural indebtedness remains the cost of the children's education - Table 9.2.

Improving Vocational Education and Apprenticeship: Moreover, in many cases, economic development in the rural areas has actually meant booming growth in the trade sector. This probably means that agriculture is commercializing under demographic pressures, and that employment alternatives are offered to those rural residents who trade rural goods in urban markets. Such a growth of the trade and allied services sector can be interpreted as a positive factor provided, however, that rural residents are not pushed out of agriculture to undertake petty trading activities, but, instead, improve their source of income. Observations made in the field seem to confirm the latter in several instances. In turn, retailers (though it is not clear what percentage are urban dwellers moving to rural areas) open shops in the hinterland where, in spite of the continuing indebtedness of many households (Table 9.2), the rising incomes of a significant share of the population have created a steady demand for retailing goods.

However, while trade and the allied services sector are booming, industries have not grown proportionately, especially in rural areas and along some urban corridors in the Regency of Bantul. The reason for this is a combination of lack of relevant training and education, and perhaps the relative ease with which profits can be made in the booming trade sector for those with capital to invest. It appears, therefore, that efforts should be made to reinforce vocational education and specialized technical training in the hinterland of the D.I.Y. in those fields such as agricultural engineering or construction materials technology, for instance, which

Figure 9.1   **Household Heads' Perception of the Degree of Importance of Six Main Alternatives versus Owning Land** (the communities of the Plain of Bantul are not included)*

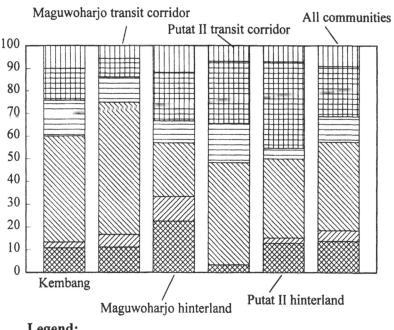

In Percentage

Legend:

▨ Securing a permanent revenue from agriculture

▤ Owning an enterprise   ▦ Cultivating land

◹ Sending children to school   ▥ Other alternatives**

▨ Securing a permanent revenue from trade

*   Part of the questionnaire annexed in Brookfield, *et al.*, *The City in the Village* (Singapore: Oxford University Press, 1991), was used for this figure.
**   See following Figure 9.2.

Source: Primary data processed by Vincent Rotgé using SAS (fieldwork in 1992).

Figure 9.2 **Details of 'Other Alternatives' -**
Answer from Figure 9.1*

In Percentage

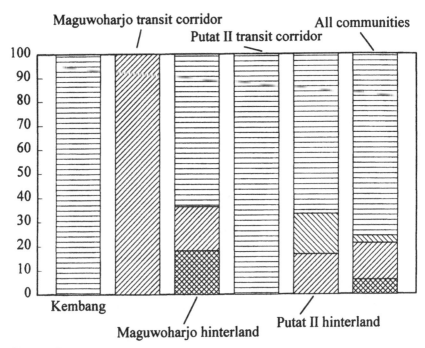

Legend:

▨ Securing a permanent revenue from a handicraft activity or
small-scale industry

◩ Owning or building a townhouse

▨ Saving money in a bank

▤ Securing a permanent revenue from another type of activity

*   Part of the questionnaire annexed in Brookfield, *et al.*, *The City in the Village*
(Singapore: Oxford University Press, 1991), was used for this figure.

Source: Primary data processed by Vincent Rotgé using SAS (fieldwork in 1992).

could lead to the establishment of new and innovative industrial activities in rural areas. Policy could partly consist in providing students from poor rural households with scholarships that could be granted at local level in those relevant fields that may benefit local development.

Rural Credit Policy

Villagers's attitudes were studied in the lowland communities of the Plain of Bantul concerning their readiness to borrow from the informal banking sector. This resulted in the following:

(1) When compared with their respective rural hinterland, an overwhelming

majority of rural residents borrowing money from credit or banking institutions live in the corridor areas. (This remark concerns only *KUPEDES, e.g. Kredit Umum Pedesaan*, General Rural Credit, from *BRI, e.g. Bank Rakyat Indonesia*).

(2) The same trend seems to occur for savings accounts in the nonsuburban hamlets of Celep and Piring in the village of Murtigading-Srigading, but the contrast is much less pronounced in the relatively suburban hamlets of Karanggondang-Cepit and Bandung in Pendowoharjo village. (This remark concerns only *BRI* savings schemes: mainly *SIMPEDES, i.e.* Rural People Savings Scheme, and *TABANAS, i.e.* National Development Savings Scheme).

(3) Rural residents borrowing money from *BRI* through *KUPEDES* schemes in Piring and Celep are farmers (sixty-seven in Celep), traders (thirty-nine in Celep) and civil servants (six in Celep and one in Piring). In Bandung and Karanggondang-Cepit they are: civil servants (twenty-five in Karanggondang-Cepit and ten in Bandung) and traders (twelve in Karanggondang-Cepit and seven in Bandung).

(4) Some villagers use also various credit facilities provided by village cooperative units (*KUD*, such as *Kredit Industri Kecil* or *Kredit Modal Kerja Pembangunan*).

(5) Traditional systems of saving (including rotating credit system, *Arisan* or *Simpan Pinjam*) are much sophisticated and can perform social activities which go far beyond the grant of credit alone, but on the other hand usually offer small loans.

From the above observations, it appears that a large share of credit schemes offered by the *BRI* local branches and the village cooperatives

(*KUD*) in the studied lowland communities of the Plain of Bantul are used by rural residents for trading activities, but few, if any, for small-scale industries. Kuroyanagi has observed that the hinterland communities of Bandung and Piring tend to show that a large share of villagers borrow money from formal credit and banking institutions, and also from informal sources to spend on the education of their children, or on food/clothing, and the improvement of their houses - Table 9.2. The share of borrowers spending money on food/clothing, and the improvement of their homes is even higher in Piring (double that in Bandung) which seems to reflect the fact that villagers in Piring probably live more at subsistence level than villagers in Bandung do. At the same time, from various field observations and the evidence of the geographical distribution of *BRI* savings accounts, it appears that capital formation is rather low in an area located away from main roads *and* in a deadlocked region such as Piring, but significantly higher in an area located away from the main road but located near Yogyakarta, as with Bandung. Also, in both cases, capital formation seems higher in transit-corridor than in hinterland communities.

Expanding Rural Savings and Credit

Many farmers in the D.I.Y. live at subsistence level. Most of the farmers' small savings, if any, and/or borrowing go to the purchase of indispensable goods and expenditures on clothing, tools, housing, and also on children's education. Accordingly, while a significant number of farmers are indebted to varying extents, little money is left for savings and investment in fixed capital.

Strengthening Capital Formation in the Hinterland: It is recommended that governments take necessary steps in order to enable capital formation in the rural areas. This means, firstly continuing and expanding policies for strengthening savings in rural areas, but also raising rural income and productivity. The most likely way to achieve the latter objective is to take steps towards the diversification of the agricultural sector and also of the rural economy overall, so that it includes a larger share of 'productive nonfarm activities'. In designing policies aimed at the latter objective, decision makers should be conscious that for many farmers who are either landless or whose agricultural plot is becoming too small through the mechanisms of inheritance, the necessary shift to nonfarm activities - which may be gradual and partial when farmers and their family undertake

Table 9.2   Reasons for Borrowing Money and Source of Loans in Piring and Bandung*
(percentages in parentheses)

a: Piring Sources of credit**	Food, clothing and shelter	Consumables and commodities	Pressing needs (diseases, etc.)	Important events (child birth, marriage, etc.)	Religious ceremonies	Education	Investment	Other	Total
BRI	4	·	1	·	·	3	6	3	17 (36.9)
KUD/BPD	·	·	·	1	·	2	·	·	3 (6.5)
Simpan Pinjam of Ronda	3	·	1	·	·	6	1	2	13 (28.3)
Simpan Pinjam of PKK	3	·	·	·	·	4	1	·	8 (17.4)
Friends or relatives	·	1	·	1	·	2	1	·	5 (10.9)
Total (per cent)	10 (21.7)	1 (2.2)	2 (4.3)	2 (4.3)	·	17 (37)	9 (19.6)	5 (10.5)	46 (100)

*   The 1989-90 research hamlets of Piring and Bandung included the hinterland communities, but not the transit corridors, that Rotgé studied in 1991.

** BRI (*Bank Rakyat Indonesia*): People's Bank of Indonesia; *KUD* (*Koperasi Unit Desa*): Village Unit Cooperative; *BPD* (*Bank Pembangunan Daerah*): Regional Development Bank; *Simpan Pinjam*: Savings and Loan Organization; *Ronda*: Organization for Surveillance and Security; and *PKK* (*Pendidikan Kesejahteraan Keluarga*): Education for Family Welfare.

Table 9.2 (continued)

b: Bandung Sources of credit**	Food, clothing and shelter	Consumables and commodities	Pressing needs (diseases, etc.)	Important events (child birth, marriage, etc.)	Religious ceremonies	Education	Investment	Other	Total
BRI	3	·	·	·	1	2	10	9	25 (40.3)
KUD/BPD	2	·	1	1	·	4	·	·	8 (12.9)
Simpan Pinjam of Ronda	1	·	·	·	·	·	·	·	1 (1.6)
Simpan Pinjam of PKK	9	3	1	1	1	2	1	1	19 (30.7)
Friends or relatives	5	·	·	·	·	·	3	1	9 (14.5)
Total (per cent)	20 (32.3)	3 (4.8)	2 (3.2)	2 (3.2)	2 (3.2)	8 (12.9)	14 (22.6)	11 (17.8)	62 (100)

**   Same as above.

Source: Quoted from Haruo Kuroyanagi, 'Source of Livelihood, Mutual Help Credit, and Saving Systems in Two Villages of Yogyakarta Special Region' [paper presented at the second Country Seminar on Regional Development and Planning of Daerah Istimewa Yogyakarta, Yogyakarta, August 1991]. Kuroyanagi's original table gives a different literal meaning for 'PKK' (see notes above).

several concomitant activities - should definitely entail a net increase in the household's total income, which even if modest would constitute a positive trend. In other words, diversification, as a policy target, should not encourage the proliferation of low-productive nonfarm activities constituting last-resort solutions in the face of growing landlessness. Nonetheless, the often vital importance of certain low-return activities should not be overlooked and neglected either, in view of securing subsistence means for very poor households. Observations in urbanizing communities of the hinterland confirm that the development of rural-urban linkages stimulates the growth of productive activities and capital formation in the hinterland.

Consolidating Traditional Savings and Self-help Credit Groups' Activities: Second, traditional savings and credit systems should be linked with decentralized formal banking institutions in rural areas. In particular efforts such as those initiated by the German Agency for Technical Cooperation (*Deutsche Gesellschaft für Technische Zusammenarbeit*: *GTZ*) / Indonesian joint 'Pilot Project Linking Banks and Self-help Groups' could be promising. Traditional credit and saving systems, indeed, are those which are the most responsive to villagers' genuine needs. By participating in savings or credit activities of traditional self-help groups, villagers do not have to deal with bank officers from outside the village, but with fellow villagers who are likely to better understand their needs. Also, in doing so, villagers do not have to follow long and tedious formalities that are usually requested by formal banking and other credit institutions. Moreover, traditional credit systems can allow some repayment flexibility in the face of events that could unexpectedly happen to the borrower, making him temporarily unable to repay. For villagers used to living at subsistence level, the experience of taking out a loan is usually both novel and disquieting. Any inability to repay in time may entail very severe consequences for the borrower and his family or acquaintances. The piece of land - the villager's own land or that of a relative or close acquaintance - which is usually used as collateral may have to be resold in order to repay the loan. Deposit and saving accounts can be used for collateral as well, but they seem to be rare, especially in rural areas. In that sense, traditional credit systems help reduce what can probably be regarded as one of the most important sources of inhibition for villagers to take out loans. At the same time, traditional credit and saving systems usually constitute only one component of a larger self-help system. The latter includes the organization of inspection tours of the village at night, special social events for women or youth, or even the establishment of local retailing shops. Supporting traditional systems can constitute a pivotal component of a wider policy aiming at supporting community life and community-based programmes. Also, an important reason for linking traditional self-help groups with formal credit institutions is that in so doing, the principal weakness of traditional systems can be ameliorated, *i.e.* the paucity of their financial means and in particular of their initial capital.

Improving the Efficiency of Application Procedures for Loans: Third, the efficiency of the procedure to obtain a loan should be upgraded. In particular, the procedure should be speeded up, without harming the process of reviewal of project proposals by prospective candidates for loans.

Subsidized Credit for Rural Small-scale Industries: Recent developments in the rural areas of the Regency of Bantul show a persistently low level of expansion of the small-scale industry subsector which has not been commensurate with a booming expansion of the trade and allied services sectors. Based on our observations in the lowland areas of the Regency of Bantul in the early 1990s, it does not seem that such a situation stems from competition for credit between the small-scale industry subsector and the trade and allied services sectors. Therefore, there is probably no current need to establish local-level regulations governing the intersectoral allocation of loans of public banking and credit institutions in rural areas.

Instead, it seems that the comparatively low level of development of small-scale industries, excluding cottage industries, in rural areas stems from a combination of factors, some of which are not related to credit at all. These additional factors are likely to be a basic lack of marketing possibilities; insufficient appropriate training and education of the rural population; certain types of trade activities appear to rural residents to be more profitable and also 'easier' to undertake than small-scale industries. It is therefore recommended that a set of integrated policy measures should be undertaken for the development of small-scale activities, including subsidized credit, and simultaneously small-scale industries in rural areas should be provided. This could possibly include the provision of subsidized credit at low rates of interest, as well as extended advisory facilities concerning technical but also financial and managerial aspects, such as book keeping and accounting. Wim Stoffer and Agus Sutanto in a study of small-scale industries in both upland (peripheral to the central plain) and lowland areas of the Regency of Bantul point out interregional and scale differences in small-scale industries, noting that certain rather scattered small-scale industries have no access to credit facilities.[15] When various factors hinder access to credit for certain small-scale industries, specific solutions should be studied in order to overcome them. However, it should be mentioned that existing credit schemes for small-scale industries are the *KIK* (small-scale investment credit) and the *KMPK* (permanent working capital credit). Both are part of the *KUPEDES* scheme.[16] An important question relates to why this policy does not yield more effective results.[17]

Regarding Villagers' Debt: Great care should be given to ensuring that the expansion of credit facilities in the rural areas will not contribute to a worsening of villagers' indebtedness. Accordingly, banks or other credit institutions should always take great care not to grant loans to villagers for unrealistic projects. Banks should carefully evaluate project proposals of candidates for loans and should avoid granting excessive loans when land is used as collateral or when candidates for loans plan to use the money for certain types of non-essential expenditures, *i.e.* certain type of consumer goods. Effective guarantees should be required from candidates for loans so as to make sure that loans are used for their declared purposes. On the other hand, credit and banking institutions which provide subsidized credit for development purposes should avoid providing credit *too narrowly* for specifically 'productive' activities. In particular, subsidized credit should be provided to poor households for educational purposes (since education-related expenditures constitute an important cause for farmers' indebtedness) as well as for professional internships. As mentioned earlier, vocational education, training and apprenticeship are necessary for residents of rural areas to start certain activities such small-scale industries. Also, subsidized credit should be provided, at low interest rates and in combination with other forms of possible assistance including grants for social welfare purposes, to some households which face exceptional events, so as to help them meet short- and longer-term needs. One should always keep in mind that, although the contribution of cottage industries to GRP is probably smaller than the contribution of small-scale industries, the socioeconomic function of cottage industries is extremely important, since many cottage industries are subsistence activities. Cottage industries, therefore, should not be denied access to credit.[18]

Widening the Range of Services Offered by Banking and Other Credit Institutions: Bank employees working in rural areas should be provided with specialized educational or professional training so as to make them better acquainted with specific rural problems and needs. This would make possible a new conception of banking services: advising on potential activities and assessing more earnestly those activities which may qualify for a loan. Such a step may also constitute an advantage for both credit institutions and their customers. It may contribute to increasing the ability of bank staff to assess the feasibility of projects being submitted to them from candidates for a loan. However, banks should not duplicate the work of other development institutions but should try to increase their co-operation with them. Finally, the wages of bank employees working in rural areas could be raised in order to make such positions more attractive to qualified personnel.

Linking Credit Policies with Regional Development Planning: Areas and activities should be delineated in which priority subsidized credit should be provided after the local potentials and needs for expansion of such activities have been identified, and after feasibility studies have been conducted from which guidelines for banking officials in charge of managing such subsidized credit can be formulated. Moreover, The possibility for providing special banking services in the least accessible parts of rural areas should be studied. This is especially important since it has been noticed that interest rates for credit are very high in some upland areas of Southeast Asia, for instance, where the limited supply of credit remains concentrated in the hands of a few private lenders.[19]

By and large, policies for the provision of rural credit should be linked with regional development policies, since credit needs and availability are influenced by factors of a geographical and locational nature.[20] Similarly, studies should be undertaken of the industrial concentration processes which are occurring within urbanizing corridors. A comparative study of the patterns of industrialization further away from transit corridors within hinterland areas should be also conducted. Relevant local credit policy implications should be drawn from the latter, taking differences in types and patterns of industrialization into account, in the same manner as advocated by Stoffer and Sutanto[21] for small-scale industries depending on whether they are located in lowland or upland communities.

Defining Local Initiatives for Diversifying Agricultural Production and Assessing Marketing Potentials

Background: Low Diversification of Agriculture and of Non-rice Cash Crops: Whereas the D.I.Y. exports very little outside its boundaries, it imports a great deal of agricultural produce. Thus, many fruits and vegetables sold in the large Yogyakarta fruit market originate from other Provinces. Also, from general observations made in the field, it appears that most farmers in lowland areas generally grow two crops of rice and one *palawija* (non-rice) crop, usually soybeans, a year (more rarely five crops of rice and one of *palawija* in two years), unless they have to grow sugarcane for Madukismo - the local sugar factory. Each sugarcane crop requires a sixteen- to eighteen-month cycle. Soybeans frequently constitute the most popular *palawija*. For instance in the hamlet of Piring, the most popular *palawija* were as follows: soybean, onion, pepper, and garlic. Soybeans are not the most valuable of such *palawija*. It is, however, the most popular among farmers. The reason is that other crops require much care and that growing them would probably require hiring additional labour. This would ultimately reduce initial price differentials with soybean. At the same time, observations made in Celep and Bandung (transit-corridor hamlets in the Plain of Bantul) revealed that foreign-imported soybeans are used by local small-scale agroprocessing (milling) and cottage-food making (soybean cakes - *tempe*) industries, because they are preferable to local varieties of soybean which reportedly would 'have a thicker skin and would be more watery'. This would tend to show strong limitations for recycling locally-produced soybeans into local agroprocessing industries and by and large some marketing limits of locally produced soybeans. However, as seen in the case studies, a very positive observation is that cacao and other fruit trees have been introduced in some upland and piedmont areas of the D.I.Y., including the village of Kembang and the hamlet of Putat II.

Cattle- and Poultry-raising, Fish-breeding: Field observations in all studied communities of the Plain of Bantul, showed that some rural residents who are using capital accumulated through a primary activity - such as trading and/or producing construction materials, or agroprocessing activities - often undertake an additional secondary activity such as 'zero-grazing' cattle-fattening. The principles of which are simple:

(1) A few head of cattle are purchased at a relatively low price usually in Gunung Kidul Regency. Animals are selected which are young and healthy but skinny;

(2) The animals are then fed on a special fattening diet with maize straw and the husks of soybeans available from the local mills;

(3) The animals are then resold a few months later at the market to be sent and slaughtered outside the D.I.Y.

The monthly return from this activity can be quite high. A significant number of rural residents with sufficient capital at their disposal, therefore, undertake this activity. Some are even gradually undertaking the latter activity as a primary activity, while their formerly primary activity gradually becomes secondary.

In the upland community of Putat II, many farmers raise cows as a part-time activity. But shortage of fodder, especially during the dry season, constitutes a serious impediment. Hence, such farmers charter motor vehicles to collect fodder in lowland areas. In fact, some of the cattle raised in Putat II are probably resold directly or indirectly to farmers in the lowland areas, who quicly reap some value-added by fattening this cattle on the diet.

Some farmers in lowland communities and in Kembang operate fish ponds. But these schemes are usually very limited in size (often farmers raise a single large cat-fish a year), though in the suburban community of Maguwoharjo a more elaborate form of fish raising can be found, including the raising of a large variety of selected and valuable species of fish, which target a broad segment of the urban markets including urban restaurants (*gurami* for example). In addition, some rural dwellers raise large numbers of poultry (between fifty and a few hundred head), like ducks for selling the eggs and the animals to urban markets. However, mostly the people involved in these activities are servants either active or retired, or householders who have been able to accumulate the initial capital through one or several anterior activities.

To sum up, field observations clearly demonstrated that capital formation constitutes an essential prerequisite to agriculture diversification in the studied lowland communities. Most, if not all, successful cases of agricultural diversification that could be seen in the studied communities of the Plain of Bantul are 'spontaneous' or self-initiated ones on an individual basis (versus community-based projects). They have always been realized by rural residents who have been able to accumulate sufficient capital either through urban or international remittances, or through initial activities in trade and construction.

Policy Implications

Against the current situation of quasi monoculture (rice) in the D.I.Y., projects should be introduced aiming at the diversification of agriculture. This would concern high value-added crops, cattle-fattening, fish breeding, and treecrops (gardens) or plantations for which marketing potentials can be identified at regional and/or national level. In attempting to diversify agriculture, emphasis should be put on encouraging farmers to grow cash crops whose net return is superior to that of paddy. Such crops may include vegetables, treecrops, and fish breeding that increasing urbanization would probably fuel the demand for. Numerous human as well as technical problems that may reduce or even cancel attractive price differentials should be taken into account. Certain disincentives for farmers to grow such crops should be taken into account such as those relating to the volatility of the market prices which may fluctuate very broadly as a function of the level of the production in the region during the past season. It might be desirable, therefore, to study the feasibility of establishing some intra- and inter-regional mechanism(s) that would enable some price regulation and offer some guarantees to farmers who are ready to grow alternative crops.

Farmers should be encouraged to grow alternative cash crops through community-based and other mutual assistance associations through which subsidized credit could be provided to 'small farmers' (those who tenant wetland significantly below 0.5 ha in wetland communities, or pieces of land, either dry and/or wet, which are too small for meeting the needs of their households).

J-L. Maurer, in a study of socioeconomic conditions in villages located in the D.I.Y. suggested that small intensification programmes, promotion of fertilizers, pesticides, high-yield variey of seeds, appropriate management, and credit, be set up for crops other than rice.[22] In this author's view, such programmes could be of the same nature as intensification programmes established throughout the 1970s and 1980s for rice, but on a smaller scale. Barbier, in turn, contends that such intensification programmes would be too costly to be realistically implemented on a large scale and above all would be conducive to further environmental degradation, recommending the promotion of agroforestry and of innovative farming systems and crops in particular in uplands.[23]

Further obstacles for the development of alternative crops to be seriously considered are risk aversion: at subsistence level farmers usually prefer growing rice (as noted by Hardjono,[24] rice-growing provides a regular harvest for home consumption). Specific steps should be undertaken in order to better understand and identify the underlying causes of risk aversion and then reduce such causes.

Cattle- and poultry-raising and fish-breeding constitute important potentials for the D.I.Y. which could be expanded. Cattle-raising could be developed for exports in particular, but should also be associated with the parallel strengthening of relevant agroprocessing industries such as dairy products industries. In this sense, cattle raising could come to constitute over time a regional specialization of the D.I.Y. Cattle-raising needing space (apart from the 'zero-grazing' type and whose expansion in lowland areas might prove ultimately limited) should be expanded on the dry land of the Regencies of Gunung Kidul and Kulon Progo, where it constitutes a welcome alternative to dryland cropping. The latter solution is being actively promoted and advocated by the 'Yogyakarta Rural Development Project' sponsored by the World Bank.

Thus, specific steps should be taken towards the expansion of cattle-raising and fish-breeding in both lowland and upland areas. For instance, new types of fodder should be introduced. Their marketing should be promoted particularly in poor upland areas of the D.I.Y. Subsidized credit schemes should be established in parallel, so as to enable poor farmers, who are already involved in cattle-fattening, to purchase such fodder, thus enabling them to raise their return through the improvement of their animals' diet. At the same time, short-term credit, possibly subsidized, should be made increasingly accessible to farmers willing to start cattle-fattening but who lack initial capital. Such farmers should be granted advisory assistance in financial matters by banking or other credit institutions, so as to help them repay loans taken out for raising the initial capital, and becoming more rapidly financially independent. Similar steps should be initiated for the expansion of fish-breeding and of poultry-raising. Public efforts should be channeled through self-help groups and directed towards supporting schemes on a variety of scales. Such efforts should be addressed in particular to the diffusion of information and to the training of rural residents in such relevant activities as fish-breeding for instance, which concerns breeding and the selection of suitable food especially for the young fish.

National and regional needs for sugar production in the D.I.Y. should be also carefully assessed. As noted by various scholars and as confirmed though observations realized in the field, renting out their land for growing sugar cane is economically disadvantageous for farmers. The length of the agricultural cycle of sugar cane, as already noted, is about sixteen months. Then one additional month is needed in order to remove bulky roots left deep in the soil by the cane. The point is that during a period of sixteen to eighteen months, farmers would have been able to grow three crops of paddy and one of *palawija* (intermediary non-rice crop) whereas rent levels paid to the farmer by the sugar factory do not offset the resulting loss of income for farmers, even when the farmer succeeds in working as agricultural hired labour during the time that his land is cultivated for sugar cane by the sugar factory (usually farmers can work only a very short period of time as hired labour when the demand for labour is at its highest during harvest time). A comparison of the monthly revenue that a farmer derives from his land when he is growing paddy and when he is growing sugar cane shows very important income level differentials. It should be noted that sugar production is a very protected sector and that sugar domestic prices in Indonesia are significantly above international prices - still 50 per cent higher in 1988 according to Shawki Barghouti, *et al.*, in a World Bank technical paper on rural diversification in Asia.[25] The point is that, as contended in the same publication: 'High-cost sugar displaced other crops, including rice, cassava, corn, or other secondary crops that received little protection'. Why not redirect some of the resources being allocated to sugar cane to crops which are more advantageous for farmers to grow?

The Need for Community-based Initiatives in Favour of Agricultural Diversification

It is true that attempts have been made to introduce certain types of cash crops such as vegetables and treecrops in respectively lowland and upland areas of the D.I.Y. Some of these programmes involve credit and land registration institutions together with other partners, besides individual farmers. However, field interviews reveal the extent of many farmers' reluctance in collaborating with some diversification programmes. In some cases (regarding the cultivation of garlic in lowland areas for instance), farmers questioned the feasibility of the programme itself as well as their economic purpose in joining it. Many farmers are also afraid of ultimately losing their land which is often used as a collateral to secure loans which were essential to obtaining some of the necessary inputs, if such programmes fail. Instead, community-based programmes based on the voluntary collaboration of farmers, though with possible public incentives or assistance in a way that would not limit the strict spontaneous decision to join such programmes from the part of individual farmers, would better serve both the interest of local community development and of individual farmers. Together with local empowerment, the development of such programmes would strengthen a sense of entrepreneurship among farmers and reduce risk aversion while farmers would be free to take advantage of opportunities created by the urban demand for certain types of cash crops (such as fruits and vegetables).

Strengthening Marketing Outlets

Even if socially and technically possible, diversifying agriculture will remain necessarily limited in scope, if marketing outlets cannot be found for the new range of agricultural produces. It would be useful if public bodies promoted the diffusion at the community level of information on marketing potentials of a range of agricultural or cottage- industries' products.

Regional Policies for Employment Expansion

Spatial Policies

The government of the D.I.Y. is designing a strategy to reduce the regional urban primacy of Yogyakarta, by reinforcing secondary centres (such as the capital of Regencies: Wonosari, Wates, Bantul, and Sleman). However, in so doing, the evidence arising from both the international and national experiences should be recognized, *i.e.* that in order to succeed, strategies for strengthening the role of secondary towns or new town strategies must be coupled with policies for creating employment within or in the vicinity of designated growth poles or new towns.[26] That is to say that the evidence that the regional growth role of small towns will remain weak or nonexistent if better integration with their hinterland is not realized and if specific policies to support the development of their hinterlands are not undertaken, should be acknowledged. A relevant illustration can be drawn from the research study. While the towns of Wonosari and perhaps Wates, are probably distant enough from Yogyakarta to constitute subregional centres, it is questionable whether the town of Bantul is either too close to Yogyakarta to constitute itself a regional subcentre, or too distant to constitute its outskirts. Such a location and the fact that the town of Bantul remains mainly an administrative centre could explain the low growth rate and the town's very low attraction for urban commuters living nearby, who, apart from a few local civil servants, very often commute to Yogyakarta. In turn, practical ways should be studied for establishing rural-urban linkages between the abovementioned secondary urban centres and their hinterland. It is therefore essential to study ways of diversifying the administrative functions of capitals of Regencies, so that such centres can include a wider range of functions in the framework of a better integration of such towns with their hinterland (marketing, industries, service and education, for example).

Employment Policies

Sectoral policies should be studied to ascertain whether the experience of existing traditional subcontracting systems in the *batik* industry can be applied to further activities with a higher economic potential. Steps should be taken to make externally-funded infrastructural projects benefit local employment. The latter includes explicitly designed employment creation policies (some possible policies are suggested in the following section). Guarantees should be taken for public projects related to the development of secondary urban centres to definitely benefit employment in peripheral areas. Simultaneously, efforts should be pursued for the establishment of labour-intensive public works programmes in the hinterland.[27]

Certain subsectors such as construction which is growing rapidly and is likely to further benefit by expanding urbanization could be encouraged. The health subsector could also receive special attention. By and large, this subsector is well-developed in the D.I.Y.[28] Its importance in rural employment was confirmed by field observations. It appears that a significant number of people living or being born in the studied communities (such as the hamlet of Piring) are involved in the health subsector locally, or even outside the D.I.Y. (in Bekasi near Jakarta, for instance). A possible way to strengthen this subsector would be through expanding educational facilities in the D.I.Y. in the field of medicine and pediatrics and for the training of midwives, so that the Special Region becomes a national centre in the field of health. Training and educational facilities should be set up in the rural areas for both regional and national trainees.

It is also recommended that the number of candidates qualifying every year for the programme to work abroad sponsored by the Indonesian government should be definitely increased at District (*i.e.* Regency) and Subdistrict levels with a focus on the poorest areas. It must be emphasized that controls exercized by Indonesian officials at the places where expatriates work should be made efficient to ensure that the latter's working conditions are always decent. The fear of being mistreated by employers in host countries constitutes a strong disincentive, especially for female labour.

Transportation Policies

For rural households, a short distance between the place of residence and Yogyakarta, and also - particularly as such a distance increases - the ownership of a motor vehicle entails profound socioeconomic consequences. This is because, in the existing situation of scarcity of well-paid employment opportunities in the rural areas of the D.I.Y., accessibility to an urban job constitutes a decisive economic advantage. But wide disparities exist in the patterns of vehicle ownership in the studied communities. At the same time, fares of existing public transport can be considered as reasonable in terms of the average income of many commuters, but may still prove beyond the ability to pay, for some of the poorest rural dwellers who must rely on petty urban (often part-time) employment for a livelihood. Commuting also remains very time-consuming.

The issue of providing subsidized public transport or providing easier subsidized or nonsubsidized credit for the purchase of individual vehicles which are needed for commuting, as well as for expanding productive activities (carrying goods), may be considered. It is true, however, that enabling the direct acess of rural producers to urban markets might affect the activities of *makelar* (intermediate traders). Also, it may be worthwhile investigating possibilities for farmers to carry their crops to more distant markets by trucks chartered by cooperatives. The latter would enable the decrease of individual transportation costs, and allow farmers to increase the amount of produce that they can sell at the market. Mounting traffic congestion, however, is occurring in the D.I.Y., particularly as a result of increasing commuting and rural-urban linkages. Hence, would not it be wise:

(1) To design efficient public transportation policies, and;
(2) To help expand employment throughout the D.I.Y., in order to reduce daily traffic flows from Yogyakarta to the hinterland and *vice versa*?

This is to say that, though commuting impacts positively upon rural growth, it also presents side-effects such as increasing traffic congestion, and therefore should not be given too much importance in a regional strategy for employment creation. This is especially true for commuting by means of individual vehicles (motorcycles), but also of mini-buses which are abundant on the roads of D.I.Y.

The Growth of Tourism in the Context of the Integrated Rural-Urban Approach to Regional Development in the D.I.Y.

The Balinese Experience

Tourism in the D.I.Y. has shown continued growth in recent years. Considering its possible potentials but also side-effects for regional development tourism should be definitely addressed by policymakers. A brief examination of the more than two-decades-long Balinese experience in planned tourism development might prove enlightening in the abovementioned respect. A plan for tourism development in Bali was initiated in the early 1970s (known as the SECTO report). It stated that 'tourists would be contained in designated resort areas and certain excursion routes', while the construction of luxury hotels was scheduled near certain coastal beaches.[29] Hotel occupancy rates dropped during the 1980-84 period.[30] To boost the development of tourism, the Indonesian government took the decision to introduce a system of visa-free entry for citizens from a large number of countries. A second decision, more effective according to Jayasuriya and Nehen,[31] allowed international flights to Bali in 1985. According to the same authors, neither expected nor planned was the growth of the so-called 'budget tourist sub-sector'. The links established by this sector with the Balinese domestic economy have proved intense, in contrast with luxury tourism for which food is not infrequently imported and labour often hired from outside Bali.[32] A few observations concerning the impact of tourism upon the Balinese economy are noteworthy.

First, while tourism has constituted the 'most visible external stimulus to growth', it should be stressed that, as pointed out by the same authors, agriculture has actually contributed the most to the increase of gross regional domestic product (GRDP) in Bali.

Second, according to the same study, the economic effect of the development of tourism in Bali is to be counted as a positive one, mainly in the following respects:

(1) A direct effect has been the revenue generated by tourism which has increased overall GRDP;

(2) Indirect effects have been generated through linkages established between the tourist sector - especially the 'budget tourist sub-sector' or homestay tourists - and other (food, supply, etc.), and upon employment (in the tourist sector and in allied supply sectors);

(3) 'Dynamic' effects such as upon the garment subsector of the manufacturing industry through the exposure of international standards of quality of clothing to Balinese textiles, and the contacts established by local producers with tourists who in some instances turned to importing Balinese garments and became 'buyer/consultants' for the nascent garment industry.[33]

The study of such 'dynamic' effects was undertaken by Wheeler, Cole and Irianiwati.[34] These authors stressed the very positive effect of '(the combination of)... Indonesian labor skills and material inputs with skills and information provided by foreign buyer/consultants'. Nonetheless, the same authors also stress that after an initial phase of heavy reliance on foreigners (prior to the 1981 recession), the Balinese have now become more independent.[35] Furthermore, the same authors point out positive repercussions of the expansion of the Balinese garment industry upon income and employment in rural areas of Bali. Java would have also benefited since the Balinese garment industry has placed orders in Java and also subcontracted Javanese labourers whose wages are lower than in Bali (*batik* from Central Java, and cotton and rayon fabric from Bandung and Surabaya have been imported to Bali).[36]

But Jayasuriya and Nehen[37] identify also negative economic side-effects of the expansion of tourism upon other economic sectors, as follows.

(1) Tourism increases the demand for labour and simultaneously the level of wages. Part of the income of 'domestic residents', indeed, which itself has been increased as an effect of tourism expansion, is spent on 'domestically produced goods and services'. This in turn is likely to cause an increase in wages.[38] The possible resulting increase in wages 'has a negative effect on other sectors that compete with tourism for labour'.[39] The importance of such a negative side effect is, however, played down by Jayasuriya and Nehen who point out that the abundant supply of cheap labour in nearby Java is likely to very significantly reduce its level of importance, and;

(2) Tourism competes for capital with other sectors. Jayasuriya and Nehen, however, emphasize that the importance of the latter side effect is likely to be reduced by, firstly 'an inflow of capital from the rest of Indonesia', and secondly 'regulations governing intersectoral allocations of state bank lending'.[40]

Possible Lessons for the D.I.Y.

Several general conclusions can be cautiously drawn from the Balinese experience in tourism for the D.I.Y. To start with, luxury tourism has a relatively weak impact upon the domestic economy, and probably none upon the rural economy (this is confirmed for D.I.Y. in Table 9.3). Efforts should be made to establish linkages between such a category of tourism and the domestic economy of the D.I.Y. This could be achieved through making incentives for luxury hotels and restaurants in the region to purchase domestic produce, and on the supply side, in encouraging farmers to grow vegetables, fruit, breed fish, and develop other food products of high quality as part of a general policy of agricultural diversification. Attempts should be made to introduce some traditional types of domestically produced food into dishes served in such hotels. Additionally, incentives should be provided to encourage luxury hotels to recruit local staff if it would appear that luxury hotels in the D.I.Y. would tend to hire their staff from outside the Special Region.

Secondly, as recommended above for the construction subsector in general, regulations should be introduced to ensure that a 'fair' share of regional construction projects undertaken by the private sector in connection with the building of tourism infrastructure is secured by small-scale construction enterprises or individuals from within the D.I.Y. including those based in Yogyakarta's hinterland. This might create the need for revising current practices of hiring labour in connection with larger-scale projects, which often lead to an increase in the number of middlemen. With each middleman's commission, wages received by construction workers at the end of the chain are depressed. This in turn seems to drive middlemen to search for workers living in the poorest hinterland areas of the D.I.Y.

Whereas such a system might benefit the poor in some rural areas, it is also likely to make projects unavailable to local labour, and ultimately to reduce the level of real wages granted to construction workers in general. Indeed, it appears from various interviews that independent construction workers were paid about Rp. 3,500 a day in 1991 (US$1.75 at the early 1990s exchange rate, or US$0.50 at the mid-December 1999 exchange rate) in connection with the construction of private residences, against about Rp. 1,500 in 1991 (US$0.75 at the early 1990s exchange rate, or US$0.21 at the mid-December 1999 exchange rate) for construction workers hired through middlemen in connection with large-scale development projects.

Thirdly, steps should be taken in order to ensure that the supply of capital in the region will not be excessively strained by borrowing, on the part of the tourism sector, and also to regulate the intersectoral allocations of state bank lending, so as to prevent the possible adverse side effects of competition of tourism with other sectors for capital from harming the growth of other sectors of the regional economy.

Fourthly, as we have seen, Bali experimented at the beginning of the 1970s with steps aiming at restricting tourism development to certain confined sites, so as to confine the adverse effects that tourism usually inflicts upon traditional forms of social organization, and upon the cultural heritage and the environment. It seems, however, that such attempts have failed considering how tourism has actually developed along the transit corridors between Denpasar and Ubud or Kuta Beach and Legian. In such areas, indeed, tourism development has deeply transformed the original environment and perhaps also traditional forms of social organization - often in a disruptive manner - though it is difficult to assess to what extent changes would have occurred in the absence of tourism development.[41] In the D.I.Y., it is not yet clear whether physical development associated with the growth of tourism is going to encroach significantly upon rural areas in the short term. This is also true in the vicinity of resort areas which are located in the hinterland areas of Parangtritis or Samas beaches along the southern coast (Figure 3.2). Still, it would be wise to take steps to define conservation areas in the D.I.Y., where the building of hotels, restaurants and other infrastructure related to tourism, including the so-called 'budget tourist sub-sector' would be prohibited. This could be implemented through a procedure for reviewing applications for construction permits by special committees including local, regional, and perhaps national governments' representatives, as well as other local representatives of various professional and community-based associations. Moreover, an advisory master plan for the spatial development of tourism in the D.I.Y. could be drawn up. The use of such a plan in association with the process of granting building permits might offer more flexibility than simply a zoning system. Simultaneously, special protection zones in which new construction would be strictly regulated should be defined around landmarks of particular historical and cultural value.

Fifthly, the development of tourism in the D.I.Y. should not be considered as an all-out solution. The Special Region should continue developing in a planned and cautious manner, avoiding the widening of rural-urban disparities. Also, governmental intervention for tourism development should not lead to the development of other sectors being overlooked, in particular a diversified agricultural sector, manufacturing, and health and education services. In that respect it is worth repeating the fact that in Bali, agriculture and not tourism has, in the 1980s, constituted the largest contributor to GRDP increase.

In particular, even though our fieldwork revealed that the only tailor in Celep received orders from an Australian tourist who noticed the tailor's business on a main road while he was going to Samas Beach, it remains questionable whether some of the positive side-effects of tourism development upon the garment industry recorded for Bali in Wheeler, *et al.*,[42] and Jayasuriya and Nehen[43] could possibly occur in the future with the same magnitude in the D.I.Y. The development of the Balinese garment industry, indeed, began slightly more than two decades ago when international and national competition was still rather low. Still, Balinese production had to be shifted overtime from cheap mass-produced garments to more expensive high quality clothes to face growing competition. Could the D.I.Y. today engage in mass-production, or could it find a niche for high-quality exports in the absence of well-developed related skills within the contemporary international and national context of competition? Additionally, giving any excessive importance to the development of tourism within a general strategy for regional economic development in the D.I.Y. might inhibit the process of diversification of the regional.

Finally, if attempting to increase the inflow of international tourists by allowing direct international flights to Yogyakarta airport is to be considered, this should be instituted with caution. If such a step succeeds in contributing to significantly increasing the number of tourists in the D.I.Y., would the Special Region be able to cope with such an increase, especially in terms of safe-guarding the environment and cultural heritage? Second, would there be sufficient demand on the part of international tourists, for two international airports at such a short distance distance from each other - Solo[44] and Yogyakarta. In other words, could airline companies generate a profit in operating a direct international connection to Yogyakarta?

To sum up, the development of tourism in the D.I.Y. should be considered:

(1) Within the framework of global regional and economic development and growth, *i.e.* in giving due respect to other sectors and to sectoral and spatial linkages in the region, and;

(2) As a transitional solution towards, and as a way of boosting, a diversified and more endogeneous type of development.

Side-effects of Rising Rural-Urban Linkages and the Spread of Urbanization

The main thrust of the approach being followed in this Research Report is that the strengthening of rural-urban linkages in the D.I.Y. could impact very favourably upon the regional economy as a whole and the diffusion of growth throughout the region. All things being considered, the latter ought not to obliterate specific side-effects associated with the strengthening of rural-urban linkages. One particular concern relates to preserving a sound environment in the D.I.Y. Possible adverse side-effects are reviewed below.

Table 9.3   Involvement of the Labour Force (primary activity) in the Tourist Industry, by Research Areas

Hamlets / Villages	Works directly for the tourist industry			Works partly or occasionally for the tourist industry			Does not work for the tourist industry			Does not know		
	Males	Females	Total	Males	Females	Total	Males	Females	Total	Males	Females	Total
Piring	1	2	3 (1)	.	.	.	119	150	269 (89.3)	11	18	29 (9.6)
Celep (transit corridor)	1	.	1 (1.6)	.	.	.	23	3	54 (87.1)	5	2	7 (11.2)
Bandung	.	.	.	.	.	.	241	192	433 (94.7)	13	11	24 (5.2)
Karanggondang-Cepit (transit corridor)	.	.	.	.	.	.	44	54	98 (96)	3	1	4 (3.9)
Kembang	.	.	.	.	.	.	82	62	144 (60.5)	49	45	94 (39.5)

Number of cases (per cent in parenthesis)

Table 9.3 (continued)

Hamlets / Villages	Works directly for the tourist industry Number of cases (per cent in parenthesis)			Works partly or occasionally for the tourist industry Number of cases (per cent in parenthesis)			Does not work for the tourist industry Number of cases (per cent in parenthesis)			Does not know Number of cases (per cent in parenthesis)		
	Males	Females	Total	Males	Females	Total	Males	Females	Total	Males	Females	Total
Maguwoharjo (transit Corridor)	.	1	1 (1.3)	.	.	.	41	23	64 (86.4)	3	6	9 (12.1)
Maguwoharjo (hinterland)	4	.	4 (2.1)	1	.	1 (0.5)	100	76	176 (93.6)	3	4	7 (3.7)
Putat II (transit corridor)	.	.	.	.	.	.	18	12	30 (53.5)	13	13	26 (46.4)
Putat II (hinterland)	.	.	.	.	.	.	30	13	43 (28.2)	60	49	109 (71.7)
All	6	3	9 (0.5)	1	.	1 (0.06)	698	613	1311 (80.4)	160	149	309 (18.9)

Note: Forty-seven miscoded answers are discounted.

Source: Primary data processed by Vincent Rotgé using SAS (fieldwork implemented in 1991 for Piring, Celep, Karanggondang-Cepit and Bandung, and in 1992 for Putat II, Kembang and Maguwoharjo).

Table 9.4   Examples of Average Price of Land (Rp/m²)

Location vis-à-vis road infrastructure	Along roads					Hinterland	
Land characteristics	Main road			Kabupaten (Regency) road	Village road		
	Land with building permit	Agricultural land		Land with building permit	Land with building permit	Land with building permit	Agricultural land
Name / Characteristics of area	Pekarangan (garden)	Tegal (dryland)	Sawah (wetland)	Pekarangan (garden)	Pekarangan (garden)	Pekarangan (garden)	Sawah (wetland)
South Ring Road sector (Bantul Regency)*	Rp. 50,000 to 60,000	Not recorded	Not recorded	Not recorded	Not recorded	Rp. 8,000	Not recorded
Karanggondang-Cepit*	Rp. 20,000 to 30,000	Not recorded	Not recorded	Rp. 10,000 to 15,000	Rp. 4,000 (?)***	Rp. 4,000 (?)***	Not recorded
Piring*				Not recorded	Not recorded		
Putat**	Rp. 5,000	Rp. 3,000	Rp. 3,000 to 5,000	Not recorded	Not recorded		Rp. 1,500
Maguwoharjo**	Rp. 75,000 to 100,000	Not recorded	Rp. 25,000	Rp. 15,000	Not recorded	Rp. 20,000	Not recorded
Kembang**	Not recorded	Not recorded	Not recorded	Not recorded	Not recorded		Rp. 8,000 (?)***

*   1991

**   1992

***   Question mark indicates a rough approximate.

Source: Interviews with villagers and land dealers, Vincent Rotgé (1991 and 1992).

Background

The strengthening of rural-urban linkages entails accelerated physical urbanization. Such a process has been occurring for some time in regions of Java or Bali which have been urbanizing at a much faster pace than the D.I.Y. where the following types of urbanization are taking place:

(1) Peripheral physical urbanization, or urbanization of urban fringes mainly around Yogyakarta;

(2) Linear physical urbanization, or expansion of urban corridors along the most important roads (occurring especially in areas crossed by the Klaten-Yogyakarta-Wates thoroughfare which are those with the highest population growth rates), but also along roads of minor significance;

(3) 'Diffused' physical urbanization throughout the countryside due to the relatively slow but continued growth in human density (until a possible state of nearly stationary population is reached); the general sectoral shift to nonfarm activities, and the booming construction subsector resulting in particular from urban remittances.

Demand for land under the pressure of urbanization is reflected in land price gradients - Table 9.4. Land prices are higher along main roads and, in particular, within expanding corridors, but land price levels are also rising along secondary roads in areas surrounding Yogyakarta. Land price increases have been especially rapid following the opening at the beginning of the 1990s of a ring road circling Yogyakarta. One consequence of such a dynamic is that some apparently small-scale farmers are selling tracts of agricultural land which are located along main roads and other such corridors, and using the proceeds to purchase larger tracts of agricultural land located further away from important roads. They may also simply look for a land exchange with the simultaneous aim of making of a profit.

In hinterland areas close to Yogyakarta where land prices are rising rapidly, some cases were reported of farmers selling their agricultural land and purchasing coffee estates in areas of Sumatra where land prices are significantly lower than in Java, often to which all or part of the household have emigrated. Thus far, the latter process can be seen as a positive one, as long as the farmers can expand the size of their property and as long as the supply of alternative locations on reasonably good agricultural land either in the D.I.Y. or outside the region remains subordinate to the demand, as is probably still the case.

The implications of such a dynamic need to be examined from the point of view of their possible adverse effects and the consideration of when and if it is to significantly gain in magnitude over time. Thus, in the abovementioned case of land exchange, the farmer's initial plot of land which is usually of a particularly good agricultural value[45] is being converted to nonagricultural use by the purchaser subsequent to the transaction. In other reported cases, rapid urbanization has occurred in the vicinity of the ring road, which was under construction in places where land has a particularly high agricultural value.

It can be argued that the conversion of the best agricultural land (in terms of soil, irrigation, slope, etc.) of the central Subdistricts of Bantul and Sleman to nonagricultural uses may seem illogical from the point of view of allocation of resources, when the revenues of farmers in some other Districts of the D.I.Y. are limited by mediocre soils or irrigation, or unsuitable gradients such as in the District of Gunung Kidul. This is probably true from an agricultural point of view and also from the point of view of optimal regional allocation of land-use.

This process is not specific to the D.I.Y. In reality, it can be observed in other parts of the world. Urbanization, indeed, very often takes place around existing urban settlements, while many urban settlements, especially in regions with human settlements dating back to preindustrial times, originally developed within an agrarian context in lowland or gently sloping areas which are the most fertile areas and those which have the highest carrying capacity. Urbanization also takes place along existing transportation routes particularly, as it appears, in those regions of Monsoon Asia where wet-rice cultivation is practiced.[46] The crux of the matter is that main roads are usually located in valleys and basin areas and along main irrigation canals, and therefore are also located in some of the most fertile areas. It is a process that cannot be avoided in many cases, but that can be at most mitigated and spatially adjusted through the implementation of local and regional policies. At the same time, public policies such as for the provision of infrastructure which is likely to fuel urbanization, should avoid worsening such a trend.

Conditions under which Possible Adverse Effects of Urban Encroachment upon Farmland May Be Reduced

Such a potential diminution of the total cultivated area subsequent to urban encroachment would not be necessarily detrimental, provided that:

(1) Farmers continue being in a position to choose (as opposed to being economically forced) to sell their land located in urbanizing areas, and use the return of the transaction to start up a new economic activity, which leads to an increase in their income;

(2) When land is exchanged as mentioned above, relocation alternatives are located on land of reasonably good agricultural value. Farmers are not moving to uplands where they would further contribute to the degradation of the environment by using land too intensively and by contributing to deforestation. Related problems of environmental degradation were discussed in reference to Jakarta Metropolitan Region by Clarke and by Douglass;[47]

(3) More employment opportunities and a more even access to such opportunities are offered in nonfarm activities in newly urbanized areas, than would have been possible through the use of such areas as farmland;

(4) The reduction of agricultural production resulting from the loss of cultivated areas (assuming that such a reduction cannot be offset either by technical innovation or by increasing returns subsequent to agricultural diversification alone) leads to a reduction in the share of GRDP of agriculture. But simultaneously, the growth of one or several other sector(s) compensates for this reduction. Also, provided that increased regional expenditures spent on agricultural produce that the region no longer produces, as a consequence of the resulting loss in cultivated area, and must therefore import, do not offset the increase in GRDP brought about by the growth of nonfarm sector(s); and;

(5) The abovementioned process of land exchange does not engender a dynamic which would entail adverse social effects.

On the policy side, several measures should be taken to mitigate the adverse effects of urban encroachment upon agricultural land:

- Various steps should be taken to create greenbelts or areas in sectors of particular agricultural value, where land fragmentation would be deterred and urbanization discouraged. This could be realized at local levels through land-use planning and fiscal policies, and to some extent through regional policies aimed at attracting urbanization outside designated green areas into areas whose land is of lesser agricultural value;

- Areas of reforestation are established in catchment areas of rivers where new settlements conducive to deforestation should be strictly prohibited;
- By and large, land-use planning should always be linked to fiscal and transportation policies.

Moreover, a long-term and consistent policy of public land acquisition or land banking could be possibly implemented in urbanizing areas of the D.I.Y., the purpose of which would be:

- To tame land price increases and speculation;
- To create green reservations in the periphery of Yogyakarta and in areas located along expanding corridors or in secondary urban centres;
- To purchase land, when prices are still relatively low, that will be made use of in the future for planning purposes, such as for low-income housing.

It is also recommended that further studies be undertaken in the D.I.Y. to assess the precise impact of urbanization upon employment generation and changes in income and subsistence levels in urbanizing areas, and upon the displacement of farmers from urbanizing areas.

Notes

1   Gourou, 1984.
2   See for instance World Bank, 1988.
3   In Buchari Zainum, 1988 (Vol. 3), p. 103.
4   See Devas, Autumn 1989.
5   In Uppal, 1986.
6   See Booth and Damanik, 1989.
7   See Uppal, 1986.
8   See Claval, 1981.
9   See for instance, Hamer, *et al.*, 1986.
10   Booth and Damanik, *op. cit.*
11   Brookfield, Hadi, and Mahmud, 1991.
12   Haruo Kuroyanagi, 1991.

13   I am grateful to Haruo Kuroyanagi for drawing my attention to this fact, for which he deserves full credit.

14   Concerning communities in the Philippines, see Pernia, 1978.

15   Stoffer and Sutanto, 1990.

16   *Ibid.*

17   See also Dawan Rahardjo and Fachry Ali, 1986.

18   This proposal is similar to an earlier proposal which was made by Stoffer and Sutanto, *op. cit.*

19   See for instance on this matter in the case of Thai communities: Ammar Siamwalla, *et al.*, 1990.

20   This is also suggested in Stoffer and Sutanto, *op. cit.*

21   *Ibid.*

22   Maurer, 1986.

23   Barbier, 1989.

24   Hardjono, 1987.

25   Barghouti, Timmer, and Siegel, 1990.

26   See for instance: den Boer and Gill, eds, 1989, and; *NUDS Final Report* (Jakarta: Directorate of City and Regional Planning, 1985).

27   See Godfrey, 1990; Esmara, 1987, and; Patten, Dapice, and Falcon, 1980.

28   See Booth and Damanik, *op. cit.*

29   See Jayasuriya and Nehen, 1989.

30   *Ibid.*

31   *Ibid.*

32   *Ibid.*

33   See Wheeler, Cole, and Irianiwati, 1989.

34   *Ibid.*

35   *Ibid.*

36   *Ibid.*

37   See Jayasuriya and Nehen, *op. cit.*

38   *Ibid.*

39   *Ibid.*

40   *Ibid.*

41   *Ibid.*

42   *Ibid.*

43   *Ibid.*

44   Solo is also called Surakarta.

45   Plots located along important roads are also often those located near important irrigation canals.

46   Some of these problems are pointed out in UNCRD, 1989.

47   Clarke, 1987. Douglass, 1989.

Part III
Conclusion

10 The Passage from an Agrarian World to an Urban Civilization of an Original Kind

- by Vincent Rotgé -

Foreword

In the preceding pages, we have acquired a good knowledge of the regional agroecological environments and realities from which we can draw lessons within an enlarged geographical and conceptual framework. In this way, we are going to see how rural-urban linkages figure in the vast socioeconomic transformations that affect Monsoon Asia: decreasing importance of the agriculture, specialization of work, and recourse to subcontracting. We shall then examine the weaknesses of a regional growth derived from rural-urban linkages, when the economic and social landscape was greatly transformed in Southeast Asia after the start of the economic crisis in 1997. Afterwards, we shall examine how the strengthening of rural-urban linkages proceeds through the re-composition of lifestyles and the slipping of a traditional agrarian world towards an urban civilization. We shall see that this process is a variant of that of the growth of metropolitan areas in full flight in the world, to which the cultures and environments of Monsoon Asia confer a very strong originality and identity.

Decreasing Importance of the Agriculture

The strengthening of rural-urban linkages was rendered possible in large measure by programmes of agricultural modernization and the economic, social and political evolution which they set in motion. It is useful to grasp the principal stages of this evolution through a review of the studies that were devoted to them. The work of Peter F. McDonald and Alip Sontosudarmo, *Response to Population Pressure: The Case of the Special Region of Yogyakarta*,[1] published in 1976, several years after the start of the agricultural modernization programmes, was the forerunner in this matter. These authors assumed that the growth of secondary and tertiary economic sectors would lead to a containment of the explosion in unemployment and underemployment in the countryside and would forestall the risks of 'agricultural involution'. But they recognized the still important role of outward migration as a regulating mechanism. Moreover, they observed a form of prospective industrialization 'along the main arteries linking the cities of Java' where 'a wide variety of small, labour intensive industries [... were] springing up'.

The conclusions of this study of rural-urban linkages in the Special Region of Yogyakarta (D.I.Y.) are in agreement with the work of Gavin W. Jones, *Structural Change and Prospects for Urbanization in Asian Countries*,[2] published in 1982, whose scope was more economic and urban. In this work, Jones foresaw the coming transformations in the structure of employment within Asian rural areas, and underlined the role of population growth in urbanization and the necessity to control the birth-rate. Jones took up the theses of Anne Booth and R.M. Sundrum,[3] according to which the share of agriculture in employment was doomed to decline in Indonesia, by extrapolating the structure of employment in countries with more advanced economies. Based on recent statistical sources, one can observe that the share of agricultural employment is in slow but constant decline in Indonesia since the 1970s (59.6 per cent of the active population in 1971, 58 per cent in 1980 and 55 per cent in 1990; compared with 11.8, 12 and 14 per cent in industry in 1971, 1980 and 1990, respectively).[4] It is to be noted that the share of the active population engaged in agriculture in Indonesia in 1990 corresponded roughly to the percentage in the United States in 1870 (50.8 per cent, but already 23.5 per cent in industry).[5] Nevertheless, the meaning and scope of these comparisons are limited. For one thing, the population of the United States at that time was much smaller than that of Indonesia today, and American agriculture was in large measure extensive and completely different than the rice agriculture practised in Java. Moreover, in today's world, services have a greater weight in advanced economies, but also in an economy such as that of Indonesia, although the structure of services is clearly not the same in the two types of economies. Indonesian employment statistics, in particular, obscure the importance of part-time work, since many rural residents exercise one or more non-agricultural activities along with their agricultural employment. In addition, Gavin Jones advanced the reasons for the decline of the share of agriculture in employment. According to him, this diminution would be due to the productivity gap between agriculture and the non-agricultural sectors, and to the income elasticity of demand for food and agricultural products - that is to say mainly agricultural food products, including rice products, in the countryside.[6] Over time, this elasticity would tend towards zero; that is to say that income would increase faster than the demand for basic food products. As support, Jones cited the hypothesis that with an increase in the level of development of a country, the share of agriculture within the structure of employment would tend to diminish in favour of industry, which, in turn, would diminish to the benefit of services.[7] This contemporary study of rural-urban linkages within the D.I.Y. indicates that the situation described by Jones has been attained in this region today through a particular process that we shall analyse later.

The principal conclusions of this work are also in accordance with the macro-economic analyses of Anne Booth (*Agricultural Development in Indonesia*[8] and 'Indonesian Agricultural Development in Comparative Perspective')[9] according to which the agricultural modernization programmes in Java have had clearly beneficial effects. This author estimated that because of an annual increase of the GDP of at least 5 per cent, a large proportion of this growth would come from non-agricultural sectors.[10] But Anne Booth also observed that if non-agricultural labour did not increase sufficiently (at least 7 per cent per year):

> [...] then agriculture (together with activities such as petty trade) will have to continue to be the employment sector of last resort. There is likely to be a decline in productivity, incomes and living standards in rural areas, unless agricultural growth is sufficiently rapid to take up the slack.[11]

In addition to the studies cited above, it is useful to mention the works of Jean-Luc Maurer,[12] of Chris Manning, and of Joan Hardjono,[13] the principal conclusions of which are supported by this work on rural-urban linkages in the D.I.Y. These authors have observed the global effects of agricultural modernization programmes that, according to them, have had a positive impact on growth. Nevertheless, Maurer has stated that the poor have benefited less than the rich from these programmes, and that, at the end of the day, the disparities will be larger than before their introduction.[14] In a more recent 1991 publication, 'Beyond the Sawah: Economic Diversification in Four Bantul Villages, 1972-1987',[15] Maurer tackled the question of non-agricultural activities in the villages on the plain inside the Special Region of Yogyakarta, where he had previously studied agricultural modernization programmes and their effects. For this author, the diversification of employment in the rural milieu of Java has become a reality thanks to agricultural modernization programmes and energetic policies of rural development and infrastructure, as well as to the funds drawn from the country's natural resources and to the international aid that allowed the Indonesian authorities to manage effectively this development option.[16] Maurer, himself, relied substantially on the theses of the economist, Harry Oshima (presented since 1983 in *Transition to an Industrial Economy in Monsoon Asia* and then adapted in 1987 in *Economic Growth in Monsoon Asia*)[17] the principal points of which it is appropriate to state precisely. This exercise will permit us to introduce the notion of the specialization of employment and its implications.

'A Factory without Chimneys'[18]

The keystone of the work of Harry Oshima is that the development of agriculture within Monsoon Asia constitutes a decisive intermediate step towards the passage of an economy 'in which the industrial labor force exceeds the agricultural labor force'.[19] In his presentation, this author relies on a collection of geographic and economic elements forming the framework of a development scenario suited for Monsoon Asia. Oshima observes that an industry operating throughout the year with fixed labour and important equipment was impossible in Monsoon Asia, in his opinion, because of the major labour that rice cultivation required compared with the cultivation of wheat. There would have been a connection between this particularly intensive form of agriculture and the development of heightened levels of population density. In addition, monsoon weather would have necessitated the mobilization of a large part of available labour for agricultural work during the wet season, which, by default, would have deprived industry of this labour. During the dry season, this labour would have been available for work in small industry or in the service sector, which it needed to support itself and to hold on until the next wet season. Simultaneously, the high level of population density would have led to the fragmentation of land and to the atrophy of animal husbandry because of the scarcity of pasture land, which would have reduced even further the possibilities offered by agriculture during the dry season. This would have contributed to the keeping of rural populations in a state heavily marked by poverty and to a hindering of the development of an industrial revolution along western lines. Oshima returns to the long-term impossibility of the emergence of heavy industry in Monsoon Asia. Traditionally, the industries in this part of the world would not have the necessity of a very large prior accumulation of capital. In addition, the seasonal character of activity would have favoured the proximity of the work place with the place of residence. Oshima compares this situation with that in the West, where harnessed transport was available and where urban centres appeared, while in Monsoon Asia, where draft animals were rare, the types of land use (residential/industrial) were much more mixed. These factors would have led the societies of Monsoon Asia to search for very stable political systems - indeed even rigid in the sense that one gives to this adjective - based on the life of the community and co-operation within the group to which one belonged, without, for all that, eliminating competition between groups. This type of society would not have been more favourable for technological innovation, all the more so because these societies had reached a very high level of development of agricultural technologies well before the West and would no longer have tried to go beyond them, or could not have gone beyond them because of the constraints raised above.[20] Moreover, the agricultural technological innovations of the West would have almost all gone in the direction of an extensive agriculture and 'were either non-applicable [to Monsoon Asia] (as in the case of drainage) or, if applicable, would cause per hectare yields to fall drastically and unemployment to rise substantially'.[21]

At the threshold of the 1990s, Oshima foresaw the realization of a phased development scenario within the poorer countries of Monsoon Asia, close to that already followed by certain emerging Asian countries (Korea, Taiwan) and even Japan. He judged as essential the augmentation of rural incomes due to agricultural modernization programmes and infrastructure in the countryside, structures of land, diffusion of credit, etc. The diversification of agriculture and of non-agricultural employment, particularly during the dry season, seemed to him to be even more important. The objective of these improvements is to stabilise income while augmenting it and to mitigate the negative effects of seasonality. One can very seriously question the possibility that the poor countries of Asia will follow the same path of development as Japan and other emerging countries, within a very different political, historical and economic environment, where the economic competition between countries has become very severe, without even speaking of the major cultural differences within Monsoon Asia. Thus, one can often find the theses of Oshima to be too mechanistic and sometimes a bit caricatured. Nonetheless, this researcher puts forward a frequently convincing argument - despite the evident limits and weaknesses - which illuminates the conditions of the passage from an agrarian world to an industrialized and urbanized society in Monsoon Asia.

The Special Region and the Theses of Oshima

To judge from the improvements made in agriculture within the D.I.Y., the situation described by Oshima was verified in the province from the first years of the 1990s. On the other hand, a persistent defaulting exists in the matter of programmes that adjust land tenure systems. Much could yet be accomplished through punctual adjustments in land tenure reallocations and, most certainly, the registration of property titles for the numerous peasants who have a life interest in land without official title to it. This situation retards economic development in the countryside and weakens the inhabitants within the context of rapid urbanization, where land stimulates the desire of real estate agents. It represents equally a very serious risk of a social explosion.

This study of rural-urban linkages within the D.I.Y. also shows that the seasonal character of agricultural employment has greatly diminished in the plain for several reasons. Very good irrigation using canals has reduced for decades the dependence of rice cultivation on rain patterns. The introduction of new varieties of less photosensitive rice has resolved the problem of reduced sunshine during the rainy season. In return, agricultural income remains entirely in rhythm with the agricultural calendar, since farmers are paid after the monsoon. The savings of agricultural households are consequently reduced as the season of harvest approaches and that of the previous harvest recedes into the past. At this time, the household members must frequently search for supplementary sources of income in urban areas. Furthermore, the bulk of work for a given field remains concentrated in the periods of planting and harvesting, and the farmers of the same community often select, though not obligatorily, the same agricultural calendar. In addition, harvests are more and more frequently sold on the spot to teams of professional harvesters outside the village. At the same time, a connection exists between a reduction in the seasonal nature of rice cultivation and the development of animal husbandry on the plain. In effect, the absence of pasturage is compensated for, to a certain degree, by the possibility of collecting throughout the year the straw used as fodder on the plain. In short, the traditional seasonal character of agricultural employment on the plain has greatly diminished. But it remains very present in the mountains, where dry fields are numerous. Furthermore, non-agricultural employment, urban in particular, has assumed much importance as a principal or even supplementary activity. Thus, the conditions required for the attainment of the *first phase* of development defined by Oshima are to a large extent present today within the D.I.Y.

The *second phase* of development described by Oshima corresponds to an augmentation of interior demand, especially for industrial products made within the country and those for which the fabrication process is labour-intensive. Also, country people would purchase manufactured products that they formally produced themselves by traditional methods. This would reduce demand still further. This phase is partly attained in Java and within the D.I.Y., as the study presented in this work shows. The *third phase* coincides with an increase of real, urban incomes. This follows the increase in real rural incomes that would push the increased mechanization of industries established in town. Exports would increase. There would be a beginning of a shortage of urban employment. The mechanization of agriculture would accelerate because of the migration of the young population from the countryside, while industries looking for labour would settle in small towns. At this stage, the transition process to an industrial society would be very advanced. The D.I.Y. and even the greater part of Java had not attained this stage before the economic crisis that began in 1997. We shall return later to the consequences of this crisis.

Specialization of Work

An economic process of specialization of employment may be found in the D.I.Y. which is in keeping with the development scenario proposed by Oshima. Rural-urban linkages play a decisive role in this process which, at the very least in the plain, is accompanied by the increase of productivity and real income, and by inter-sector transfers to the most productive activities. However, the productivity level of numerous traditional cottage industries remains very low. Many of these activities are performed by part-time female agricultural workers. They have an uncertain future because of the disaffection of their traditional *clientèle*, and of the competition of products manufactured in urban or suburban areas. These activities, however, are replaced by others situated at the centre of rural-urban exchanges or are linked to urbanization: shops of tailors and of repair, construction, fabrication of baskets for the urban market, etc. These new activities often require specialized knowledge. They cannot be carried out by the workforce who lived from traditional product activities, because it has different qualifications and is frequently too old. Nevertheless, most of the time they are involved in a growing specialization of employment and a shift from the agricultural activities previously exercised by the individuals or their parents and into higher-return service activities. By default, they at least offer a possibility of economic survival to inhabitants who would probably have no other possibility, except maybe that of leaving the region. A 1989 article by Anne Booth and Konta Damanik on the D.I.Y. ('Central Java and Yogyakarta: Malthus Overcome?') underlined nonetheless the often unacceptable levels of nutrition, housing and income, and conditions of employment often marked by 'long hours of work and weak productivity'.[22] But rural-urban linkages can also have the inverse effect and encourage the multiplicity of employment, to judge by the many country people and daily or circular migrants who simultaneously or alternately occupy urban and rural employment, in accordance with an evolution equally depicted in East and West Africa.[23]

Increase in the Marginal Productivity of Labour

This work on rural-urban linkages in the D.I.Y. tends to show, by and large, that the marginal productivity of labour would not have decreased in most of the households that stayed within the D.I.Y. But many country people continue to exercise several activities in parallel, because none is productive enough taken in isolation. In these conditions, the movement from agriculture towards other sectors of activity evidently remains very gradual. It is accompanied by a reorganization of the activities at the level of the individual or the household. The arrangement of 'first' (or 'primary') agricultural activity and 'second' (or 'secondary') non-agricultural activity, which is quite typical, also tends to be progressively inverse. Agricultural profits can be invested in non-agricultural activity. The possibility for a better education for children, or more materially, the purchase of a bicycle or a motorcycle also represents investment. However, this optimistic outlook must be tempered in view of the high level of debt of many households, which also demonstrates the financial fragility of many country people. Local particularities, of geographic or other origin, clearly influence the levels of productivity with which the inhabitants must be satisfied. For example, where the average income is very low, jobs in local services are very limited in number. It has been noted, moreover, that the local population is disadvantaged by its level of education and training, the means of motorized transport at its disposal, etc. It thus occupies few urban jobs, and the weakness of local agricultural production limits the possibilities that are offered to it in agricultural trade. It results that numerous inhabitants, when they do not migrate, go back, particularly in the dry season, to cottage-industry activities - woodwork, making of charcoal, etc. - frequently of extremely low productivity. This is one of the reasons that cottage-industry activities are at the same time numerous in the mountains but also of very low productivity.

Organization of Work and Sub-contracting

The organization of work and especially sub-contracting constitute another important facet of rural-urban linkages, which is also related to the characteristics of the agroecological environment. In this regard, a comparison with the West is useful. In the long-industrialized western countries, in effect, the implementation of new organizational forms of work has generally coincided with the re-examination of the preceding arrangements called 'Fordist', which formerly structured industrial space. Their disintegration leaves the field open for new systems, called 'flexible production', which have penetrated long-industrialized regions and others located on their periphery. These systems have also gained in regions of emergent countries, where, as in the peripheral regions of the western world, the traditions and work cultures based on the small household enterprise still survive. According to certain researchers, the presence of these traditional cultures, left unchanged by the 'Fordist' industrial arrangements that their regional environment has not or only very partially known, favour the development of new systems of production and for the organization of work.[24] The following observation of Charles Sabel

('Flexible Specialisation and the Re-emergence of Regional Economies') is very clear:[25]

> The explanation of the origins of trust in the regional economies focuses on the relation between pre-industrial land-tenure patterns and traditions of artisanal by-employments with their connections to world markets. In the Third Italy, Jutland and Baden-Wüttemberg, [...] agrarian conditions were similar to those which gave rise to flexible specialisation in the regional economies of nineteenth-century France. Land holdings were so small that proprietors had to supplement agricultural income with income from artisanal work (weaving, knitting, furniture making) or industrial employment (in, say, the urban construction industry during the agricultural off-season). The property regime and connection to international trading networks which fostered these relations were different from case to case. *Mezzadria*, or sharecropping, combined with handicraft production exported via trade routes first opened by the Renaissance city states, were typical of parts of the Third Italy. In Jutland, eighteenth- and nineteenth- century state regulations kept peasants tied to the land, allowed them to capture the return on their investments, but not to enlarge their holdings. This situation combined with proximity to the old Hanseatic sea routes to produce similar incentives and opportunities. The common results were the formation of entrepreneurial families which survived by shifting resources quickly from activity to activity, and the creation of local institutions such as banks and small merchant houses which helped the families move rapidly into national and international industrial markets when the opportunity arose. By contrast, [...other regions], where large estates were cultivated by farm labourers or peasants with scant possibilities for familial accumulation through astute management, have not produced modern industrial districts.

Conditions favourable to 'flexible specialization' are present in the countryside of the D.I.Y.: small fields which prompt the peasants progressively to leave agriculture, and, simultaneously, the opening of new opportunities, a tradition of supplementary employment, and the beginning of the accumulation of capital, which nevertheless remains socially and geographically limited. These conditions also encourage men to organise themselves better in order to take best advantage of economic possibilities. This can be noted through the subcontracting links between urban partners and batik craftsmen in the plain and those of masks (*topeng*) and *marionettes* (*wayang golek*) in the mountains. Many cases of sub-contracting also exist in the periphery of Yogyakarta: the manufacture of sport bags, braided bamboo baskets used in urban markets, etc. However, these links sometime reflect a situation of 'dependent growth' of the periphery with the urban centre which is Yogyakarta. This signifies that the communities of the periphery, above all those most distant, are often restricted to furnishing labour at costs unmatched in urban areas. But their inhabitants have no control over production or marketing. On the other hand, this labour has minimum power to negotiate on the prices charged and only receives a very small part of the profits realized by the urban partner. It is urgent that producers in rural communities organise themselves into co-operatives in order to collect the necessary capital and means of transport and to access directly, when this is possible, urban markets, rather than passing through urban intermediaries who generally abuse their advantages acquired as a kind of situation revenue. The appearance of subsidiaries of urban companies within the urban periphery or strategic sectors (for example, along the peripheral highway or at important regional crossroads) is equally very significant. The causes of the process in which the town often plays the role of an 'incubator' have been examined. It permits the hive-off in the hinterland of service or small industrial enterprises, which could not be born without the financial aid and frequently the facilities granted by the urban mother-company. This assistance takes diverse forms: loans, sharing or exchange of raw material or finished products, provision of transport, exchange of know-how, utilization of common channels of distribution for the marketing of products, etc. The owners of the mother-company and its affiliates are frequently connected by family ties, and one sees the reproduction of an economic strategy based on family co-operation, but on a larger scale.

Viability of a Form of Growth Derived from Rural-Urban Linkages

However, a serious question remains in suspense: would not the diversification of employment be accompanied by a form of 'involution', extended this time to non-agricultural sectors? After the programmes of agricultural modernization have offered for a time an important gain in productivity thanks to the increase in profits, would not the process of fragmentation of agricultural parcels continue under the impact of an increase in population, and would it not now drive the inhabitants of the countryside to undertake less well compensated employment outside of agriculture than the agricultural employment they have left?

Within the D.I.Y., however, this pessimistic scenario seems to be contradicted by a cluster of indices before the political and financial crisis, which began in 1997. First of all, the net regional product per inhabitant had appreciably increased during ten years, and the rural-urban socioeconomic disparities were not aggravated.[26] Another favourable factor was the growth of consumption.

In return, there are dangers linked to urbanization: loss of agricultural land, bringing into question self-sufficiency of rice at the national level, and pollution.[27] Other risks flow from the increase in disparities and the polarization of poverty within an urban landscape in formation. It is therefore important that policies specifically take into account a reduction in disparities and of their polarization.

Another question concerns the durable and viable character of a form of growth derived from rural-urban linkages. What are, in effect, the consequences of a prolonged contraction of the national economy on rural-urban linkages? A large part of the growth in rural areas finds its source outside the rural communities concerned: diverse public assistance, urban demand for goods and labour, and investments, frequently of an urban origin. Now the factors of exogenous growth greatly depend on the overall macro-economic situation and the level of exports, and therefore on international demand for petroleum, gas and other extractive products, for products of forests and plantations or industrial products, on the value of the Indonesian *rupiah* in US dollar, on the level of foreign investment,[28] on international competition in capital markets, and, in the matter of production, on the share of other developing countries, on the national and regional political situation, and, of course, on financial markets, etc. If sufficiently high annual growth of non-agricultural labour cannot be maintained during a prolonged period, a degradation of living conditions in the countryside may be feared, unless 'sufficiently rapid' agricultural growth takes over.[29]

Some say that the warning of Jean-Luc Maurer on the dangers of too great specialization of employment makes sense in the context of the economic and political turmoil of the late 1990s. To the extent that the economy of the countryside is linked more and more with that of urban centres and is derived from urban demand, and that it is restructured to satisfy the latter, should not one fear for the effects of a reversal of macro-economic factors that would affect the urban economy first and then that of the countryside, directly through a lowering of State subsidies but also because of a decrease in rural-urban exchanges? Within the context of a prolonged crisis in urban employment, it is reasonable to think that the countryside will play a role of refuge, as Jean-Luc Domenach has underlined in *L'Asie en danger (Asia in Danger)*, published in 1998:[30]

[...] everything leads us to believe that the rural world will again play a very important role in the near future. In the short term - one sees this very well in Indonesia today - because it is going to bear a large share of the burden of the economic crisis, and that the extent of popular protestations will very much depend on the countryside. Equally because *its ability to stabilise village labour will be of determining importance in the circumstances of an urban employment crisis.* Finally, and perhaps above all, because of the essential role of the countryside in the matter of customs and national identity. [emphasis added]

To confront this situation, national and international public aid policies must take greater aim at reinforcing the factors of endogenous growth in the countryside, and especially the development of agriculture, local industries, and in a general way the increase of purchasing power and the raising of the living standards.[31] Certainly, the forced cutting off of a certain form of economic dependence of the countryside in relation to urban areas could stimulate the creation of local industries and by necessity favour agricultural diversification. If such a trend would continue in a once again favourable macro-economic environment, then this crisis could have positive effects for the countryside. In the immediate future, however, the countryside does not benefit more than before from employment possibilities in urban areas, nor from urban outlets for the products of agriculture and small industry. One can even ascertain a strong inflation hitting certain basic necessity products, the production or distribution of which is slowed by the crisis. For the D.I.Y., the potential consequences of this crisis are multiple. First of all, one can fear a slowing down of student attendance in studies paid for in large measure by upper middle class families distributed throughout Indonesia. If this evolution does not coincide with the installation of lasting political troubles, it is possible that tourism will not find itself much affected in the medium term. Barring a generalized international recession or always possible serious political troubles, a very low Indonesian *rupiah* could even attract a greater number of foreign tourists. But a contraction of the national economy would also influence domestic tourism, which is more and more important. Moreover, the construction sub-sector would be affected, especially in the urban and suburban areas where activity has been intense and speculative during the 1990s. All of this would contribute to a lasting contraction of the urban economy. However, it is not certain that rural-urban linkages would diminish abruptly in terms of the flow of goods, people and information. One can appear more circumspect concerning the flow of capital. On the whole, the nature of these relations would no doubt change. The African experience is interesting in this regard. The researchers, Jamal and Weeks, for example, have assumed that the deterioration of the African economy would lead to an increase in rural-urban linkages in certain countries and to a contraction of rural-urban disparities, because the urban dwellers were more directly affected and impoverished by the economic crisis than the rural population and should find extra-urban outlets.[32] Baker and Claeson observe that this hypothesis contradicts Todaro's model,[33] frequently cited, but whose reductive character shows very substantially its insufficiencies on the ground. But the effects that a contraction of the economy could have on the disparities between urban and rural zones depend greatly on the specific conditions of the economy and of the region concerned. Therefore, in the D.I.Y., the important number of urban jobs or jobs associated with rural-urban linkages and held by residents of the countryside signifies that the contraction of the urban economy would also lead to the impoverishment of rural areas. But, as Booth indicates,[34] it is probably that labour would be increased within the agricultural sector, but that productivity would diminish at the same time. It is therefore possible that a portion of the flow of labour is reversed, and that a return to the countryside begins more or less temporarily in accordance with the way in which circumstances evolve.

Another weakness of a type of development derived from towns is related to the financing of local governments. An article of Anne Booth and Konta Damanik on the D.I.Y. ('Central Java and Yogyakarta: Malthus Overcome?')[35] recalls that the reasons of socioeconomic success have largely depended on the reinvestment of tax revenues on petroleum and gas products. This article raised the difficulty of pursuing this effort in the future at the time that 'these revenues diminish in absolute value'. The very great dependence of local public finances compared with the central government is obvious. On the other hand, if one judges on the basis of the first half of the 1990s, the relative share of petroleum and gas revenues in the revenue of the state (between a little less than 30 and 20 per cent) has in effect decreased but has not very much oscillated in absolute value during the same period.[36] However, one has distanced oneself from the considerable levels of 1978-1979, or after the second increase of the price of petroleum in 1979, in 1980-1981, when 43.54 and 60.9 per cent, respectively, of these revenues came from hydrocarbons, and 19.53 and 14.22 per cent from international assistance.[37] The Indonesian economy has thus become much more mature, with a larger share of state revenues represented by taxes on economic activities, especially industrial activities other than petroleum, gas and others related to the extraction and exploitation of natural resources.

However, a major problem remains that of the great dependence of a region like the D.I.Y. in terms of public finance, which results in large part from the weakness of its economy, and which will render necessary for a long time the existence of very important transfers from the central government. At the level of districts (*kabupaten*), if it were conducted in an imprudent manner, an eventual enlargement of local fiscal competencies which are still very narrow could lead to disparities between the areas that are still very rural and without a fiscal base - indeed the old urban areas - and, on the other hand, the urban corridors where new activities are installed. The present tendency is for the public powers to involve the private sector more by making it participate in equipment expenditures. The nature of these expenditures is also changing. One has seen in this work that because of differences in the demographic evolution at the interior of the regional territory, certain equipment becomes useless within remote areas, while needs are centred in the urbanized areas, and in those in the process of becoming urbanized, along the principal inter-urban arteries of communication (situated between two important urban centres). The volume of land taxes collected must also be increased. As a result, Booth and Damanik (above) have solid reasons to insist on the difficulty of achieving a form of growth which, for this region like the other Indonesian provinces, will be necessarily different than past models. In this regard, the warning of the economist Rémy Prud'homme about certain dangers of an ill-considered decentralization (*On the Dangers of Decentralisation*)[38] is very useful in a country like Indonesia, where the demand for decentralization is strong - in every sense of the word: spatial, industrial, political, administrative and of markets - but also where the disparities are very large in the matter of resources and the standard of living between the different administrative and geographic units that make up the country.[39]

In return, one can observe that the political stature of the D.I.Y. at the national level has been reinforced during the events that accompanied the fall of Suharto.[40] Sultan Hamengku Buwono X, who has been reigning over the Special Region for a decade, has gained a political aura there equal to that of his father, Hero of Independence. The aid given by the central government for the development of the province is not about to dry up in the medium and long term, as long as Indonesian public finances are not lastingly affected by the crisis.

There are other political and social risks related to the land and real estate aspects of urbanization. Thus, before the beginning of the economic crisis that started in 1997, the construction of deluxe housing developments and golf courses in the Special Region constituted another possible source of social instability. These developments are perceived to be bad by the poor population and certain intellectuals. They render disparities even more visible in the high circles of the Javanese culture, where a certain sobriety on the part of the rich was obligatory, and in any case, prudent until recently. They only serve to fan the conflicts related to the control of land, and especially the conversion of fertile agricultural land into deluxe housing projects, which accentuates still more the frustration of the poor and those without land. It would be regrettable if a form of urban development, whose effects on local employment are very questionable, and a very great part of whose profits are not reinvested locally, places in doubt the relatively balanced state of development which has been attained in this region between rural and urban areas in the course of the last thirty years before the crisis. It is true that the crisis has probably frozen a large portion of these developments realized within the context of exceptionally sustained growth. These models of land and real estate development must be strongly reconsidered when growth resumes.

The departure from agriculture of an increasing number of rural people and its implications for the question of self-sufficiency of the country in rice may constitute another subject of concern. In effect, one can only hope that this self-sufficiency, attained over the years at the national level, continues to be satisfied by the increase of production. Before the serious draught that raged in Java in 1997, productivity in the irrigated perimeter during these last years had attained a level difficult to surpass in the present state of agronomic knowledge. On the other hand, the opening of new land is very much slowed down in the so-called 'outer islands' of the country.[41] Now, within the D.I.Y. and elsewhere in Java, the area in *sawah* (wet fields) is decreasing. There is no doubt that physical urbanization is partly responsible. In these conditions, the authorities must avoid all laxity and all temptation, taking into consideration the real estate interests in play, in granting the concession of permits to convert *sawah* into land for building. To do this, it is necessary to reconcile the necessities of economic growth, which has a need for land for building and for keeping the cost of this land low enough (thus the supply of it large enough), with the imperatives of food self-sufficiency and the protection of agricultural land. This is very difficult in the Javanese context of very high population density. The authorities can more or less avoid aggravating the rhythm of land conversion and refrain from economic infrastructure projects such as roads within the most sensitive areas, unless they are indispensable. This problem is surmountable in part through the importation of rice,[42] but it can become worrying in the event of a serious and prolonged slowing of growth, or of recession. In return, it is true that the rhythm of physical urbanization is likely to slow down in the urban periphery.

Urbanization and Rural-Urban Linkages

The processes of socioeconomic transformation have numerous spatial implications. The spatial framework influences their implementation by a reaction effect. Therefore, socioeconomic and spatial analyses cannot be separated, and we shall stick to the process of urbanization in its spatial dimension. We shall introduce this process by means of the two theories of rents and central place familiar to urban geographers, which allow us to link the dynamics of the departure from agriculture, of which we have spoken above, to the processes of urbanization and its morphological aspects.[43] The theory of rents rests on an analysis of the advantages which the inhabitants of urban areas and the users of urban services take from urban areas as a function of their location, and, taking it from there, it puts forward an interpretation of the structure of urban space. To determine these advantages, the theory is founded on an analysis of the interactions between given places and one or several urban centre(s) in the interior of the metropolitan area. Let us look in detail into what it consists of. To this end, it is useful to consider the inhabitants of a region as producers or consumers. The inhabitants are generally both at the same time, but this does not harm our reasoning.

There are advantages that the 'possibilities of communication' represent for these producers and consumers.[44] To define these advantages, one knows that the theory of rents is based on the works of Johann Heinrich von Thünen, who studied the plain of Hamburg, Germany at the beginning of the 19th Century. This forerunner had assumed that a given town had its own field around it depending on the distance to the town (the market) and on the type of production. The assumed transportation costs were tied to the distance at the same time that the costs and the value of production (taking into consideration the value or rent of the land) determined a kind of zoning in the hinterland of the towns: cultivated, high value-added products, though perishable and fragile and thus difficult to transport, were situated in the belt around the town; the others were thrown back to the periphery in accordance with a gradient determined by the same parameters. If one considers isotropic space - that is to say identical in its physical characteristics at any point which one finds - the geometric transposition of this model corresponds to a ring-shaped zoning. This form of reasoning can be extrapolated to other types of land use (residential, industrial: manufacture of machine tools, for example, etc.). It then leads to a radio-concentric schematization of urban and metropolitan space, with which, for example, the model proposed in 1925 by R.E. Burgess, which corresponds to an ideal image of the American industrial town of the first half of the century, has something in common.[45] Other models that are not radio-concentric have been suggested. The one that Homer Hoyt defined in 1939 on the basis of an empirical analysis of American towns placed its accent on a model of development by sectors, where the growth of residential areas followed the lines of communication.[46] In 1945, Harris and Ullman proposed a model in which urban space would be made up of several urban cells, which are much like the hubs of different categories of activity.[47] These models correspond to that which Paul Claval defined within the framework of the theory of rents as 'linear developments', 'ribbon structures',[48] and 'peripheral centres'.[49] According to this geographer, the first developments correspond to 'linear configurations of the field of externalities', and more precisely to 'a deformation of the theory of rents and a linear extension of central functions to these borders'. The second developments appear within a town sufficiently vast where there are different needs, all of which do not need to be satisfied in the principal intra-urban activity centre(s). Thus, smaller urban sub-centres of 'elementary services' destined to satisfy the nearby population are built up on the periphery. The models of Burgess, Homer Hoyt, and Harris and Ullman corresponded to development stages and geographic situations frequently specific to the United States. Moreover, as is the case for many models, they simplified reality and often corresponded to the complexity of actual situations only in a very imperfect fashion - a schematic. Each model crystallises a body of theory at a given moment and at a given place. When these change, the model becomes obsolete. It therefore becomes necessary to come back to the principles that underlay the model in order to confront them with the new conditions and, if necessary, to amend or complete them, if they, themselves, no longer fit. In the United States, the models of which we speak above only describe the contemporary situation in a very partial manner, if not even at all. The model of Burgess, for example, has only historic value. Nevertheless, it permits us to explain the traces that the past dynamics of urbanization have left. The recall of these models permits us, however, to illustrate the theory of rents, and it introduces comparative elements that can be useful. Moreover, the principles of the theory of rents remain valid, and show different morphologies adapted to the milieu and to the era.

How can the preceding discussion clarify the dynamic urbanization observed in Java? It is essential first of all to understand that a major historic difference exists between the rapid urbanization that took place in the West from the end of the 19th Century to after the Second World War, and that which one can observe at present in the D.I.Y. and in the populated rice-growing plains of Monsoon Asia. In the West, urbanization[50] corresponded to a movement of population concentration in, and around, urban cells, which were in large part nourished by international immigration (United States) or coming from the countryside and, indeed, sometimes both, as in the case of the most important cities (Europe, United States). But the population density in the countryside around these urban cells was weak in terms of the type of agriculture, extensive as opposed to the cultivation of rice in Monsoon Asia, which was generally practised beyond the belt of market gardens. On the contrary, in the rice-growing plains of Monsoon Asia, one witnesses today an urbanization that extends to a countryside where densities have attained considerable levels (2,000 inhabitants per square kilometre, or even more, is not rare). It involves an urbanization *in situ*, that is to say that the original peasant population increases to the point where it must begin to diversity its activities and progressively to leave agriculture. If many European towns and cities and even some in North America - one thinks, for example, about the old orchards of the Silicon Valley or about the gardens of New Jersey - were originally small market towns, whose population increased around a primitive nucleus, the urbanization of the countryside in Monsoon Asia represents a phenomenon that has not existed in the West, either in this form or on this scale.

This urbanization in the rice-growing plains of Monsoon Asia is characterized by an intense development along the important arteries of communication which cross the countryside. One has seen that movements of population can be observed there: urban dwellers move in when farmers sometime sell their fields and retreat from the corridor, indeed outside of Java, where they can acquire a larger property. The hierarchy of land prices reflects the pressure of urbanization along the lines of communication, which varies according to the importance of these arteries.

Among the inhabitants of urbanized corridors, consumers profit from locational advantages, while producers take advantage of external economies. Why? Because the former find less expensive housing than in town and with almost equivalent if not equal on-the-spot access to most current merchant or other services. The producers, for their part, profit from the external economies of both the town and the hinterland, since they are situated at the interface between the two. Moreover, the majority of the inhabitants who, with the exception of some pensioners of public service or of the army, are at the same time consumers and producers, find a cumulative advantage in residing in the corridors of urbanization. But the progress of transport is not alone in illuminating this type of ribbon urbanization. It is also explained by the spatial characteristics of agricultural development. In effect, on a rice-growing plain whose soils are almost identical, which is the case of most of the central part of the D.I.Y., the thing that makes the difference in the matter of agricultural profits is the proximity of the principal irrigation canals. The closer one is, in effect, the greater the flow, and therefore water is abundant. But very often, the more important canals follow the principal roads. The sectors situated on the periphery of these axes have often been the first to profit from the improvements provided by the programmes of agricultural modernization, if only because the forwarding of inputs and the outflow of harvests was facilitated there. All this has led to more rapid development along the principal road axes. It is also in these corridors that population densities are the highest. Moreover, certain categories of infrastructure favourable for development are particularly present in these corridors (credit institutions, bus stops and other communication networks, etc.). It follows that urbanization progresses at the interior of the countryside at the heart of a milieu which is not absolutely identical in each geographic point but on the contrary is humanly and physically differentiated, as one has seen. This is especially true as the urbanization of a place is not only influenced by its locational characteristics (its distance from the town), but by a large number of factors, including the level of economic development, etc. The urban areas exercise beneficial effects on the hinterland which translate into advantages for the original inhabitants (access to external economies) and the newcomers who, we have seen, are often of urban origin (situation revenue).

The growth process of the suburbs is very spectacular in this regard. It was described in the D.I.Y. at the beginning of the 1990s (Vincent Rotgé, *Rural Employment Shifts in the Context of Growing Rural-Urban Linkages*)[51] and in Jakarta (Michael Leaf, 'The Suburbanization of Jakarta, A Concurrence of Economics and Ideology').[52] It concerns a genuine process of acculturation which integrates foreign concepts - American in particular - of physical and commercial planning. This is not surprising, since Indonesian urban specialists and architects have frequently received an education influenced by American techniques, even when they have not studied in such countries as Australia, Canada and the USA, or when foreign agencies or consulting firms do not intervene directly. This school of physical planning places a lot of importance on *condominium* and villa (single detached housing) development, where a road system in the form of a star or *cul-de-sac system* dominates, all having been frequently organized in an autonomous 'village'. In this way, appendages such as commercial centres (*malls*), swimming pools, golf courses, etc., are associated with housing. This type of physical planning encourages urban sprawl, and it is essentially addressed to upper middle class households who are financially solvent. One can also see this type of development in the town of Chiengmai in Thailand, for example, during the 1990s before the financial and stock market crisis, all of whose implications are not known at the time that we write this conclusion. This city and Yogyakarta are major historical and cultural centres which today attract middle class households whose professional activity is located in parts of Thailand and Indonesia that are most active economically. The heads of these households are not infrequently natives of the region who had to migrate for economic reasons and who are now returning to their birth place. Some of these households purchase a secondary residence within the kind of residential development described above. There they keep close to the senior executives who work there but do not necessarily originate from the place. In any event, these costly lodgings appeal to a minority *clientèle* within the local population. This type of development leads to a style and framework of life separated from the village communities. In this way, these members of the middle class liberate themselves from the numerous social obligations of village life well removed from their lifestyle, which more closely approaches that of comfortable western suburbs, or of the modern 'suburban villages' of the United States, where the well off inhabitants are gathered together by socioeconomic affinities. This form of development is frequent in Southeast Asia within certain countries were socioeconomic disparities are very strong. Frequently, the members of the middle class who adopt this new lifestyle and accommodation communicate with other members of the middle class elsewhere in the world, but are disconnected from the social realities of their own metropolitan environment. In sum, this constitutes an aspect of a certain form of globalization. Within the D.I.Y., this form of development starts to flourish along the most active urban corridors in the north of the region and in the immediate periphery of Yogyakarta. There, where the changes are less rapid, the mix of the new commuters with the original population is less brutal, more progressive and more harmonious. Their houses are distinguished from those of the original inhabitants only by their more opulent aspect and urban decorative motifs.

Morphological Characteristics

One has seen that a kind of ribbon development prevails in the countryside along the important road axes. This phenomenon, whose causes one has just studied, is very marked. It is also very different from the western situation and deserves to be considered in some depth. If one considers a large enough sector of one or another parts of the lines of communication, one can see that the types of land occupancy there are very mixed together. Zoning (United States) and similar land-use planning techniques (*e.g.* '*Plan d'Occupation des Sols*' in France), based on the type of occupation, show through very clearly here and orient physical growth. But this is not the only reason. Seen from closer up, one can ascertain in fact that a very clear differentiation exists between the spaces contiguous to these lines of communication and their hinterland. Over a maximum depth of some tens of meters, which in general corresponds to the band formed by the first range of properties bordering the most important regional routes, the workshops, merchant and other services are concentrated. Most often, this concerns a concentration of specialized activities, sufficiently productive, to which the household members devote themselves full time. Behind this band, one notices traditional rural communities where households performing non-agricultural, non-delocalized activities are more widely dispersed. There one finds household activities of traditional small industry widespread in the rice-growing communities of Monsoon Asia. Daily migrants also live there: they are inhabitants of old stock or newcomers more or less numerous according to the degree of proximity to the town. In sum, this is above all a residential sector. This contrast is once again explained by the theory of rents, because the services, especially merchant services, are in search of a commercial *façade* and maximum exposure to a potential *clientèle*, at a time when the young families of urban employees seek tranquillity for themselves and their children.[53]

One sees that today the very simple carving-into-sectors proposed by followers of von Thünen is not verified absolutely in the countryside of the D.I.Y. A supplementary reason for this is that the lands under cultivation are not totally planted with cash crops, far from it. They are frequently used to grow subsistence food, and the households that produce them are engaged in activities that are principally non-agricultural or supplementary. Another characteristic of contemporary spatial development in the countryside, particularly in the areas being urbanized, is the near absence of separation in land-use categories. In his thesis on industrialization in Monsoon Asia, of which we have spoken above, the economist Harry Oshima considers that the conditions of a separation between agriculture and artisanal work or small industry, such as in England, for example, have not been present in Monsoon Asia since the 18th Century,[54] and that this absence of separation has persisted up until today. This has become a characteristic as much cultural as economic and spatial in Monsoon Asia, and perhaps within other developing countries that have not passed through the industrial revolutions of western countries. This particularity presents certain advantages. It suffices *a contrario* to examine the consequences of land use planning in western countries (zoning, etc.) on the removal of both industry and employment in residential areas, which are circumstances that aggravate unemployment, poverty and its spatial polarization (Vincent Rotgé, *Some Remarks Concerning the Social and Regional Development Impact of Land Control, Drawn from an Analysis of the U.S. Experience - With Further Reference to the Recent French Experience*).[55] In return, this mixing of land uses also presents certain inconveniences: the pollution of water used for irrigation, the exposure of residential areas to industrial dangers, congestion of transportation routes, etc. The 'divide between urban and rural areas has become blurred', as stressed by Terry McGee (below) and some other geographers. This is also reflected in gradients of density. Within a western context, Paul Claval very justly observed that:

> In a rural area, the hierarchy of the centres is ordered by a population whose density depends on the agricultural economy, and thus is uniform over quite vast spaces.

Within urban space, it is not the same thing: the distribution of population is determined by the general field of externalities. It is thus based on an uneven gradient of density, decreasing from the centre outwards, that the network of secondary service centres develops. [56]

This differentiation does not truly apply in the rice-growing plains of Monsoon Asia, as one can see within the D.I.Y. In these regions, the highest densities are situated in the old urban centres, but the corridors of urbanization form areas of high population density throughout the countryside where population affected by immigration continues to be concentrated. But the theory of rents illuminates only a part of the urbanization process in Monsoon Asia. In order to understand this well, one must also consider the growing role of communications.

Communications and the Central Place Theory

Here again, the theoretical work of Paul Claval is very useful. This geographer remarks that:

For the activities linked to exchange and communication, not to be at the centre constitutes a penalty; it is unequally heavy depending on the sectors.[...] [57]

It is true that the appearance of urban corridors where services and small industry flourish would seem to contradict this remark. In fact, it is nothing of the kind. This ribbon urbanization, in effect, is explained not only by the theory of rents, but also by the role of the axes of communication. These, much more than the places of transit, have become very important centres of activity and exchange in the rice-growing communities of Monsoon Asia. For someone who is not very familiar with this geographic area, this fact can be difficult to understand in its human reality. Behind an apparent commonplace - the important role of communications - hides a veritable economic and spatial revolution as well as a revolution of mentalities. This role of the axes of transport as a place of intense social and economic activity can be observed in other countries of Monsoon Asia - in Bangladesh, for example, whose economic and social development is, however, behind in comparison with that of Java. In the southeast quarter of Bangladesh, for example, south of the Ganges and west of the river born from the union of the Ganges and the Brahmaputra, human densities are on the same order as those in the Javanese countryside. Since very recently, asphalt roads cross this region, which is also traversed by waterways that must be crossed by ferries because bridges are frequently unusable. The 'Green Revolution' has permitted an increase in rice-growing income, but electricity has not been installed throughout the country, and the principal indices of socioeconomic development are appreciably lower than those of Java. At night, the inhabitants gather together and concentrate along the principal roads, site of a very important social life. Why is this that way? Because in this very densely populated countryside, but with dispersed accommodation, meeting places remain scarce. In these conditions, the roads offer themselves as a natural place, easily accessible to maximum social interaction. In the rice-growing plains of Java, accommodation is not dispersed. It is a 'country' of accommodation grouped at the very least on the plain [58]

This work on the D.I.Y. also shows that the villages of the plain, located away from the corridors of activity, are like the hinterland and form secondary centres of activity. The intersection of the roads that lead to these villages and corridors are at the same time nodes of communication and important places of an activity as intense as it is picturesque: a bus stop and small payable parking spaces for bicycles for the daily migrants who continue on their way in public transport, stops for rickshaws, small restaurants for the use of these same daily migrants, markets, etc. In sum, the corridors are the places of intense interaction and exchange, which extend the central urban areas. The services, especially merchant services, and the workshops that sell their production directly settle along these corridors, where they benefit from a front of maximum interaction close to the inhabitants of the hinterland and passers-by originating from more distant communities. Less when the corridor leads to a cul-de-sac, this interaction is larger when it is situated between two towns and the flow of passengers is more important for this reason. Moreover, according to the respective distance of the two towns, the corridor can be affected by the cumulative influence of the two urban areas. For certain activities, this represents a considerable advantage (wholesalers who diversify their sources of supply, traders who enlarge their range of action, etc.). Curiosity is not the least thing attracting rural people to the corridors, where a little piece of the social life of the streets of the important urban centres is reconstructed. Better, these corridors possess their own hinterland, predominantly agricultural and residential, because these functions do not need an interaction so great, or at the very least of the same nature: the recent resident of urban origin who fled the town searches for tranquillity and finds it there apart from the congested places; the social life of the agricultural communities aims to reinforce cohesion and collaboration among their members, something which is not necessarily compatible with an over-large extraversion. The young who frequent the corridors can escape a little from the social pressure of their communities of origin. Within the D.I.Y., the new peripheral boulevard or 'ring road' represents a particular case of an urban corridor. One has seen above how it also profits from the theory of rents and attracts real estate development. All in all, an exceptional rural-urban interface and the circular extension of the urban corridors are at the heart of the zone of expansion of older urban areas.

The *Kotadesasi* Process

All of this is not without considerable theoretical implications. One sees, in effect, that the contemporary dynamics of urbanization in the D.I.Y. and other fertile rice-growing plains of Monsoon Asia are explained more by the work of the geographer Jean Gottmann on megalopolises (*Megalopolis: The Urbanized Northeastern Seaboard of the United States*)[59] and those that he has later inspired, than by recourse to the central place theory or the models derived from the theory of inherited localization from the work of von Thünen. In 1961, Jean Gottmann described a new process of urbanization, both because of its scale and the mechanisms that govern it. This geographer showed how metropolitan areas of the north-east seaboard of the United States between Boston and Washington D.C. were developed on their periphery until there was only a single vast agglomeration, including numerous still-rural areas. One of the motors of this evolution was the appearance of lighter industries and offices established outside of the old centres, thanks to the development of communications. It had become more interesting for an enterprise to be located between two old urban centres close to an important communication node, an airport, etc. These conclusions have inspired the work of Terry McGee[60] on urbanization in Monsoon Asia. McGee analyses the appearance in this part of the world of vast semi-rural, semi-urban areas, which he calls *desakota* (from the Indonesian *desa* = 'village' and *kota* = 'town/city'; the term *kotadesasi* corresponds to the process of transforming agricultural regions into *desakota* zones). McGee summarises the characteristics of *desakota* zones as follows:[61]

(1) a past marked by the cultivation of rice in small holdings and the development of transport,

(2) the development of non-agricultural activities,

(3) an 'extreme [...] mobility of the population' and goods,

(4) a mixture of land use categories even more marked than in the case of the American megalopolis, which has positive and negative effects (pollution) at the same time,

(5) an important participation of women in economic life, especially non-agricultural life, and,

(6) the absence or scarcity of regulations, and the predominance of the 'informal sector'.

The bringing together of the theories of Harry Oshima on the departure from agriculture of the agricultural economies of Monsoon Asia and those of Jean Gottmann on the growth of the great metropolises of the advanced economies has proved to be fruitful. The theory of *kotadesasi* is only an hypothesis today, but it is well enough supported. It proposes a description based on an empirical approach, but which reveals itself as being very accurate in usage, to a process whose unfolding development in the D.I.Y. is confirmed by this study. It also requires the precision and in-depth analyses that new studies, to which the works of McGee open the way, will have to bring. Promising areas of investigation are, for example: in-depth analysis of the transition between economic theories and morphological aspects, the development of a more differentiated approach which takes into consideration the internal processes at the interior of *desakota* zones and between these and their periphery, the taking into account of the characteristics of the agroecological environment, as well as the existence of other more or less ancient urban networks, which can be superimposed on the 'structural' role of *desakota* zones (markets, administrative centres, towns situated outside of the plain, etc.). Another interesting point concerns the differences established by McGee between the *desakota* zones. This author considers the *desakota* zone of the D.I.Y. as belonging to a category ('*desakota* Type 3') characterized by '[high densities of population] in which economic growth is slow', the proximity of 'secondary urban centers [the town of Yogyakarta, in this case], [...], surplus labour, and persistent low productivity in both agriculture and nonagriculture'.[62] This study of the D.I.Y. confirms this. It indicates, however, that the region's population growth is not rapid (according to McGee, this is one of the characteristics of this category of *desakota* zone), but it is, on the contrary, very moderate for a developing country. This is explained in part by the particularly efficient birth control in the region. This study of the D.I.Y. also makes possible an interesting observation on the characteristics of the *desakota* zone of the Special Region. In the first place, it is important to keep in mind that a weak GDP and slow growth are not synonymous with a weak level of economic exchanges. Even the contrary occurs within the D.I.Y., where the weak GDP is explained by the average level of household income which is very low, in part precisely because of the low productivity of work, and also due to the fact that the rural economy of this region is often one of subsistence and even of survival.[63] This last point poses the question of not taking into consideration the production of certain goods, which are exchanged, self-consumed or not accounted for in this largely 'informal' economy (one also thinks of the small contracts by mutual agreement in the construction sub-sector, etc.). The relative weakness of the GDP of the D.I.Y. is also explained by many other economic factors, including, for example, the weak local reinvestment of profits that are earned locally from tourism. In this way, an important portion of the infrastructure of tourism and top level real estate development profits from the situational income that the advantages of place procure, but if it creates a dynamic of growth, this remains limited on that account, above all in the countryside.[64] The moderate level of average local income rightly obliges many inhabitants to take up many activities. Among the communities of the D.I.Y. studied in this work, for example, it is within the poorest village in the mountains where activity is the most extroverted and the multiplicity of employment of the inhabitants among the highest. In a general way, the volume of exchanges between the rural and urban areas is high in a region like the D.I.Y., whose GDP is low. Because, in addition to the insufficiencies of the GDP per inhabitant, which make other indicators more reliable to express the levels of life, a positive relationship exists here between the weakness of productivity and income and the importance of rural-urban linkages. Augustin Berque, great connoisseur of Japan, reached a similar conclusion on the subject of rural Japanese (called 'alternates') who, during the 1970s, carried out urban activities alternately with agricultural tasks. He observed that:

> The analysis reveals an [...] original characteristic. It is not the regions where industries abound nearby which have the most of these 'alternates', as one would

expect from the examples of Lorraine and the Saar. [...] In absolute numbers, it is the slightly urbanized regions that, for lack of local employment, send the greatest mass of 'alternates' to the towns; which is to say that for many of them, it means [...] a long-distance migration and an absence of six months and more. [...][65]

All this is perfectly coherent. Within regions only slightly rich in high-productivity employment, which can provide full-time activities whose remuneration suffices to cover the needs of households, it is logical that the inhabitants diversify their activities in time (multiplicity of employment) and space ('bi-localism' rural/urban). In more urbanized and better endowed regions with full-time non-agricultural employment, which display higher levels of productivity, employment tends in return to stabilise, and eventually to become settled, due to the spreading out in space (over-spill) of urban activities or to urbanization *in situ*, which creates local employment outside of agriculture, or to be transformed into more stable activities which are accessible by daily migration. The Special Region is situated in an intermediate phase, but it continues to be very close to the situation described by A. Berque. However, the D.I.Y. is also a region where urbanization has become rapid, contrary to certain accepted ideas that generally bear on the period before the 1980s. It is that which shows the surface importance of 'rural' areas in 1980, in accordance with the criteria of the Indonesian Central Bureau of Statistics, which have become 'urban' in 1990, according to the definition of this same organization. The progression of this urbanization is impressive in terms of both surface and percentage. But the extent of urbanized areas here is much weaker in absolute value than in the other regions of Java. Moreover, urbanization here is less spectacular or visible than in the other large metropolitan areas principally in the north of the island. In effect, the type of urbanization that one finds in the vicinity of Yogyakarta is shown by changes in the structure of employment, an increase in population density, and improvements in networks and infrastructure. The expansion of the built-up areas appears in the regional statistics. But new construction is often scattered in the existing landscape and thus poorly visible, and the presence of professional premises of small areas inside housing contributes without doubt to rendering this urbanization still more difficult to perceive. In order to understand well the general significance of the preceding discussion, it is useful to bring together the present situation of the D.I.Y. with observations on 'under-urbanization' made in 1982 by Gavin Jones (Structural Change and Prospects for Urbanization in Asian Countries). To judge this 'under-urbanization', Jones relied on an index of the proportion of the urban population in non-agricultural employment. Applied to several Asian countries, this index allowed Jones to estimate if a country is 'under-urbanized' or 'over-urbanized' in relation with another, and to remark:

> As a broad generalization, the poorer, more agricultural countries [... among a group of selected Asian countries with different levels of development] appear 'under-urbanized' by comparison with the wealthier countries. [...] The tendency in most of the countries is for the index to increase over time (*i.e.* for urbanization to grow rather faster than the shift out of agriculture). [...] [66]

He observed moreover that:

> [...] the decline in agriculture's share of the labour force certainly does not have to be followed by an equivalent increase in urbanization. [... The] shift out of agriculture does not have to be accommodated by shifts in the rural/urban residential composition of the labour force, but could alternatively be accommodated by changes in the occupational structure of the labour force. [...] Basically, just as developing countries have 'sidestepped' the stage in the Clark-Fisher model,[67] where employment in industry increases at the expense of agriculture and have moved straight to the stage at which labour shed by agriculture shifts directly into services, so too can they modify the traditional urbanization/occupation nexus during the structural transformation of the economy.[68]

If one applies the preceding to the situation of the D.I.Y., one can deduce the unfolding of the following scenario during the last three decades:

(1) In a situation of modernization of rice growing, rural-urban linkages have favoured the departure from agriculture of an important portion of the population.

(2) At this stage, the neighbouring areas of the grand axes of communication already show a high concentration of non-agricultural activities (for the reasons evoked above), but they remain 'under-urbanized'.

(3) The following stage was clearly attained within the D.I.Y. during the 1980s; it corresponds to the concentration of activities and to the physical urbanization of these areas, according to the definitions of the Indonesian Central Bureau of Statistics. One has seen how this physical urbanization is more than a simple statistical reality. It also corresponds to an increased density of equipment and building made possible by an increase of the capital invested in infrastructure. In other terms, the rapid departure from agriculture does not necessarily

signify that a process of urbanization is being realised, but in a non-involuted situation[69] it constitutes a phase of development which leads to urbanization like that realized in the D.I.Y. But this urbanization also obeys morphological characteristics very different than those of the old urban centres.

Old Urban Centres and Suburbs

Within the D.I.Y., without doubt the central place theory would illuminate the localization of sugar factories at the centre of the sectors that formerly divided the regional territory. It meant at that time to find an economic and spatial system of agricultural organization to collect, transform and export the production of a single-culture plantation in the most rational manner possible. The constraints and the solutions were relatively simple, with the economy planned in a centralized and authoritarian manner. The situation was completely shattered by the end of colonization and the destruction of many sugar factories, the revolution in transportation and individualization connected with the increase in the means of individual transport, the passage to an economy less and less agricultural, and more and more commercial, centred on small family holdings, the development of credit sources, etc. In these conditions, the hypothesis of the *kotadesasi* process allows a clarification of the urbanization process on the plain. This does not mean that the old town centre no longer had a role to play, on the contrary. In the United States, for example, the formation of a megalopolis on the north-east seaboard coincided with the process of de-concentration of the residential function towards the suburbs. Certain old cities have nevertheless retained very important central functions in the interior of the megalopolis. Nothing permits us to affirm that the old Javanese cities follow or will follow such an evolution. They do not yet posses, or still to a small enough degree, heavy polluting industries in their heart, which could, as was the case in the United States earlier in the century, make the comfortable social classes flee and urban violence to remain limited. Moreover, the role of externalities must not be underestimated. In effect, if the old town exercises a field of externalities on its periphery, the inverse is equally true. The presence of many low-priced building sites on the extended periphery of the old urban centres can also contribute to the creation of centrifugal forces, and to empty the centres of a part of the members of the comfortable middle class. We see that already in the D.I.Y.

and elsewhere in Java,[70] the phenomenon of the growth of residential suburbs inhabited by the middle class is important. It is certain that, in these conditions, the functional relationships between the old centres and their periphery - including urban corridors - continue to be adjusted, and that they will be translated into reasonable modifications in the occupation of intra-urban land. But the old Javanese cities, also because they are situated at the intersection of urban corridors, will conserve an administrative, touristic, commercial, political, symbolic and religious role. Also because the Javanese have a rich urban culture to which they remain very attached. It suffices to observe at the centre of Yogyakarta the intense flow of motos driven in the evening by the young to understand that the heart of this city retains a central role as a place of diversion. In a certain measure, this flow constitutes somewhat the counterpart of the flowing back that at about four o'clock in the afternoon marks the return towards the countryside of the urban workers who live in the country. In return, the flow in the morning towards Yogyakarta, in which the same workers participate, is directed not only towards the heart of the city, but also towards peripheral quarters where the growth of activity is rapid. It remains for us to turn to the small 'rural towns' in the context of rural-urban linkages.

Small 'Rural Towns'

The potential role of small towns in the economic growth of the countryside, and as a tool of political decentralization (devolution) has been an important research theme since the end of the 1970s and the beginning of the 1980s.[71] Very useful studies in Java have shown the growth of systems of towns in the countryside (cf. Manuelle Franck),[72] and the ties that small towns maintain with their hinterland (*cf.* De Wouter de Jong and Frank van Steenbergen).[73] Graeme Hugo has studied the possibilities offered to the daily migrants who work in town ('Population Distribution and Urbanization in Indonesia: Recent Trends and Some Policy Issues for the Fifth Five Year Plan').[74] All of these studies accentuate the functional relation between secondary cities or even smaller towns and their hinterland, and/or between these urban centres within the same region.

In this work, the study of rural-urban linkages is certainly not limited to the interaction between the countryside and the capital of the region,

Yogyakarta. It has shown a certain level of interaction with other, smaller towns. Nevertheless, we have seen at the same time that the exchanges between the countryside and small towns remain well below those which exist between the countryside and the capital of the region in the majority of cases and above all in the plain. But we have also seen that the volume of these exchanges is very dependent on the geographic characteristics of the surroundings 'englobing' these towns and on their situation in relation to communication networks, as well as on the function, or principal functions, of these towns, themselves, which often flow from history (this is the case, for example, of the administrative capitals of the Districts or Regencies). Therefore, within the D.I.Y., the urban centres other than Yogyakarta are essentially the capitals of four administrative districts (other than that of Yogyakarta), a small number of historic and religious[75] towns including old royal sites - Courts or cemetery,[76] old sugar factory locations or sites of early-industrial establishments,[77] very small touristic towns or large villages at high altitude[78] or on the coast,[79] localities situated on the border between the plain and the mountains which are very much implicated in exchanges between the two milieus,[80] and, certainly, the seats of permanent or periodic markets.[81] Excepted the localities, which take advantage of their historical patrimony or natural exclusivity, practically all of these small towns play a privileged role in the regional system of communication. Similar observations can be made in Monsoon Asia elsewhere than in Indonesia.[82] This observation of Paul Claval is empirically verified in this way:

> [... the towns] are in essence the nodes of the communication system. It is for this reason that they form networks and are not arranged by accident.[83]

One can also observe that, within the D.I.Y. and after Yogyakarta, the four capitals of administrative districts are the only urban centres of a certain importance because of the size of their population - Figures 3.1 to 3.4. The town of Sleman, situated in a *desakota* zone in the north of the region, is experiencing important demographic growth. Wonosari is, as we have seen, a particular case: the town, in the centre of an enclosed basin far from Yogyakarta, constitutes a genuine obligatory passage for commercial activity in its district, and possesses moreover a market specialized in the products of the district, especially livestock. In return, Wates at the extreme south-west of the D.I.Y. is essentially an administrative town whose economic base remains only slightly diversified. Even though it is situated on a national axis of communication of a certain importance, it represents a town in transit, which does not belong to a *desakota* zone, and whose hinterland is very enclosed. As for Bantul, it is a market town situated on a rich rice-growing plain, but its demographic growth is relatively weak. It belongs to a *desakota* zone, but this still remains too little developed to create a sufficient level of activity, which would have significant repercussions for this town. Also, different from Sleman, it is not located between two important towns, but 'in a dead end' between the coast and Yogyakarta. Even though it has a market, it is so close to Yogyakarta that numerous traders in the hinterland of Bantul prefer to return to Yogyakarta or in the immediate periphery of the capital of the D.I.Y. The case of certain towns or large villages on the border between the plain and the mountains is equally interesting. We have seen that these towns benefit from the commercial exchanges between the two milieus, and serve as a relay in the regional system of communication. They could be led to play a still more important role, if the standardization of motorized transport does not progressively contribute to their marginalization to the profit of the large regional towns and the *desakota* zones. According to the particular geographic conditions, it may also be that they become the 'bridgeheads' of the urban network of the plain, whose central column would be made up of the *desakota* zones, including the regional capitals in their nodal points. All small town development policy should take their potentialities into account. To invest in the growth of certain towns because of their administrative stature or in order to 'stitch' space in a regular fashion in order to approach, for example, the 'ideal' hexagonal 'grid' of Christaller and Lösch, whose insufficiencies are known today, would constitute an act doomed to failure, because it would go against the real economic, social and, without doubt, also cultural forces described above.

The Passage From an Agrarian Society to an Urban Civilization of an Original Kind

In Monsoon Asia, programmes of the Green Revolution type have raised incomes in the countryside, where many roads and other categories of infrastructure have been constructed. Urbanization and rural-urban linkages have progressed within the areas of high population density. The major problem is no longer one of choosing between the urban and rural areas as a priority place of investment, but one of assuring openings for rural products within, or through, towns, and of providing rural people with the services they need. These services, if only for reasons of economy of scale, cannot always be 'near at hand'. Nonetheless, in the secondary cities and smaller towns, they remain accessible to the daily migrations, something that encourages the rural population to stay in the country. An increase in rural-urban linkages is not only an objective of development policy, which would have given birth to a purely technocratic idea. It already constitutes a reality. Confronted, in effect, with a situation where resources are scarce, but also disposing new means (agricultural surpluses, transport, credit, etc.), inhabitants of the countryside have managed to optimise their resources by diversifying their production in terms of both quality and space at the same time. For this, they have known how to make use of the considerable possibilities offered by urban areas and the dynamics of urbanization. The vital character of possibilities for urban employment for rural people has been noted also in Africa.[84] In the shade of the great metropolises of Monsoon Asia, rural people engage on a daily basis in veritable acts of heroism, in order to optimise their very limited resources by integrating the parameters of time, space, technology, human structures of organization, and other things, with very great flexibility and with the ability to adapt to circumstances. Their survival depends on the success of their strategies, and resources are too scarce not to make use of everything to which their resourcefulness can enable them to have access. It is evident that their strategies follow a very strict and precise logic, and without doubt even more so in communities where the possibilities are more limited and productivity weaker. In these conditions, agricultural development policies can, and must, play a role that remains essential. But they have everything to gain by being designed to: encourage - and not discourage, which is at present very often the case - existing strategies, especially individual, family and co-operative ones, and go together with urban policies.

To this effect, it is necessary to have agricultural diversification and the production of food near urban areas, as well as more democratic and transparent access to the means of production, including, but not limited to, land. In effect, too large a concentration of resources often encourages the expenditure and investment of capital within urban areas, outside the rural communities concerned. That being the case, it is acutely desirable that the public powers deploy the means necessary to face up to the menaces to the environment, which represent on the other side the urbanization of the countryside. It is also necessary to hope that the experience of past agricultural policies will not be placed in question by land speculation, corruption, and the absence of democracy, which prevent the inhabitants from taking full advantage of existing possibilities. The development of rural-urban linkages can constitute a factor of change in this regard. Provided that the transformations that accompany this development do not destabilise too much positive community structures or do not leave a void which could lead to political and social *malaise*, it can help reduce certain real weights of the past by overthrowing ancient agrarian hierarchies. It can also encourage the sense of enterprise at the individual and household level, or within a co-operative framework more liberally chosen to bring together often-limited resources. The sense of enterprise could take a larger and larger place in the face of certain patterns of work organization whose attainments one has often seen - probably rightly - in the past, but whose burdens begin to break through in a contemporary world. These changes could even contribute to the bringing into question of certain current forms of the political control, which is being exercised on village communities.

After further thought, the role of the state will no doubt continue to be important in the events, because it is indispensable. But it is necessary first and foremost that it disengage itself everywhere that it slows down, needlessly or because of corruption, the growth of exchanges by the obligation to submit to numerous fussy and costly administrative authorizations, by the imposition of prices fixed in advance for certain agricultural products, etc. In return, it is essential that the public powers carry out their duties and exercise energetic control over the dis-economies connected with the urbanization of the countryside: pollution, loss of agricultural land, etc. It is equally important that they look for ways to give to the largest number the means to profit from new possibilities (credit policies for small producers, etc.) in a manner that will reduce the polarization of poverty in the communities left on the margins of the growth process, as well as social stratification to the detriment of those unwanted because of their insufficient capital, lack of education (whose cost is often prohibitive), absence of a recognized, stable and permanent right to the land that they occupy or cultivate, or for any other reason. In this domain, as in others, what is necessary is a completely new way to conceive of governance, an essential concept even though one brought into disrepute by the excessive usage, which is made of it today. It is important to act quickly while the country is being profoundly transformed, and before directions are taken which will mark for a long time the urban and rural landscape and will condition the future. Moreover, if there are reasons to hope provided that adequate measures are taken, poverty and income gaps give reason for great concern in this country, and they are the source of political and social troubles, of which a large number of observers are aware. In the hope that a political consensus is possible, it will be necessary to attack at their sources efficiently.

One has seen that new possibilities already stand out in an environment where urbanization and rural-urban exchanges progress rapidly. A far-seeing policy must be adopted to take advantage of these changes. It should also avoid a situation in which these changes aggravate spatial and social disparities, and it must conserve a liveable, high quality environment for man. This objective is still more pressing in a metropolis which, like the D.I.Y., incarnates much of the culture and the memory of a people, and at a time in which cultural, ethnic and religious factors correspond in the world to outbreaks or to more durable rises - one does not know which - of identity crises founded on economic mutations probably more rapid than any which have previously existed. The financial and stock market crisis that descended upon eastern Asia at the beginning of 1997 gives a supplementary relief to certain of the dangers that we have mentioned above. This crisis may also have the merit of deflating 'financial bubbles' and real estate speculation, and of permitting the return of a form of growth saner from the point of view of morals, human rights, and of equality, and more durable in political and economic terms. One must hope, however, that the transition towards this type of more balanced growth, as well as less corrupt democratic political forms, can really be made without major political crises, tensions, indeed inter-ethnic and other conflicts, which, alas, are not improbable. A period opens now with its share of new possibilities but also dangers. The urban peripheries, because they are places of intense economic activity, where a large part of the riches and exportations of the country are produced, and because they are the very important places of contact in cultural, ethnic and socioeconomic terms, are certainly directly concerned by the changes to come, in which they are called upon to play an essential role.

Notes

1   1976:

2   1982.

3   In *Labour Absorption in Agriculture*, Department of Economics, Research School of Pacific Studies, Australian National University, Canberra, (cited by Jones, *op. cit.*, with omission of date).

4   The data for 1971 are taken from Jones, *op cit.*, p. 17. Those for 1980 and 1990 come from the *Rapport sur le développement dans le monde en 1996: De l'économie planifiée à l'économie de marché*, World Bank, Washington D.C., 1996, Table 4: *Population et population active*, p. 226.

5   Data taken from: Castells, 1989, Table 3.1: Percentage distribution of the labour force by industry sectors and intermediate industry groups 1870-1980, p. 128.

6   It is expressed as follows: Variation in % of the quantity of food demanded
                                                     Variation in % of income

7   Hypothesis of Clark-Fisher; Jones, *op. cit.*, p 20. *Cf.* Colin Clark, *Conditions of Economic Progress*, McMillan, 1957 (third edition); cited by Jones, *op. cit.*

8   1988.

9   1989.

10   The annual growth of the GDP was 6.1 per cent in 1980-90 and 7.6 per cent in 1990-94; see the *Rapport sur le développement dans le monde en 1996: De l'économie planifiée à l'économie de marché*, World Bank, *op. cit.* Table 11: *Croissance de l'économie*, p. 240.

11   1989, *op. cit.*, p. 1250.

12   1986.

13   Manning, 1988; Hardjono, 1987.

14   *Op cit., 1986.*

15   In Alexander, Boomgaard and White, eds, 1991.

16   This author shares the view according to which Java has undergone alternating phases of development and contraction of economic development and of rural industries.

17   Oshima, 1983, and, 1987.

18   The expression, 'A factory without chimneys' was applied to Burma by Furnivall (in Margaret Mead (editor), *Cultural Patterns and Technical Change*, New York, 1955, p. 53; cited by Macfarlane, 1978, p. 196). In other respects, Indonesia makes up part of Monsoon Asia except certain islands of the South-East of the Archipelago, as recalled by Oshima (*op. cit.*, 1983, p. 4).

19   Taken from the summary of this study; Oshima, *op.cit.*, 1983.

20   Here the reasoning of Oshima reveals a weakness to the extent that he does not say how these societies had attained these high levels of technology.

21   *Ibid.*, p. 14.

22   In Hill, ed., 1989.

23   *Cf.* the Introduction of Baker and Claes-Fredrik Claeson in Baker, ed., 1990, p. 15.

24   Of course, 'flexible production' systems have appeared in other environments.

25   Sabel, 1989, p. 46.

26   See Part I of this book. It is true that this tells us nothing about the possible increase of the disparities at the heart of the countryside. Taking into account that the Gini indexes that we have calculated in the villages studied remain very high (between about 0.5 and 0.6), the increase in disparities at the interior of the countryside constitutes a very worrying tendency. Indexes of this order of size have been noticed elsewhere by Harry Oshima, for example (1987, p. 307), who, starting with data of 1976, underlined the exceptionally raised character of the Gini coefficients in the Indonesian countryside compared with the rest of Monsoon Asia and with urban areas, especially in Java. It would therefore be useful to study how the Gini indexes have evolved. Of course, an increase of the Gini coefficients, and therefore of income disparities, would not necessarily signify that the poorest section of the population grew poorer. It could equally signify that the richest sectors were enriched more quickly than the others. But a reduction in Gini indexes and a simultaneous elevation of incomes, including the lowest socioeconomic sectors, would undeniably constitute excellent news.

27   *Cf.* Douglass, 1989.

28   These depend clearly on the economic and financial state of the investors, including Japan.

29   Booth, 1989, *op. cit.*, p. 1250.

30   1998, p. 307.

31   *Cf.* Douglass, 1991.

32   Vali Jamal and John Weeks, 'The Vanishing Rural-Urban Gap in Sub-Sahara Africa' (*International Labour Review*, 127, 3, 1988), cited by Baker and Claes-Fredrik Claeson in Baker (editor), *op. cit.*

33   Todaro explains the migratory flow by the income differentials and the conditions of the work market between the places of depart and destination concerned. See: Todaro, 1971.

34   1989.

35   In Hill, ed., 1989, *op. cit.*

36   28.67 per cent in 1991-92; 25.56 per cent in 1992-93; between 18.69 and 20.25 per cent in 1993-94; between 18.2 and 20.26 per cent in 1994-95; Source: *Statistik Indonesia, 1995*, Biro Pusat Statistik, Jakarta, Table 9.1.2, p. 432.

37   *Cf.* Papanek, ed., 1980, Table 1.9, p. 26.

38   1994.

39   *Cf.* also Chapter 9.

40   Pomonti, 29 August 1998.

41   Booth, 1989, *op.cit.*, p. 1249.

42   International co-operation agreements also exist between the countries of the region, which permit, in case of need (in particular, bad harvests) exchanges between the rice reserves of these countries.

43   *Cf.* Claval, 1981.

44   See *ibid.*, p. 79.

45   Park, Burgess and McKenzie, 1925.

46   Hoyt, 1939.

47   Harris and Ullman, 'The Nature of Cities' (*The Annals of the Academy of Political and Social Science*, Volume No. 242, 1945) cited in Schwab, 1982, pp. 276-8. Schwab's book also gives an analysis on the well-known works of Burgess and Hoyt.

48   Claval, *op. cit.*, pp. 99-100.

49   *Ibid*, pp. 97-9.

50   Before the subsequent appearance of contra-urbanization movements.

51   Article presented on the occasion of 'The International Conference on Geography in the Asean Region', Gadjah Mada University, Yogyakarta, 31/08-03/09 1992.

52   1994.

53   *Cf.* Claval, *op. cit.*, p. 85: 'Le champ urbain des différentes catégories d'agents'.

54   *Op. cit.*, 1983, pp. 4-5.

55   1991.

56   Claval, *op. cit.*, p. 90.

57   *Ibid*, p. 85.

58   See Demangeon, 'La géographie de l'habitat rural', *in Problèmes de Géographie Humaine*, (pp.159-205), p. 167, see also p. 163.

59   1961.

60   1987.

61   McGee, in Ginsberg, Koppel and McGee, eds, 1991, pp. 16-17. This publication is in a form adapted from that mentioned in the preceding note.

62   *Ibid.*, pp. 8-9. *Cf.* preceding note.

63   One knows that these two are not synonymous. One recalls that the subsistence economy is '[a form] of economic organization oriented to the direct satisfaction of material needs. [in this form of organization] Restricted organization units (families, homes, villages) consume an important part of their production. Economic exchanges are restricted, confined to scarce goods and without general monetary mediation [...]. The subsistence economy characterises first of all the primitive societies, and, in a certain measure, traditional agricultural societies (in these latter, exchanges are more developed and the usage of money is more widespread). A subsistence economy is not the same as an economy of scarcity. [...].' (*Dictionnaire d'économie et de sciences sociales*, under the direction of E.C. Echaudemaison, Nathan, Paris, 1993, p. 141).

64   *Cf.* for example Mubyarto, 1993.

65   Berque, 1973, p. 335.

66   *Op. cit.*, p. 20, The author recognized, however, when this article was written that India was an exception, and that elsewhere, 'in half of the countries [studied], [... this] tendency [... was] too weak to permit the identification of a significant transformation, taking into account the unreliability of the data'.

67   See note 7, above.

68   *Ibid*, pp. 24-25.

69   That is to say, where in parallel the productivity of work increases more rapidly than the population.

70   *Cf.* the article of Leaf on the growth process of the suburbs of Jakarta, *op. cit.*

71   *Cf.* for example, the numerous works that Dennis Rondinelli has written on the question during the 1980s.

72   1993.

73   1987.

74   When we had access to the manuscript, it was understood that it had been published in *Mobilitas Penduduk dan Pembangunan Daerah*, Wirosuhardjo Kartomo (editor), 1988.

75   Example, Prambanan.

76   Examples, Imogiri, Kota Gede. Kota Gede is situated so close to Yogyakarta that it has coalesced with it.

77   Example: Kalasan.

78   Example: Kaliurang.

79   Examples: Parangtritis, Sanden.

80   Examples: Kembang, Piyungan.

81   Examples: Niten and often the localities included in the other categories.

82   However, in certain countries, Bangladesh for example, it would be suitable to add the urban centres situated along waterways.

83   Claval, *op. cit.*, p. 64.

84   *Cf.* Baker, ed., *op. cit.*; or Gaile, 1992; this article bears on the Kenyan programme RTPC: Rural Trade and Production Centre, *cf.* also: OECD / Club of Sahel - ADB (African Development Bank) - CILSS, *Pour préparer l'avenir de L'Afrique de l'Ouest: Une Vision à l'horizon 2020, Synthèse de l'étude des perspectives à long terme en Afrique de l'Ouest*, December 1994.

Glossary

Adang-adang: Intermediate trader purchasing produce along the road, usually in the very early morning, and selling it to a market.

Arisan: A traditional system of (rotating) credit and savings.

Batik: A piece of fabric with either stamped or hand-painted colour patterns. As their use as traditional clothing material has been receding for decades, the nature of *batik* has changed and *batik* are now increasingly sold to tourists as decorative 'paintings',

Bawang merah: Onion.

Bawang putih: Garlic.

Becak: Rickshaw.

BIMAS (acronym for '*Bimbingan Masal*'): Programmes of modernization of the agriculture started in the second half of the 1960s.

Cabe merah: A variety of pepper.

Colt (or *Kolt*): A type of mini-bus.

Cukupan: (From '*cukup*' = 'enough') 'Self-sufficiency', when speaking about a household which has access to an acreage of farmland large enough to secure the household's basic needs, assuming that the household derives all its income from farming.

   Cukupan levels are a function of such variables as: agricultural yields, the selling price of the share of crops which is not consumed, the cost of inputs. Authors like Penny and Singarimbun consider the case of farmers cultivating a certain acreage of both wet and dry land; see D.H. Penny and M. Singarimbun, *Population and Poverty in Rural Java: Some Economic*

Arithmetic from Sriharjo (Ithaca, New York: Cornell International Agricultural Development Mimeograph 41) (1973).

Therefore, several definitions of *cukupan* can be given as a function of farmland acreage, depending on a variety of local conditions. Also, these definitions can vary over time depending on the fluctuation of the market prices.

In this book, we did not deem to recalculate *cukupan* levels to match very precisely the local characteristics of the studied communities. For the wetland communities of the Plain of Bantul, we re-used a definition given by Hardjono for a family which would derive all of its income from wetland farming (*i.e.* 0.5 ha of wet land); see Joan Hardjono, *Land, Labour and Livelihood in a West Java Village* (Yogyakarta: Gadjah Mada University Press, 1987).

In the communities studied in this Research Report, empirical evidence clearly indicates that many households cannot meet their basic needs merely by cultivating the land to which they have access. This is because population pressure is very high and farmland is fragmented. But in many cases, rural-urban linkages generate opportunities for an additional nonfarm income which supplements the household's agricultural income, if any. In this case, farming either remains the main source of income, or even becomes a secondary source.

Daerah Istimewa: Administrative division meaning literally 'Special Region' equivalent to a province (*'Propinsi'*). With the exceptions of the two 'Special Regions' in Indonesia - Yogyakarta and Aceh - and Jakarta which is called a 'Special Metropolitan District', Indonesia is administratively divided into 'Provinces'.

Desa: Literally, 'village'. The administrative division immediately below the *kecamatan* (subdistrict).

Dukuh (formerly *Dusun*): Literally, 'hamlet'. The administrative division in rural areas below the *desa* (village).

Emping melinjo: Traditional chips made from the processed fruit of a common garden tree (*Gnetum gnemon* in Latin).

Gotong royong: A system of mutual assistance encompassing a variety of forms and fields of social life.

Gurami: A variety of freshwater fish, much appreciated for dishes in restaurants.

Kabupaten: Administrative division immediately below the 'Special Region' or 'Province' level. In this book, it is referred to as a 'district' or 'regency' (the two terms are synonymous here). Originally, a *Kabupaten* encompassed a still predominantly rural area in contrast with the territory of cities called '*Kotamadya*' (see below). Today, this terminology has remained, but in Java, large tracts of suburban *Kabupaten* are turning 'urban' according to official statistical definitions.

Kacang panjang: 'Yard long beans' or 'cow peas' (a sort of very long string bean; English translations used by the Indonesian Central Bureau of Statistics (*Biro Pusat Statistik*) in *Survei Pertanian, Produksi Tanaman Sayuran di Jawa* (Agricultural Survey, Production of Vegetables in Java) (Jakarta, 1989; table 7.4., p. 123).

Kecamatan: Administrative division below the *Kabupaten* (*i.e.* 'District' which stands for either 'Regency' or 'Kotamadya'). In this Research Report, *Kecamatan* is referred to as a 'Subdistrict'.

Kedelai: Soybean.

Kotamadya: Municipality. An administrative division in an urban area. Its equivalent in a rural area would be the *Kabupaten* (see '*Kabupaten*', above).

K.U.D.: Acronym for the village cooperative (*Koperasi Unit Desa*).

Lebaran: Day following the Moslem fasting month. During this period, many Javanese living in town return to their village of origin to visit their relatives. It is a period of intense, though short-duration, flows of circular migrations throughout Java. The function of *Lebaran* is important in keeping contacts between urban migrants and their relatives in the countryside.

Lele: A very common variety of catfish grown in inland fishponds.

Makelar: An intermediate trader purchasing from small rural producers and selling to regional markets (including in town).

Mandor: A foreman recruiting labour for construction sites, the *mandor* works for contractors. Usually, the *mandor* pays the wages to the labourer after taking a commission, and the bonds between the *mandor* and the labourer are based on a patron-clientèle system.

Maro: A type of sharecropping arrangement, whereby half of the harvest goes to the cultivator and the remaining half to the landlord. Costs are also shared. This sharecropping system is very widespread in wetland communities. It is virtually the only sharecropping system in use in the communities of the Plain of Bantul which are studied in this Research Report (see also *mertelu*, below).

Mendong: A variety of long grass which is woven to make mats called *tikar* (it is a handicraft in the region of Kembang, the foothills community studied in this Research Report).

Mertelu: A type of sharecropping arrangement, whereby a third of the harvest goes to the cultivator, and the rest to the landlord. Also, the 'cultivator pays all costs' (Hardjono, *Land, Labour and Livelihood in a West Java Village*).

Palawija (also commonly *Polowijo*): Intermediary non-rice crop between rice crops. The usual annual cropping pattern in lowland areas for a piece of farmland is two rice and one *palawija* crops. In the most fertile agricultural areas, five crops of rice and one of *palawija* are possible over a period of two years.

Pasar: Literally 'market'. *Pasar* refers to markets which are open on an either permanent or periodic bases.

Pekarangan: The garden compound surrounding the dwelling (dry land planted with trees; its role in the rural domestic economy is very important).

Ruko: A neologism for '*perumahan dan pertokoan*'. It is a type of building combining retail-trading on the ground floor and the housing of the traders's household on the upper floor. It is very common in urban commercial districts. It is also typical along urbanizing transit corridors.

Salak: A fruit.

Sambat-sinambat: Traditional system (gradually receding) of agricultural mutual assistance whereby assistance is rewarded by reciprocation of services and food allowance in lieu of cash.

Sawah: Irrigated ricefield (with canalized irrigation; rainfed ricefields are called: *sawah tadah hujan, i.e.* literally 'tank' or 'reservoir' *sawah*).

Simpan Pinjam: A traditional system of credit and savings.

Tahu: *Tofu*, soybean curd.

Tegal (or *Tegalan*): Dry field (as opposed to *sawah*).

Tempe: A sort of fermented soybean cake eaten in various ways (such as fried).

Toko: A wholetrade or large retailing shop (larger than a 'warung' which is a smaller convenience shop, see below). *Toko* are found in urban or urbanizing areas such as transit corridors.

Warung: A grocery or small convenience shop. The owner often operates it on a part-time basis. It is usually located in the same building as the dwelling, or next to it. It can include a small restaurant or coffee shop. *Warung* are found in both rural and urban areas.

Bibliography

(A complete list of all reference material used in the preparation of this report, both cited and uncited in the notes following each section)

Abey, Arun, Booth, Anne, and Sundrum, R.M., 'Labour Absorption in Indonesian Agriculture', *Bulletin of Indonesian Economic Studies* (March 1981).

Alexander, Jennifer, 'Information and Price Setting in a Rural Javanese Market', *Bulletin of Indonesian Economic Studies* (April 1986).

Alexander, Paul, Boomgaard, Peter, and White, Ben, eds, *In the Shadow of Agriculture, Nonfarm Activities in the Javanese Economy, Past and Present* (Amsterdam: Royal Tropical Institute, 1991).

Archief voor de Suikerindustrie in Nederlandsch-Indië, Deel III, Jaargang 1931, no. 1 a/d 31, Soerabaia (Plaat I) (in Dutch).

Arndt, H.W., and Sundrum, R.M., 'Employment, Unemployment and Under-Employment', *Bulletin of Indonesian Economic Studies* (December 1980).

Asian Productivity Organization, *Farm-level Animal Feeding Systems in Asia and the Pacific* (Report of APO Seminar 23 July-3 August 1990, Tokyo) (Tokyo: APO, 1991).

Asian Development Bank, *Appraisal of The Small Towns Urban Development Sector Project in Indonesia* (Manila: ADB, 1993).

Baker, Jonathan, and Claeson, Claes-Fredrik, in Baker, Jonathan, ed., *Small Town Africa, Studies in Rural-Urban Interaction* (Seminars Proceedings no. 23, The Scandinavian Institute of African Studies) (Uppsala: The Scandinavian Institute of African Studies, 1990).

BAPPEDA/Faculty of Geography of Gadjah Mada University, *Perencanaan dan Pengembangan Pelayanan Sosial Dasar di Propinsi Daerah Istimewa Yogyakarta, Laporan Akhir* (Yogyakarta, February 1993) (in Indonesian).

Barbier, E.B., 'Cash Crops, Food Crops, and Sustainability: The Case of Indonesia', *World Development*, 17 (6: 1989).

Barghouti, Shawki, Timmer, Carol, and Siegel, Paul, *Rural Diversification, Lessons from East Asia* (World Bank Technical Paper no. 117) (Washington DC: The World Bank, 1990).

Barwell, I., *et al.*, *Rural Transport in Developing Countries* (London: Intermediate Technology Publications, 1985).

Beek, Aart van, *Life in the Javanese Kraton, Images of Asia* (Singapore: Oxford University Press, 1990).

Beers, Howard W., ed., *Indonesia, Resources and their Technological Development* (Lexington: The University Press of Kentucky, 1970).

Bemmelen, R.W. van, *The Geology of Indonesia, Vol. IA, General Geology* (The Hague: Martinus Nijhoff, 1970).

Bendavid-Val, 'Rural-urban Linkages: Farming and farm Households in Regional and Town Economies', *Review of Urban and Regional Development Studies* (July 1989).

Berque, Augustin, 'Les campagnes japonaises et l'emprise urbaine', in *Etudes rurales*, Ecole Pratique des Hautes Etudes (sixième section) (January-June 1973) (pp. 321-52) (in French).

Bintarto, R., 'A Trial for an Urban Transport Zonation for Yogyakarta City', *The Indonesian Journal of Geography*, 14 (48: 1984).

--------------, 'Man, Rice and Problems in Jogjakarta', *The Indonesian Journal of Geography*, 3 (October 1961-December 1963).

Boer, J.W. den, and Gill, R.G., Proceedings for the symposium on 'New Settlement Development Policies, the Feasibility of New Towns in Indonesia' (Faculty of Civil Engineering, Department of Planning, Design and Management) (Delft: POO-Memorandum, 1989).

Boer, John de, *et al.*, 'The Economic Role of Sheep and Goats in Indonesia: A Case Study of West Java', *Bulletin of Indonesian Economic Studies* (December 1983).

Booth, Anne, 'Accomodating a Growing Population in Javanese Agriculture', *Bulletin of Indonesian Economic Studies* (August 1985).

--------------, *Agricultural Development in Indonesia* (Asian Studies Association of Australia Southeast Asia Publications Series, no. 16) (Sydney: Allen and Unwin, 1988).

--------------, 'Indonesian Agricultural Development in Comparative Perspective', *World Development*, Vol. 17 (1989) (pp. 1235-54).

Booth, Anne and Damanik, Konta, 'Central Java and Yogyakarta: Malthus Overcome?', in Hill, Hal, ed., *Unity and Diversity, Regional Economic Development in Indonesia since 1970* (Singapore: Oxford University Press, 1989).

BPS (Indonesian Central Bureau of Statistics), Statistik Indonesia (Jakarta, various years).

----------------, *Peta Indeks Kecamatan per Desa/Kelurahan Propinsi Jawa Tengah dan D.I. Yogyakarta* (Jakarta, 1980 and 1990).

----------------, *Penduduk Indonesia* (Series L1) (Jakarta, 1991).

----------------, *Pendapatan Regional Propinsi-Propinsi di Indonesia menurut Lapangan Usaha, 1983-1990* (Jakarta, 1992).

Braun, J. von, Haen, H. de, and Blanken, J., *Commercialization of Agriculture Under Population Pressure: Effects on Production, Consumption, and Nutrition in Rwanda* (Research Report 85) (Washington DC: International Food Policy Research Institute, 1991).

Brookfield, H., Hadi, A.S., and Mahmud, Z., *The City in the Village - The In-Situ Urbanization of Villages, Villagers and their Land around Kuala Lumpur, Malaysia* (Singapore: Oxford University Press, 1991).

Carapetis, S., et al., *The Supply and Quality of Rural Transport Services in Developing Countries, A Comparative Review* (World Bank Staff Working Paper, no. 654) (Washington DC: World Bank, 1984).

Carey, Peter, *Voyage à Jocja-Karta en 1825*, Cahier d'Archipel no. 17 (Paris: Association Archipel, 1988). (Main text in French by A.A.J. Payen: *Journal de mon Voyage à Jocja Karta en 1825*, commented in English by Peter Carey).

Casley, Dennis J., and Kumar, Krishna, *The Collection, Analysis, and Use of Monitoring and Evaluation Data* (Baltimore and London: Johns Hopkins University Press, published for the World Bank, 1988).

Castells, Manuel, *The Informational City, Information Technology, Economic Restructuring and the Urban-Regional Process* (Oxford, UK, and Cambridge, USA: Blackwell, 1989).

Cervero, Robert, 'Acessibility and Third World Rural Development: A Case Study of Sumatra', *Review of Urban and Regional Development Studies* (July 1990).

Charras, Muriel, *De la Forêt maléfique à l'Herbe divine, La transmigration en Indonésie: Les Balinais à Sulawesi*, (Paris: Editions de la Maison des Sciences de l'Homme, 1982) (in French).

----------------, section on Indonesia, in *Antheaume, Benoît, Bonnemaison, Joël, Bruneau, Michel and Taillard, Christian*, eds, *Géographie Universelle, L'Asie du Sud-Est, Océanie* (Belin-Reclus, 1995) (in French).

Clark, Audrey N., *Longman Dictionary of Geography* (Harlow: Longman, 1985).

Clarke, Giles, 'Supporting Co-ordinated Capital Improvements through EPM: The Jakarta Experience', *Environmental Guidelines for Settlements Planning and Management*, Vol. 1 (Nairobi: UNCHS and UNEP, 1987).

Claval, Paul, *La Logique des villes* (Paris: LITEC, Librairies Techniques, 1981) (in French).

--------------, 'L'économie de l'information et la métropolisation' (Paris, 1991) (in French).

Coedès, George, *The Indianized States of Southeast Asia* (Honolulu: The University Press of Hawaii, 1968) (Translation from the French: *Les Etats Hindouisés d'Indochine et d'Indonésie*, Hanoi, 1944).

Connell, J., and Lipton, M., *Assessing Village Labour Situation in Developing Countries* (Delhi: Oxford University Press, 1977).

Connell, Dasgupta, Laishley, and Lipton, *Migrations from Rural Areas, The Evidence from Village Studies* (Delhi: Oxford University Press, 1976).

Demangeon, Albert, *Problèmes de Géographie Humaine* (Paris: Librairies Armand Colin, 1952) (in French).

Devas, Nick, *Financing Local Government in Indonesia* (Monographs in International Studies, Southeast Asia Series no. 84) (Athens, Ohio: Ohio University Press, 1989).

--------------, 'Issues in the Financing of Local Government in Indonesia', *Planning and Administration*, 16 (Autumn 1989): 30-40.

Dick, H.W., 'Urban Public Transport, Part 1', *Bulletin of Indonesian Economic Studies* (March 1981).

--------------, 'Urban Public Transport, Part 2', *Bulletin of Indonesian Economic Studies* (July 1981).

Domenach, Jean-Luc, *L'Asie en danger* (Paris: Fayard, 1998) (in French).

Donner, Wolf, *Land Use and Environment in Indonesia* (London: C. Hurst, 1987).

Dorléans, Bernard, *L'Indonésie, Les incertitudes du décollage économique* (Paris: Les Études de la Documentation Française, 1992) (in French).

Douglass, Mike, 'The Environmental Sustainability of Development: Coordination, Incentives and Political Will in Land Use Planning for the Jakarta Metropolitan Region', *Third World Planning Review* (May 1989).

--------------, 'Uneven Urbanization in Asia: Toward an Alternative Policy of Endogenous Development of Intermediate Cities' (Honolulu: Department of Urban and Regional Planning, University of Hawaii, 1991).

--------------, 'A Regional Network Strategy for Reciprocal Rural-Urban Linkages : An Agenda for Policy Research with Reference to Indonesia', *Third World Planning Review*, 20 (1: 1998).

Duby, Georges, *L'économie rurale et la vie des campagnes dans l'Occident médiéval*, Vol. 1 (Paris: Flammarion, 1977) (in French).

Échaudemaison, E.C., ed., *Dictionnaire d'économie et de sciences sociales* (Paris: Nathan, 1993) (in French).

Effendi, T.N., 'Mobility Behaviour and Household Structures: A Case Study of Two Villages of West Java, Indonesia', *The Indonesian Journal of Geography*, 17 (53: 1987).

--------------, *The Growth of Rural Non-farm Activities at the Local Level: A Case Study of Causes and Effects in a Subdistrict of Upland Central Java* [Ph.D. dissertation submitted for the degree of Doctor of Philosophy, Discipline of Geography, School of Social Sciences, The Flinders University of South Australia, November 1991].

Esmara, 'Creating Employment through the Labour Intensive Public Works Programmes: The Indonesian Experience', *Philippine Review of Economics and Business*, 24 (September and December 1987).

Études Rurales, special issue on the urbanization of the countryside, no. 49-50 (January-June 1973) (in French).

Evers, H.D., 'Trade as Off-Farm Employment in Central Java' (Working Paper no. 124) (Bielefeld, Germany: Sociology of Development Research Centre, 1989).

FAO-UNESCO (1979), *Soil Map of the World Series*, Southeast Asia, Volume IX (Paris: UNESCO, 1979).

Farvacque, Catherine and McAuslan, Patrick, 'Reforming Urban Land Policies and Institutions in Developing Countries' (Urban Management Program Policy Paper) (Washington DC: World Bank, 1992).

Franck, Manuelle, *Quand la rizière rencontre l'asphalte..., semis urbain et processus d'urbanisation à Java-est* (Etudes Insulindiennes / Archipel: 10) (Paris: Editions de l'Ecole des Hautes Etudes en Sciences Sociales, 1993) (in French).

Friedmann, John, and Douglass, Mike, 'Agropolitan Development: Towards a New Strategy for Regional Planning in Asia', in Lo, Fu-Chen, and Salih, Kamal, eds, *Growth Pole Strategy and Regional Development Policy, Asian Experience and Alternative Approaches* (published by Pergamon Press for The United Nations Centre for Regional Development, 1978).

Gaile, Gary L., 'Improving Rural-Urban Linkages through Small Town Market-based Development', *Third World Planning Review*, Vol. 14, no. 1 (February 1992) (pp. 131-48).

Geertz, Clifford, *The Religion of Java* (Chicago: The University of Chicago Press, 1960).

----------------, *Agricultural Involution* (Berkeley and Los Angeles: University of California Press, 1963).

----------------, *Peddlers and Princes, Social Development and Economic Change in Two Indonesian Towns* (Chicago: The University of Chicago Press, 1963).

----------------, *The Interpretation of Cultures* (Basic Books, 1973).

Geertz, H., *The Javanese Family: A Study of Kindship and Socialization* (New York: The Free Press of Glencoe, 1961).

Gertler, Paul J., and Rahman, Omar, 'Social Infrastructure and Urban Poverty', in Pernia, Ernesto M., ed., *Urban Poverty in Asia, A Survey of Critical Issues* (Hong Kong: Oxford University Press, 1994) (pp. 127-94).

Ginsburg, Norton, Koppel, Bruce, McGee, T.G., *The Extended Metropolis, Settlement Transition in Asia* (Honolulu: University of Hawaii Press, 1991).

Godfrey, Martin, 'Labour Market Analysis and Employment Planning, Crisis Management in Employment Planning: The Indonesian Case' (Working Paper no. 40) (Geneva: International Labour Office, World Employment Programme Research, June 1990).

Goldblum, Charles, *Métropoles de l'Asie du Sud-Est. Stratégies urbaines et politiques du logement* (Paris: L'Harmattan, 1987) (in French).

----------------, 'Des métropoles en crise au nouvel ordre urbain', in *Antheaume, Benoît, Bonnemaison, Joël, Bruneau, Michel and Taillard, Christian*, eds, *Géographie Universelle, L'Asie du Sud-Est, Océanie* (Belin-Reclus, 1995) (in French).

Gottmann, Jean, *Megalopolis: The Urbanized Northeastern Seaboard of the United States* (New York: Twentieth Century Fund, Kraus International Publications, 1961).

Gourou, Pierre, *L'Asie* (Paris: Hachette Université, Classique Hachette, 1971) (in French).

--------------, *La Terre et l'Homme en Extrême-Orient* (Paris: Flammarion, 1972) (in French).

--------------, 'Les deltas, foyers de concentration humaine' in *Ressources naturelles de l'Asie tropicale humide* (Paris: UNESCO, 1974) (in French).

--------------, *Riz et civilisation* (Paris: Fayard, 1984) (in French).

Graaf, H.J. de, and Pigeaud, Théodore G., *Islamic States in Java 1500-1700, A Summary, Bibliography and Index* (The Hague: Martinus Nijhoff, 1976).

Hamer, Andrew M., *et al.*, *Indonesia, The Challenge of Urbanization* (World Bank Staff Working Papers no 787) (Washington DC: World Bank, 1986).

Hardjono, Joan, *Land, Labour and Livelihood in a West Java Village* (Yogyakarta: Gadjah Mada University Press, 1987).

--------------, ed., *Indonesia - Resources, Ecology, and Environment* (Singapore: Oxford University Press, 1991).

Hartmann, Betsy, 'Population, environment and security: a new trinity', *Environment and Urbanization*, Vol. 10, no. 2 (October 1998) (pp. 113-27).

Hill, Hal, 'Concentration in Indonesian Manufacturing', *Bulletin of Indonesian Economic Studies*, 23 (2: 1987).

--------------, ed., *Unity and Diversity - Regional Economic Development in Indonesia since 1970* (Singapore: Oxford University Press, 1989).

Hoyt, Homer, *The Structure and Growth of Residential Neighborhoods in American Cities* (Washington DC: Federal Housing Administration, 1939).

Hugenholtz, W.R., 'Taxes and Society: Regional Differences in Central Java around 1830', in Kartodirdjo, Sartono, ed., *Papers of the Fourth Indonesian-Dutch History Conference, Yogyakarta 24-29 July 1983*, Volume One: 'Agrarian History' (Yogyakarta: Gadjah Mada University Press, 1986).

Hugo, G.J., *Population Mobility in West Java, Indonesia* [Unpublished Ph.D. dissertation, Canberra: Australian National University, 1975].

--------------, *Population Mobility in West Java* (Yogyakarta: Gadjah Mada University Press, 1981).

Hugo, G.J., and Mantra, Ida Bagoes, 'Population Movement to and from Small and Medium Sized Towns and Cities in Indonesia', *Malaysian Journal of Tropical Geography* (December 1983).

Hugo, G.J., *et al.*, *The Demographic Dimension in Indonesian Development* (Singapore: Oxford University Press, 1990).

Huisman, H., 'Planning Environment and Rural Development in Indonesia: Some Key Aspects' (Research Report no. 4) (Yogyakarta: Faculty of Geography, Gadjah Mada University, 1991).

Huisman, H., and Stoffers, W., 'Socio-economic Conditions in Varying Settings within a District' (Research Report no. 1) (Yogyakarta: Faculty of Geography, Gadjah Mada University, 1988).

--------------, 'Households, Resources and Production. A report on the Situation in Bantul Regency' (Research Report no. 2) (Yogyakarta: Faculty of Geography, Gadjah Mada University, 1990).

--------------, 'Settlements, Services and Centrality in Bantul District' (Research Report no. 5) (Yogyakarta: Faculty of Geography, Gadjah Mada University, 1991).

Jayasuriya, Sisira, and Nehen, I. Ketut, 'Bali: Economic Growth and Tourism', in Hill, Hal, ed., *Unity and Diversity, Regional Economic Development in Indonesia since 1970* (Singapore: Oxford University Press, 1989).

Jones, Gawin W. (1982), 'Structural Change and Prospects for Urbanization in Asian Countries' [Paper prepared for the Conference on Urbanization and National Development, East-West Population Institute, Honolulu, Hawaii, January 25-29, 1982].

Jong, Wouter de, Steenbergen, Frank van, *Town and Hinterland in Central Java* (Yogyakarta: Gadjah Mada University Press, 1987).

Kantor Statistik D.I.Y. (Statistical Office of Yogyakarta Special Region), *Yogyakarta dalam Angka* (Yogyakarta in Figures), and, *Gunung Kidul dalam Angka, Sleman dalam Angka, Bantul dalam Angka, Kulon Progo dalam Angka*, statistical handbooks of various years (in Indonesian).

Kartodirdjo, Sartono, *The Pedicab in Yogyakarta* (Yogyakarta: Gadjah Mada University Press, 1981).

--------------, ed., *Papers of the Fourth Indonesian-Dutch History Conference, Yogyakarta 24-29 July 1983*, Volume One: *Agrarian History* (Yogyakarta: Gadjah Mada University Press, 1986).

Khan, Halim, 'Gunung Kidul: An Introduction to a Problem Area in Java', *The Indonesian Journal of Geography*, 3 (4-6: 1963).

--------------, 'Water in Gunung Kidul', *The Indonesian Journal of Geography*, 4 (7: 1964).

Kinsey, B.H., *Creating Rural Employment* (London: Croom Helm, 1987).

Koentjaraningrat, *Villages in Indonesia* (Ithaca: Cornell University Press, 1967).

--------------, *Javanese Culture, Institute of Southeast Asian Studies* (Singapore: Oxford University Press, 1990) (first published 1985).

Koninck, Rodolphe de, *L'Asie du Sud-Est* (Paris: Masson Géographie, 1994).

Kristiadi, J.B., 'Financing Regional Development: The Case of Indonesia' (pp. 233-53) in Prantilla, B., ed., *Financing Local and Regional Development in Developing Countries: Selected Counry Experiences* (Nagoya: UNCRD, 1988).

Kuperus, G., 'The Relation Between Density of Population and Utilization of Soil in Java' (Amsterdam: Quinzième Congrès International de Géographie, 1938) (pp. 465-77).

Kuroyanagi, Haruo, 'A Case Study of Two Villages in Yogyakarta Special Region' [Final report submitted to The Indonesian Academy of Sciences, L.I.P.I., Jakarta, March 1990].

--------------, 'Source of Livelihood, Mutual Help Credit, and Saving Systems in Two Villages of Yogyakarta Special Region' [Paper presented at the second Country Seminar on Regional Development and Planning of Daerah Istimewa Yogyakarta, Yogyakarta, 3-6 September 1991].

Lacoste, Yves, *Géographie du sous-développement* (Paris: Quadrige / PUF, 1985).

Leaf, Michael, 'The Suburbanization of Jakarta, A Concurrence of Economics and Ideology', *Third World Planning, Review*, 16 (4:1994) (pp. 341-56).

Lee, K.-H., and Sivananthiran, A., 'Le travail en sous-traitance en Malaisie: le point de vue des entreprises utilisatrices, des sous-traitants et des travailleurs', *Revue Internationale du Travail* (ILO-Geneva), Vol. 135, no. 1 (in French).

Lee, Kyu Sik, *The Location of Jobs in a Developing Metropolis, Patterns of Growth in Bogotá and Cali, Colombia* (Oxford University Press, 1989).

Lombard, Denys, 'Pour une histoire des villes du Sud-Est asiatique', *Annales Économie, Société, Civilisation* (July-August 1970) (pp. 842-56).

--------------, *Le carrefour javanais, essai d'histoire globale* (in 3 volumes, Paris: Editions de l'Ecole des Hautes Etudes en Sciences Sociales, 1990) (in French).

Louw, P.J.F., and Klerck, E.S. de, *De Java-Orloog, 1825-30*, 6 volumes (The Hague, 1894-1909).

Macfarlane, Alan, *The Origins of English Individualism* (Oxford: Basil Blackwell, 1978).

Mai, Ulrich, and Buchholt, Helmut, *Peasant Pedlars and Professional Traders, Subsistence Trade in Rural Markets of Minahasa, Indonesia*, (Singapore: Institute of Southeast Asian Studies, 1987).

Manning, Chris, 'The Green Revolution, Employment, and Economic Change in Rural Java, A Reassessment of Trends under the New Order' (Occasional Paper no. 84) (Singapore: Asean Economic Research Institute of Southeast Asian Studies, 1988).

Mantra, Ida Bagoes, *Population Movement in Wet Rice Communities: A Case Study of Two Dukuhs in Yogyakarta Special Region* [Unpublished Ph.D. dissertation, University of Hawaii, 1978].

--------------, 'Mobilitas Sirkuler di Indonesia' (Working Paper 'Widyakarya Nasional Migrasi dan Pembangunan') (1979) (in Indonesian).

--------------, *Population Movement in Wet Rice Communities: A Case Study of Two Dukuhs in Yogyakarta Special Region* (Yogyakarta: Gadjah Mada University Press, 1981).

--------------, 'Population Distribution and Population Growth in Yogyakarta Special Region', *The Indonesian Journal of Geography*, 16 (52: 1986).

--------------, 'Population Mobility and the Links Between Migrants and the Family Back Home in Ngawis Village, Gunung Kidul Regency, Yogyakarta Special Region', *The Indonesian Journal of Geography*, 18 (55: 1988).

--------------, 'Nonpermanent Population Mobility in the Rural Areas: A Strategy to Increase the Household Income - A Case Study of Two Dukuhs in Bantul Regency' [Paper presented at the second Country Seminar on Regional Development Planning of Yogyakarta, Yogyakarta, 3-6 September 1991].

Maurer, Jean-Luc, *Modernisation agricole, développement économique et changement social, le riz, la terre et l'homme à Java* (Paris: PUF, 1986) (in French).

--------------, with Billeter, J.-F., and Etienne, G., *Sociétés Asiatiques: Mutations et continuité, Chine, Inde, Indonésie* (Paris: PUF, 1985).

--------------, 'Beyond the Sawah: Economic Diversification in Four Bantul Villages, 1972-1987' in Alexander, Paul, Boomgaard, Peter, White Ben, eds, *In the Shadow of Agriculture, Nonfarm Activities in the Javanese Economy, Past and Present* (Amsterdam: Royal Tropical Institute, 1991).

McAndrews, Colin, *Land Policy in Modern Indonesia* (Boston: Oelgeschlager, Gunn and Hain, 1986).

McDonald, P.F., and Sontosudarmo, A, *Response to Population Pressure: The Case of the Special Region of Yogyakarta* (Yoyakarta: Gadjah Mada University Press and The Population Institute, 1976).

McGee, T.G., *The Southeast Asian City* (London: G. Bell and Son, 1967).

--------------, 'Urbanisasi or Kotadesasi? The Emergence of New Regions of Economic Interaction in Asia' (Working Paper 87-8) (Honolulu, Hawaii: East-West Center, 1987).

--------------, 'Industrial Capital, Labour Force Formation and The Urbanization Process in Malaysia', *International Journal of Urban and Regional Research*, 12 (1988).

--------------, 'The Emergence of Desakota Regions in Asia: Expanding a Hypothesis', in Ginsburg, Norton, Koppel, Bruce, and McGee, T.G., eds, *The Extended Metropolis, Settlement Transition in Asia* (Honolulu, Hawaii: University of Hawaii Press, 1991).

Mears, Leon A., *The New Rice Economy of Indonesia*, (Yogyakarta: Gadjah Mada University Press, 1981).

Melvill van Carnbée and Versteeg, W.F., *Atlas van Nederlandsch Indië* (Uitgave van Gualtherus Kolff, 1870).

Mitchell, J.C., 'The Causes of Labour Migration,' in *Migrant Labour in Africa, South of the Sahara* (Abidjan: CCTA, 1961).

Moedjanto, G., *The Concept of Power in Javanese Culture* (Yogyakarta: Gadjah Mada University Press, 1990).

Mook, H.J. van, 'Kuta Gedé', in Wertheim, W.F., ed., *The Indonesian Town, Studies in Urban Sociology* (Brussels: Les Éditions A. Manteau S.A., Bruxelles, 1958).

--------------, Kuta Gedé (Djakarta: Bhratara, 1972).

Mubyarto, 'Economic Change in Jogyakarta', *Bulletin of Indonesian Economic Studies* (November 1970).

--------------, 'Garis-Garis Besar Haluan Negara 1993 dan Prospek Pembangunan Ekonomi DIY dalam Pelita VI' [Paper presented at the University of Gadjah Mada, April 1993].

Mubyarto and Hill, Hal, 'Economic Change in Yogyakarta', *Bulletin of Indonesian Economic Studies* (April 1978).

Mulder, Niels, *Individual and Society in Java, A Cultural Analysis* (Yogyakarta: Gadjah Mada University Press, 1989).

Nakamura, Mitsuo, *The Crescent Arises over the Banyan Tree* (Yogyakarta: Gadjah Mada University Press, 1983).

Nibbering, Jan, Willem, 'Crisis and Resilience in Upland Land Use in Java' in Hardjono, Joan, ed., *Indonesia - Resources, Ecology, and Environment* (Singapore: Oxford University Press, 1991).

Nickum, James E., 'Of Cores and Corridors: The Pattern of Development in Hebei Province' (Working Paper no. 21) (Honolulu: Environment and Policy Institute, East-West Center, February 1990).

NUDS Final Report (Jakarta: Directorate of City and Regional Planning, 1985).

OECD / Club du Sahel - BAD (Banque Africaine de Développement) - CILSS, *Pour préparer l'avenir de L'Afrique de l'Ouest: Une vision à l'horizon 2020, Synthèse de l'étude des perspectives à long terme en Afrique de l'Ouest* (December 1994) (in French).

Ommeren, van, Caroline M., and Palte, Jan G.L., 'Marketing Patterns of Agricultural Commodities in an Upland Area of Central Java', *The Indonesian Journal of Geography* (December 1986).

Oshima, Harry T., 'The Transition to an Industrial Economy in Monsoon Asia' (Economic Staff Paper no. 20) (Manila: Asian Development Bank, 1983).

--------------, *Economic Growth in Monsoon Asia, A Comparative Survey* (Tokyo: University of Tokyo Press, 1987).

--------------, 'Underemployment, Diversification and Off-farm Employment in Indonesia', *The Philippine Review of Economics and Business* (December 1987).

Otten, Mariël, *Transmigrasi: Indonesian Resettlement Policy, 1965-1985*, (Copenhagen: IWGIA Document 57) (October 1986).

Overton, J.D., 'Infrastructure and Multilevel Development: Some Examples from Fiji', *Regional Development Dialogue*, 11 (Winter 1990).

Papanek, Gustav, ed., *The Indonesian Economy* (New York: Praeger, 1980).

Park, Robert E., Burgess, Ernest, and Mckenzie, R.D., *The City* (Chicago: University of Chicago Press, 1925).

Patten, R., Dapice, B., and Falcon, W., 'An Experiment in Rural Employment Creation: The Early History of Indonesia's Kabupaten Development Program', in Gustav Papanek, ed., *The Indonesian Economy* (New York: Praeger, 1980).

Payen, A.A.J., *Journal de mon Voyage à Jocja Karta en 1825*, reprinted in Carey, Peter, *Voyage à Jocja-Karta en 1825* (Cahier d'Archipel no. 17) (Paris: Association Archipel, 1988) (original text in French with notes in English).

Peluso, Nancy Lee, *Occupational Mobility and the Economic Role of Rural Women* (Yogyakarta: Population Studies Center, Gadjah Mada University, 1984).

Penny, D.H., and Singarimbun, M., *Population and Poverty in Rural Java: Some Economic Arithmetic from Sriharjo* (Ithaca, New York: Cornell International Agricultural Development Mimeograph 41) (1973).

Pernia, Ernesto M., 'Individual and Household Migration Decision', *The Philippine Economic Journal*, 17 (1 and 2: 1978).

Pomonti, Jean-Claude, 'L'Indonésie est secouée par des violences ethniques et religieuses', in *Le Monde* (06 February 1997) (in French).

--------------, 'L'Indonésie éprouve de plus en plus de mal à gérer la crise', in *Le Monde* (08 January 1998) (in French).

--------------, 'Les travailleurs immigrés d'Asie du Sud-Est dans la tourmente', in *Le Monde* (09 January 1998) (in French).

--------------, 'La population indonésienne défie le gouvernement. Le très populaire « gouverneur-sultan » de Yogyakarta appelle à de profondes réformes', in *Le Monde* (29 August 1998) (in French).

PPK-UGM and KMM-KLH (Pusat Penelitian Kependudukan-Universitas Gadjah Mada/Kantor Menteri Negara Kependudukan dan Lingkungan Hidup), *Faktor-faktor yang Mempengaruhi Interaksi Kependudukan dan Sumber Daya Pembangunan di Daerah Istimewa Yogyakarta* (Yogyakarta: PPK-UGM, 1990) (in Indonesian).

Prinsen Geerligs, H.C., *The World's Cane Sugar Industry, Past and Present* (Manchester: Norman Rodger, Altrincham, 1912).

Priyotomo, Josef, *Ideas and Forms of Javanese Architecture* (Yogyakarta: Gadjah Mada University Press, 1988).

Radjiman, Gunung, 'The Urban Structure of Yogyakarta, Indonesia', in *Environmental Profiles of Selected Cities in Southeast Asia*, in Sani, Sham, and Badri, M. Ahmad, eds, *Tropical Urban Ecosystems Studies* (Kuala Lumpur: UNESCO, 1988).

Raffles, Sir Thomas Stamford, *The History of Java* (London, 1817 / Kuala Lumpur: Oxford University Press, 1978).

Rahardjo, Dawan, and Ali, Fachry, 'Financial Factors Affecting Small and Medium Businesses in Indonesia', in Kenneth James and Narongchai Akrasanee, eds, *Small and Medium Business Improvement in the Asean Region, Financial Factors* (Singapore: Institute of Southeast Asian Studies, 1986).

Reid, Anthony, *Southeast Asia in the Age of Commerce, 1450-1680* (New Haven: Yale University Press, 1988).

Remenyi, J.V., 'Issues in Smallholder Tropical Dairying', *Bulletin of Indonesian Economic Studies* (April 1986).

Replogle, Michael, 'Non-motorized Vehicles in Asian Cities' (World Bank Technical Paper no. 162, Asia Technical Department Series) (Washington DC: World Bank, 1992).

Rice, Robert C., ed., *Indonesian Economic Development, Approaches, technology, Small-scale textile, Urban Infrastructure and NGOs* (Clayton, Victoria: Monash University, 1990).

Ricklefs, M.C., *A History of Modern Indonesia since c. 1300* (Basingstoke and London: The McMillan Press Ltd, 1993).

---------------, *Jogjakarta Under Sultan Mangkubumi, 1749-1792, A History of the Division of Java* (London: Oxford University Press, 1974).

Rietvelt, Piet, 'Rural Small-scale Industry in Developing Countries: Indonesian Experiences', in Giaoutzi, Maria, *et al.*, eds, *Small and Medium Size Enterprises in Regional Development* (London: Routledge, 1988).

Rijanta, Ryanto, *Off-farm Activities in Kabupaten Bantul* [Unpublished Masters thesis, The International Institute for Aerospace Survey and Earth Sciences, Enschede, September 1990].

Rimmer, Peter, *Rikisha to Rapid Transit, Urban Public Transport System and Policy in Southeast Asia* (Sydney: Pergamon Press, 1986).

Robequain, Charles, *Le Monde Malais* (Paris: Payot, 1946) (in French).

Rotgé, Vincent, 'Addressing Regional Development and Rural Employment Creation in the Context of Rising Rural-Urban Linkages - Focus on Yogyakarta Special, Region, Indonesia' [Paper presented at the second Country Seminar on Regional Development and Planning of Daerah Istimewa Yogyakarta, Yogyakarta, 3-6 September 1991].

--------------, *Some Remarks Concerning the Social and Regional Development Impact of Land Control, Drawn from an Analysis of the U.S. Experience - With Further Reference to the Recent French Experience* (UNCRD Working Paper 91-3) (Nagoya: UNCRD, 1991).

--------------, 'Rural Employment Shifts in the Context of Growing Rural-Urban Linkages: The Case of Two Villages of the Plain of Bantul, Yogyakarta Special Region' [Paper presented at the International Conference on Geography in the Asean Region, Gadjah Mada University, Yogyakarta, 31 August-3 September 1992].

--------------, ed., *Rural-Urban Integration in Java, Consequences for Regional Development and Employment* (UNCRD Research Report Series no 6) (Nagoya: UNCRD, 1995).

--------------, *Villes et campagnes en Asie des Moussons: de la rencontre à l'échange* (Paris: L'Harmattan, forthcoming) (in French).

Rotgé, Vincent, Dasgupta, Nandini, Shafi, Salma, *et al.*, *Rural Towns Development Study Report* [Report of the mission undertaken in May-June 1997 in Bangladesh on behalf of the European Commission, Dhaka and Brussels, 1997].

Rouffaer, G.P., 'Vorstenlanden', in *Encyclopaedie van Nederlandsch-Indië*, Vol. IV, 1905 (pp. 587-653) (in Dutch).

Rutz, Werner, *Cities and Towns in Indonesia* (Stuttgart: Gebrueder Borntraeger Berlin, 1987).

Sabel, Charles F., 'Flexible Specialisation and the Re-emergence of Regional Economies', in Hirst, Paul, and Zeitlin, Jonathan, eds, *Reversing Industrial Decline* (New York: St. Martin's Press, 1989).

Samuelson, Paul A., and, Nordhaus, William D., *Economics* (Singapore: McGraw Hill, 1989, 13th edition).

Sandee, Henry, and Weijland, Hermine, 'Rural Cottage Industry in Transition: The Roof Tile Industry in Kabupaten Boyolali, Central Java', Bulletin of Indonesian Economic Studies (August 1989).

Schwab, William A., *Urban Sociology, A Human Ecological Perspective* (Addison-Wesley, 1982).

Schweizer, Thomas, 'Agrarian Transformation? Rice Production in a Javanese Village', *Bulletin of Indonesian Economic Studies* (August 1987).

Scott, A. J., 'Flexible production systems and regional development: the rise of new industrial spaces in North America and western Europe', *International Journal of Urban and Regional Research*, Vol. 12 (1988).

Selosoemardjan, *Social Changes in Jogjakarta* (Ithaca: Cornell University Press, 1962).

Seraj (T.M.), *The Role of Small Towns in Rural Development (A Case Study in Bangladesh)* (Dhaka: National Institute of Local Government, 1989).

Sevin, Olivier, *L'Indonésie* (Paris: Collection Que Sais-je, PUF, 1993).

--------------, 'La riziculture javanaise des origines', in *Géographie et Cultures*, no. 2 (1992).

--------------, 'Java entre hindouisme et Islam', in *Géographie et Cultures*, no. 3 (1992).

Shand, Richard T., ed., *Off-Farm Employment in the Development of Rural Asia*, (Canberra: Australian National University, National Centre for Development Studies, 1986).

Siamwalla, Ammar, *et al.*, 'The Thai Rural Credit System, Public Subsidies; Private Information, Segmented Markets', *World Bank Economic Review*, 4 (September 1990).

Siddiqui, Kamal, *Local Government in South Asia, A Comparative Study* (Dhaka: University Press Limited, 1992).

Sinaga, R., and Collier, L., 'Social and Regional Implications of Agricultural Development Policy' (Staff Paper 75-3) (New York: Agricultural Development Council, 1975).

Singarimbun, M, and Penny, D.H., *Penduduk dan Kemiskinan* (Jakarta: Bhatara Karya Aksara, 1976) (in Indonesian).

Singh, Katar, *Rural Development, Principles, Policies and Management* (New Delhi: Sage Publications, 1986).

Smithies, Michael, *Yogyakarta, Cultural Heart of Indonesia* (Singapore: Oxford University Press, 1990).

Soemarwoto, Otto, *Analisis Dampak Lingkungan* (Bandung: Lembaga Ekologi, Universitas Pajajaran, unpublished, 1988) (in Indonesian).

Soeratman, *Transmigrasi Swakarsa* (Yogyakarta: Pusat Penelitian dan Studi Kependudukan, Universitas Gadjah Mada, 1978) (in Indonesian).

Stanback, Thomas J., *Understanding the Service Economy* (Baltimore: Johns Hopkins University Press, 1979).

Standing, Guy, *Labour Circulation and the Labour Process* (London: Croom Helm, 1985).

Stoffer, Wim and Sutanto, Agus, 'Rural Small-scale Industries and Regional Development, A Case Study from Bantul District', *Indonesian Journal of Geography*, 20 (December 1990).

Stokke, K., Yapa, L.S., and Dias, H.D., 'Growth Linkages, the Nonfarm Sector, and Rural Inequality: A Study in Southern Sri Lanka', *Economic Geography*, 67 (July 1991).

Stoler, Ann, 'Garden Use and Household Economy in Rural Java', *Bulletin of Indonesian Economic Studies* (August 1978).

Sulang, Kusni, *Le mouvement des actions unilatérales pour les réformes agraires des paysans de Klaten, Java-Centre, Indonésie, 1963-1965, son commencement, sa chute et ses leçons* [Unpublished Masters thesis, E.H.E.S.S., Paris, May 1986] (in French).

Sullivan, John, *Local Government and Community in Java, An Urban Case Study* (Singapore: Oxford University Press, 1992).

Sunarto, Hadisupadmo, *Pengaruh Remitan Migran Sirkuler Terhadap Kesejahteraan Keluarga Migran dan Desa Asal, Suatu Kajian di Desa Mulusan dan Sodo* [Unpublished Ph.D. dissertation, Yogyakarta: Gadjah Mada University, 1991] (in Indonesian).

Sundrum, R.M., *Income Distribution in Less Developed Countries* (London and New York: Routledge, 1990).

Surjo, Djoko, 'Economic Crisis and its Impact on Rural Java: A Case of the Semarang Regency in the Latter half of the 19th Century', in Kartodirdjo, Sartono, ed., *Papers of the Fourth Indonesian-Dutch History Conference*, Yogyakarta 24-29 July 1983, Volume One: 'Agrarian History' (Yogyakarta: Gadjah Mada University Press, 1986).

Sutanto, Agus, *Rural Small-scale Industry in Kabupaten Bantul: An Assessment on its Structure, Potentials and Roles in Regional Development* [Unpublished Masters Thesis, Inschede, The Netherlands: International Institute for Aerospace Survey and Earth Sciences, 1989].

Thiranagamage, Dayapala, and Dias, Hiran D., 'The Role of Small Towns in Rural Development: Some Lessons from the Uda Walawe Project in Sri Lanka', *Malaysian Journal of Tropical Geography*, Vol. 6 (December 1982).

Thirlwall, A.P., *Growth and Development* (Macmillan, 1983).

Titus, Milan J., *Migrasi Antar Daerah di Indonesia* (Translation Series no. 12.) (Yogyakarta: Pusat Penelitian dan Studi Kependudukan, Gadjah Mada University, 1982) (in Indonesian).

--------------, 'Social-Spatial Consequences of the Integration of the Serayu Region (Central Java) into the Colonial System', in Muyzenberg, Streefland and Wolters, eds, *Focus on the Region in Asia* (Rotterdam: CASP, 1982).

Titus, M.J., Steenberrgen, F. van, and De Jong, W. (1986), 'Exploratory Notes on the Economic Structure and Role of Small Urban Centres in the Serayu Valley Region', in Nas, P., ed., *The Indonesian City* (Dordrecht: KITLV, Foris, 1986).

Tjondronegoro, S.M.P., 'The Utilization and Management of Land Resources in Indonesia, 1970-1990' in Joan Hardjono, ed., *Indonesia, Resources, Ecology and Environment* (Singapore: Oxford University Press, 1991).

Tjondronegoro, S.M.P., Soejono, and Hardjono, J., 'Rural Poverty in Indonesia: Trends, Issues and Policies', *Asian Development Review - Studies of Asian and Pacific Economic Issues*, 10 (1: 1992).

Todaro, M., 'Income Expectations, Rural-urban Migration and Employment in Africa', *International Labour Review* (1971).

UNCRD, 'Emerging Urban-Regional Linkages: Challenges for Urbanization, Employment and Regional Development' [Report of the proceedings of an expert group meeting, Bangkok, Thailand, 16-29 August 1989].

UNCRD/Cipta Karya, *Regional Development of Yogyakarta*, Volume 1 (1975).

UNESCO, *Quality of Life: Problems of Assessment and Measurement*, (Socio-economic Studies 5) (Paris, 1983).

Uppal, J.S., *Taxation in Indonesia* (Yogyakarta: Gadjah Mada University Press, 1986).

Warren, Carol, *The Bureaucratisation of Local Government in Indonesia*, (Working Paper 66) (Clayton, Victoria: Centre of Southeast Asian Studies, Monash University, 1990).

Wendt, P.F., ed., *Forecasting Transportation Impacts upon Land Use* (Studies in Applied Regional Science) (Leiden: Martinus Nijhoff Social Sciences Division, 1976).

Wertheim, W.F., ed., *The Indonesian Town, Studies in Urban Sociology* (Brussels: Les Éditions A. Manteau S.A., 1958).

Wheeler, David, Cole, William, and Irianiwati, Lisana, 'Made in Bali, A Tale of Indonesia Export Success' (1989).

White, Benjamin, 'Demand for labour and population growth in colonial Java', *Human Ecology*, Vol.1, no. 3 (1973).

------------, 'Population, Involution and Employment in Rural Java', *Development and Change*, 7 (1976).

------------, 'Political Aspects of Poverty, Income Distribution and their Measurement: Some Examples from Rural Java', *Development and Change*, 10 (1: 1979).

Wit, J.B. de, 'The Kabupaten Program', *Bulletin of Indonesian Economic Studies* (March 1973).

World Bank, *Indonesia, Employment and Income Distribution* (Washington DC, 1980).

------------, *Improving Indonesia's Cities, A Case Study of Economic Development* (Washington DC,1986).

------------, The Transmigration Programme in Perspective (Washington DC, 1988).

------------, Rapport sur le dévoloppement dans le monde en 1996: De l'économie planifiée à l'économie de marché (Washington DC, 1996) (in French).

Zainun, Buchari, 'Decentralization for Rural Development in Indonesia', in *Building from Below, Local Initiatives for Decentralized Development in Asia and the Pacific* (Kuala Lumpur: Vinlin Press, 1988).

For Product Safety Concerns and Information please contact our EU representative GPSR@taylorandfrancis.com Taylor & Francis Verlag GmbH, Kaufingerstraße 24, 80331 München, Germany

Printed and bound by CPI Group (UK) Ltd, Croydon, CR0 4YY
08/05/2025
01864389-0001